STUDIES IN COMICS AND CARTOONS

LUCY SHELTON CASWELL AND JARED GARDNER, SERIES EDITORS

ETHICS
IN THE GUTTER

Empathy and
Historical Fiction
in Comics

KATE POLAK

THE OHIO STATE UNIVERSITY PRESS | COLUMBUS

Library of Congress Cataloging-in-Publication Data
Names: Polak, Kate (Assistant professor of English), author.
Title: Ethics in the gutter : empathy and historical fiction in comics / Kate Polak.
Other titles: Studies in comics and cartoons.
Description: Columbus : The Ohio State University Press, [2017] | Series: Studies in comics and cartoons | Includes bibliographical references and index.
Identifiers: LCCN 2017025900 | ISBN 9780814213537 (cloth ; alk. paper) | ISBN 0814213537 (cloth ; alk. paper)
Subjects: LCSH: Comic books, strips, etc.—History and criticism. | Empathy—Comic books, strips, etc. | Historical fiction—History and criticism. | Violence—Comic books, strips, etc. | Graphic novels—History and criticism.
Classification: LCC PN6710 .P65 2017 | DDC 741.5/358—dc23
LC record available at https://lccn.loc.gov/2017025900

Cover design by Martyn Schmoll
Text design by Juliet Williams
Type set in Palatino

9 8 7 6 5 4 3 2 1

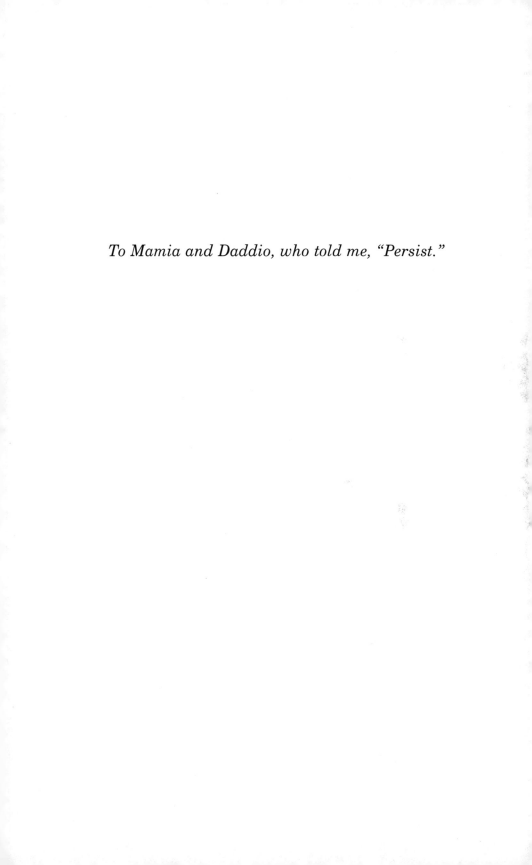

To Mamia and Daddio, who told me, "Persist."

CONTENTS

ILLUSTRATIONS

ACKNOWLEDGMENTS

I CAN'T quite believe that this project is coming to a close or that so many people spent valuable time assisting me with it. My gratitude goes first to my parents and my husband, without whom nothing would ever get done, including this book. Thanks, Mamia and Daddio, for keeping me fed, clothed, and relatively sane throughout graduate school (and beyond), as well as for listening to sections of chapters and idle book-related prattle with forbearance. Oh, and for giving me life *and* being my best friends. I love my wonderful in-laws, Maggie MacDonald, Pat O'Connor, and Scott MacDonald, who each helped this project be realized. Thanks, Scott, for all the advice on publishing. And thank you to my wonderful hubby, Ian MacDonald, whose input has been essential to this project's development and whose re-imaginings of song lyrics have kept me entertained in the rare hours not devoted to researching and writing. Moreover, thank you for ensuring that I won't die alone in any sense but the metaphysical one. You're my love.

I deeply appreciate the interest, hard work, and help of my wonderful editor Lindsay Martin, the series editors Lucy Shelton Caswell and Jared Gardner, and all of those at The Ohio State University Press. Lindsay's patience in guiding me through this process has been as valuable a resource as her exceptional ability to make me to get to the point less circuitously than I am wont. Also, thanks to Rachel F. Van Hart for her exceptional work copy editing. My thanks also to my anonymous reviewers. You made it better.

Wittenberg University has been my home since my defense, and I am profoundly grateful to the institution and to my many kind, generous colleagues. Ken Irwin, Cynthia Richards, Robin Inboden, Lori Askeland, the English Department, and the Women's Studies Department are gratefully acknowledged for their support and friendship. I appreciate Daniel Murray for his exceptional work.

I'm also indebted to the Holocaust Education Foundation and especially the Summer Institute 2011 participants (Noah and Helene, you're awesome).

Before this was a book, my longsuffering dissertation committee at the University of Cincinnati waded through countless pages, applying both praise and censure liberally. Jennifer Glaser has been an extraordinary role model for me, Gary Weissman created one of the major intellectual turning points in my life, and Beth Ash's patience with me, and amusement at me, helped make a grueling process less so. I would also like to thank Jay Twomey, Laura Micciche, Sharon Dean, Michael Griffith, Tamar Heller, and Jana Corkin for various and sundry advice, wisdom, and also for being fantastic professors.

My appreciation to also to those who have encouraged me in the professional sphere in my work on comics. Thanks to Cambridge Scholars Publishing and John Cameron, as very early version of chapter 3 appeared in *Narrative is the Essence of History: Essays on the Historical Novel*. I am also grateful for the many opportunities I have had to present versions of these chapters, including those of MLA, MMLA, NeMLA, and elsewhere.

Thank you also to my extended family for all of the love, support, and laughter throughout this process. Uncle David, Uncle Richard, Aunt Jan, and Uncle Erik, I love you. Uncle Bobby and Aunt Camille, for the years of Appalachian Festivals, even mid-graduate school. Uncle Richie and Aunt Mary, Aunt Lisa and Uncle Steve, Aunt Linda and Uncle Ralph, Uncle Jim and Aunt Pam—you had a hand in this. Finally, thanks to my friends. Megan Kokesh, whose mission in life for the past sixteen years has been to get me to take myself less seriously and to take time for leisure. You've failed, but I appreciate the attempt. Julie Berthoud, your gracious spirit is an unfailing source of light for me. Pam Geisel, your practicality and ingenuity have been a gift. My cousins Sarah Helgesen (whose creativity and delight is a constant inspiration), Lucia Palmarini (whose humor and wit have sustained me), and Emily Ulm (whose joyousness I strive to emulate) have all made my world a better, brighter one.

My thanks to many others as well. There is not enough room to list all of the boons.

HISTORY, METAFICTION, AND THE AFFECTIVE POWER OF GRAPHIC NARRATIVES

Sometimes, story-truth is truer than happening-truth . . .

—Tim O'Brien, *The Things They Carried*

EVEN PRIOR to the 1954 publication of Fredric Wertham's *Seduction of the Innocent,* comics were popularly understood as a form that promoted moral decay. From tawdry detective stories to grotesque, gratuitous horror arcs, comics seemed rooted primarily in a negative moral universe, and many critics argued that readers would unthinkingly mimic the violence represented in the pages. However, I believe that comics should be understood instead as a form that naturally lends itself to the complexities of our contemporary ethical questions, particularly those surrounding how we narrate and receive history and how we affectively engage with historical atrocity. Because of their form, graphic narratives prompt the reader to engage differently with content, particularly in terms of empathy and identification, something rooted in the imaginative collaboration that metaphorically takes place in the gutter (although, structurally, I see the gutter more as a space that creates the "room" to imagine connections, rather than the space in which connections explicitly occur).

What is the nexus between ethics and empathy in graphic narratives? Their inclusion of both words and images affects the reader's relationship to characters and to the narrative itself. Furthermore, graphic narratives

1

engage the reader's emotions and ethical norms in complex ways in the representation of historical atrocity, and fictionalized treatments seek to comment on representational ethics, the ethics of spectatorship, and how point of view creates pathways for identification. This analysis is meant to illustrate how scholars and teachers may use graphic narratives that fictionalize real-world violence as ethical projects that employ the comics form in order to comment on how we receive the content. The formal qualities of graphic narratives—including the gutter, the staging of point of view, and the textual-imagistic hybridity—make them uniquely suited to questions relating to how we negotiate representations of extremity because their staging of the gaze and their staging of questions surrounding both how and what we remember prompts readers to consider their emotional and ethical relationships to the text. This approach highlights the collaborative nature of the form but also seeks to retain a sense of the friction created by the reading process. The graphic narratives I work with place a specific set of demands on the reader that question how they relate to perpetrators and victims, how they negotiate the imaginative possibilities in the form, how history is arbitrated through a network of perspectives, and how to ethically approach fictional representations of real events.

This book seeks to explore a number of questions. First, how do writers and artists use the *form* of graphic narratives to critique the ethical dimension of reader's empathetic engagement with characters set in a historical event? Second, how are readers' affective engagements with graphic narratives complicated by focalization and point of view? Third, how does the depiction or implication of violence in visual form complicate the reader's ethical relationship to focalizing characters? Fourth, what can fictional graphic narratives offer in discussions about affect and ethical engagement with texts that deal with real-world violence? Finally, I seek to explore how fictional graphic narratives that depict historical realities engage the reader differently than the well-researched genre of autographics.

The rise of comics and comics studies can be traced back to many of the fraught questions of how best to represent extreme experience. Art Spiegelman's *Maus* is generally credited with thrusting comics into the mainstream,[1] and the 1986 publication of the first volume stands as a watershed moment in which people were not only reading comics but they were taking them seriously. This derived as much from the gravity of the topic

---

1. It is also worth noting that Alan Moore's *Watchmen* and Frank Miller's *The Dark Knight Returns* also contributed to the growing interest in comics as a form. However, I minimize their contribution here because the academic and cultural attention to *Maus* dwarfs that paid to these volumes.

(the Holocaust) and the genre (memoir) as from Spiegelman's virtuosic work. Memoirs by Holocaust survivors were already legitimate objects of study and interest.[2] In the mid-twentieth century the memoir enjoyed a rise in popularity, and by the time *Maus* was on shelves, it was a dominant cultural force,[3] and Spiegelman's masterwork was legitimated by the generic resemblance it bore to "serious" works. This initially shaped cultural perceptions of which comics were sufficiently weighty ("graphic novels") to warrant attention by scholars and thinkers and which comics were "just" comics.

Graphic memoirs in the late twentieth and early twenty-first centuries were sanctioned by critics as valid—and valuable—representations. This came partly from many graphic memoirists' propensity to acknowledge and emphasize the history and structure of the form, as Spiegelman explicitly questions the appropriateness of a comic on the Holocaust in *Maus* while Marjane Satrapi includes a comic on dialectical materialism within her own graphic memoir *Persepolis*. This habit of metacommentary on the form also communicated to readers that the artist was not "merely" illustrating but was actively negotiating representation and meaning. This is captured in the term *autographics,* coined by Gillian Whitlock in her 2006 essay, and refers to Whitlock's desire "to draw attention to the specific conjunctions of the visual and verbal texts in this genre of autobiography, and also to the subject positions narrators negotiate in and through comics" (966). Self-consciously literary autographics like Alison Bechdel's *Fun Home* (2006) emphasized the comic as a space of intellectual engagement, while Spiegelman's *Maus* and Satrapi's *Persepolis* illustrate that serious subject matter is indeed appropriate to the form. The emphasis on autographics is warranted, and many of the masterworks of the comics form are the result of the adaptation of life-writing into graphic narrative. Whitlock suggests that "perhaps they have the extraordinary potential to—as Said suggests— free us to think and imagine differently in times of trauma and censorship" (967). The potential Whitlock notes has led to works like Lynda Barry's *One Hundred Demons*, David Small's *Stitches,* Derf Backderf's *My Friend Dahmer,* Chester Brown's *Paying for It,* Joe Sacco's *Palestine,* and Phoebe Gloeckner's *A Child's Life*; this short list illustrates only a small corner of the range of topics addressed in autographics. Furthermore, many scholars have examined autographics to explore how and why we represent memory, includ-

---

2. Primo Levi's *If This is a Man* (retitled in the U.S. as *Survival in Auschwitz*) (1947) and Elie Wiesel's *Night* (1960) are in part responsible for creating the genre/subgenre of Holocaust literature.

3. For more on this, see Ben Yagoda's *Memoir: A History.*

ing Hillary Chute's *Graphic Women* and Michael A. Chaney's *Graphic Subjects*. Autographics and the associated scholarship often explore situations of extremity—disaster, war, rape, trauma, disease, and violence—and consider how the representation of the act of witness is an ethical project within the genre.

The representation of violence is not, however, limited to the realm of autographics.[4] Comics have always been deeply invested in depicting acts of violence and their consequences in genres ranging from superhero to alternative. While I believe autographics have rightly received significant acclaim and attention, this attention has sometimes been granted at the expense of fictional comics, which have a different type of "extraordinary potential" in engaging the reader's imagination. We should not forget that Alan Moore's *Watchmen* was collected only one year after Spiegelman's *Maus*, and that other fictional works have been vital in shaping the larger cultural conversation about comics. Many of these works also engage with the questions associated with autographics, asking how and why we represent the past, to what extent memory is fallible, what is and is not "representable," and what a reader can gain (or should take away from) representations of violence. Alongside autographics is another genre that deserves an investment of curiosity, a genre that incorporates both fiction and fact and comments on the construction of both. To follow Linda Hutcheon's examination of historiographic metafiction, the genre that "incorporates [. . .] theoretical self-awareness of history and fiction as human constructs (historiographic *meta*fiction)," I will refer to this genre as "historio-metagraphics" ("Historiographic Metafiction" 5).[5] Historio-metagraph-

---

4. For an excellent account of the representation of violence in nonfiction comics, see Hillary Chute's *Disaster Drawn*, in which she examines the concept of witness in the comics form. Chute asserts that "pitting visual and verbal discourses against each other, comics calls attention to their virtues and to their friction, highlighting the issue of what counts as evidence" (7). I draw less from her study than I might have, had it not been published so recently, although the fictive element is an essential component in my discussion.

5. While there is limited space for such a discussion, I chose this term in order to preserve the associations between this genre of comics and postmodernism. Attacks on postmodernism in particular shaped this investment, including objections to postmodern theorists' propensity to question scientific discourse (as with Thomas S. Kuhn's *The Structure of Scientific Revolutions*) and historical discourse (as with Jean-François Lyotard's *The Postmodern Condition*). Following Hutcheon, postmodernist engagement with history is neither "ahistorical" nor "naïve and nostalgic" (19) but rather "question[s] whether we can ever *know* [the] past other than through its textualized remains" (20), re-creating, to my mind, narrative as a prospect of acclimating readers to the provisional. The provisional nature of the postmodernist project is—I would contend—highly ethical at its core because it seeks to continue questioning and learning.

ics engage in many of the same topics as autographics and seek to represent some measure of historical reality but also do so from a fictional vantage point. This term is meant to capture—as Hutcheon's did—a range of strategies employed in order to both illustrate historical realities and to question the way in which they are represented.

Questioning how we remember and narrate the past, as well as how we feel about it, has become one of the crucial topics of the twenty-first century. Henry Giroux has framed this in terms of ignorance, arguing in an interview for *The New York Times* that "ignorance has become a form of weaponized refusal to acknowledge the violence of the past," going on to assert that "what I have called the violence of organized forgetting signals how contemporary politics are those in which emotion triumphs over reason, and spectacle over truth, thereby erasing history by producing an endless flow of fragmented and disingenuous knowledge" (1). While Giroux in this discussion places emotion at the center of ethics gone awry, emotion also constitutes one of the most important tools in mobilizing individuals to alleviate suffering. Emotion can lead to disastrous (and even genocidal) political decisions, but it can also be the means by which we remember the horrors of the past or imagine a less horrific future.

This project came about because of a Holocaust literature class taught by Gary Weissman at the University of Cincinnati, in which I assisted. When we received the first set of papers, we were disturbed to find that—rather than engaging with the issues of representation we had lectured on at length—some students instead struggled to describe the ways in which their experiences were similar to those described in the memoirs and films that constituted the course material. This was a persistent thread in discussion as well, one we both found unnerving given the gulf between our middle-class college students and survivors of the Holocaust. There was a distinct change in the tone of discussion, however, when we began to work with Spiegelman's *Maus*. Students seemed better equipped to deal with the work as an artifact, and Spiegelman's incessant questioning of his own motives and methods of relating his father's story cued the class into a more productive intellectual engagement with Holocaust representation. While they still sought to emotionally engage with characters, they seemed more aware of the pitfalls of responding to a text with emotion alone. I had already been working with graphic narratives for some time, but this made me curious as to whether there was something in the *form* that prompted a different register of initial engagement.

Was it something about the way in which the comic panel was staged that invited a response deviating from traditional models of "feeling with" a character? How did the explicit point of view created by the comic panel communicate to the reader about the complicated nature of history and knowledge? How does the combination of textual and pictorial narrative create a different way for readers to engage with the content? The tension between word and image that is among the hallmarks of the graphic narrative form echoes F. R. Ankersmit's distinction between description and representation wherein, "In a description such as 'This cat is black,' we can always distinguish a part that refers—'this cat'—and a part attributing a certain property to the object referred to—'is black.' No such distinction is possible in a representation of the black cat, a picture or photograph of it" (39). Within the graphic narrative, we are presented both with descriptions—of characters' thoughts, feelings, discussions, et cetera—and representations wherein the image stands in for a range of other descriptions. For Ankersmit, representation has the possibility of ordering reality; description refers to conditions, while representation makes narrative sense of it (56–57). Both representation and description occur from a particular point of view, and point of view is embedded in a network of values, desires, and beliefs that shape the way we receive both images and words. Point of view is an essential component of the emotions, as Peter Goldie outlines in his introduction to *The Emotions: A Philosophical Exploration*. Emotions are experienced from a given position and are directed toward an object (2, 16–17), which links how emotions are created, felt, and narrated with contemporary understandings of history as accounts that unfold from a particular point of view.[6] As Goldie elaborates in *The Mess Inside*, when we think of an emotion from a given position "it will be necessary to piece together or fill in the emotion's narrative" (181), that is, linking the person, the emotion, and the source of that emotion.

Furthermore, this can be linked to recent findings about cognition, in which neuroscientists have demonstrated certain links between language and the mental simulation of the visual field. Like Karin Kukkonen, I find a partly cognitive approach to comics useful because it "provide[s] an understanding of how readers make meaning from what they see on the comics page" (*Contemporary Comics Storytelling* 6). Benjamin K. Bergen collects this research in *Louder Than Words*, arguing that we engage with language through "embodied simulation," whereby we mentally simulate data received from language in order to create meaning. The hypothesis he explains is "Maybe we understand language by simulating in our minds

---

6. F. R. Ankersmit notes in *Historical Representation* that "we simply seem to have lost all confidence in points of view pretending to offer a synopsis of either the past itself or of how best to deal with it" (2).

what it would be like to experience the things that the language describes" (13). Embodied simulation should not be understood as a monkey-see-monkey-do cliché. In "Space, Time, and Causality in Graphic Narratives," Kukkonen notes that "to a large extent, our perception is constituted by the way we (can) appropriate the space around us" (51), that is, our point of view is influenced by the possibilities available for negotiating our environment. This means, in terms of representation, that when we view an image, the scenery and character interactions within the panel define the parameters whereby we imaginatively enter the world of the comic. That "readers of comics, too, experience bodily echoes of the motions and actions they observe" means that there are several levels by which readers perceptually connect with the comics page, including traditional physical levels (like turning or scrolling), physical-mental levels (embodied simulation and attention to point of view), as well as the imaginative levels in which readers fill in connections (53). This has repercussions for how we understand our emotional engagement with characters as well as how we understand the function of representation along the visual-verbal planes of comics.

REPRESENTING THE UNREPRESENTABLE

When employing the term "representation," I am seeking to retain its ambivalence. Representation is a term that can refer both to text and image, to fiction or fact. In *The Future of the Image*, Jacques Rancière argues that it relies on the fact that "speech makes visible, refers, summons the absent, reveals the hidden" (113), but it also masks, while images undermine the revelatory power of speech but simultaneously need speech attached to be legible.

The term "representation" is fraught with difficulties, however, when one seeks to engage with historical atrocity. The field of Holocaust studies began in part with questions about representation, between Hannah Arendt's conceptualization of the "banality of evil"[7] and Saul Friedländer's arguments that the horror of the Holocaust resisted representation in language,[8] the questions of how and whether to represent such extremity have been at the core of discussions about genocide since Raphael Lemkin coined the term.[9] Concerns about the representation of atrocity include

7. *Eichmann in Jerusalem: A Report on the Banality of Evil.* New York: Viking, 1968.

8. *Probing the Limits of Representation: Nazism and the "Final Solution."* Cambridge, Mass.: Harvard University Press, 1992.

9. Raphael, Lemkin (April 1946). "The Crime of Genocide." American Scholar 15.2: 227–30.

the potential for a representation's inaccuracy, the supposed tendency of images in particular to inure the viewer to violence, and the violation against the victims depicted in viewing them in extremity. Another important concern—one particularly important to my work in this volume—is the question surrounding the ethics of viewing representations of atrocity in order to empathize with victims.

An important tension in the writing on the representation of atrocity concerns the truth-value of the representation and how the viewer or reader receives that image. Susan Sontag, in her landmark *Regarding the Pain of Others*, remarks that "'the camera is the eye of history,' Brady is supposed to have said. And history, invoked as a truth beyond appeal, was allied with [. . .] realism, [wherein] one was permitted—required—to show unpleasant, hard facts" (52). In this phrasing, the photographic and historical representations are figured as windows into *reality*, reflecting objective conditions as they actually are. As Weissman notes in *Fantasies of Witnessing*, "Scholars and survivors frequently speak of the unimaginable, unrepresentable nature of that reality, but in practice, what can be represented of the Holocaust is often determined through a practical consideration of what is most suitable for a target audience" (10). On one hand, certain types of representation are viewed as being potentially more truthful than others. But on the other hand, there are certain things that cannot be represented for either ethical or pragmatic reasons. Weissman suggests that limitations placed on representation are partly concrete in terms of what *can* be taken in by a particular group, while Sontag emphasizes that the demands placed on certain forms show us "the Truth."

Emphasizing facticity at the expense of emotional or ethical concerns within what is represented can potentially impoverish our experience of history, and facts alone do not always sufficiently engage with the persistent ethical questions surrounding histories of violence. Because we have a "tendency to privilege and identify with those histories that resonate with one's own sense of identity" (Weissman 7), representing atrocity in a way that is accessible for at least a certain audience is necessary for deepening our understanding of others' experience. In addition, given the subject positions of most Western readers, our identification may very well hew to the perpetrators or bystanders rather than the victims. Sontag also notes that "the more remote or exotic the place, the more likely we are to have full frontal views of the dead and dying. [. . .] These sights carry a double message. They show a suffering that is outrageous, unjust, and should be repaired. They confirm that this is the sort of thing which happens in that place" (70–71). Geographical distance and cultural contexts can unwittingly depict victims of history as corroborations of attitudes that consider the victims' bodies as "natural" sites of violence (and perpetrators as "naturally savage"). The complicating element—the distance between the assumed audience's experiences and those of the victims shown in the representation of atrocity—is further emphasized by the fact that "being a spectator of calamities taking place in another country is a quintessential modern experience [. . .] Wars are now also living room sights and sounds" (18). The tension in these discussions is rooted in four distinctions. First, there is the relative distance between the experiences of the viewer and the suffering that is shown. Recognizing the differences between our own circumstances and those of the victim of a massacre is essential to any ethical project, but the victims should not be represented as so dissimilar as to be inhuman, and, moreover, their suffering cannot be framed in the same manner as "entertainment." Second, there is the question of how the commonplace viewing of such atrocities serves to expand or contract that distance in various cases. Third, there is the question of how the representation of suffering operates on one level as a reflection of truth—the reality that something has happened—and on another level in dialogue with the viewer as something that is supposed to communicate a message about how we frame and remember atrocity.[10] Fourth, there are the relationships between the reader/viewer, the author/artist, the actual historical event and the people it involved, and the representation thereof.[11] This list is meant merely to point out concerns for the sake of clarity, but I will not be treating these distinctions as necessarily separate concepts, and a list fails to capture how complicated our relationship is to historical truth and historical representation. As Nadine Gordimer ostensibly claimed, "The facts are always less than what really happened" (Toppin 76).

SITUATING THE FORM

Representational choices and awareness of audience serve to inhibit or facilitate the viewer's ability to understand and affectively relate to what is being shown. In this volume, I am particularly interested in how point

---

10. Rancière's *The Future of the Image,* particularly "Are Some Things Unrepresentable?" provides a more in-depth discussion of the philosophical questions about "unrepresentability," particularly elaborating the tension between the artistic representation and the event itself.

11. LaCapra's assertion that "it is misguided to see trauma as a purely psychological or individual phenomenon. It has crucial connections to social and political conditions and can only be understood and engaged with respect to them" is essential to understanding the relationship between historical atrocity, its representation, and the communities that receive it (xi).

of view as a representational choice can send complicated messages about how a viewer is meant to receive images. While Sontag is writing predominantly about photography and news media and Weissman is writing about documentaries, films, and survivor testimony, their remarks serve as an appropriate backdrop for the discussions that should take place in comics studies about the representation of atrocity. Unlike the above forms, graphic narratives are (in general) more obviously mediated; that is, they are composed of drawn rather than photographic images, and through the use of dialogue bubbles and text boxes, panels and frames, they are more clearly a product of a human hand.[12] Charles Hatfield emphasizes this in *Alternative Comics,* asserting that "the reader's responsibility for negotiating meaning can never be forgotten, for the breakdown of comics into discrete visual quanta continually foregrounds the reader's involvement. The very discontinuity of the page urges readers to do the work of inference" (xiv).

Before clarifying this, please bear with me through a few elementary remarks on the comics form so that the reader is aware of the parameters from which I'm working. It is generally agreed that comics are composed of static images that are often linked together by the gutter[13] (or a frame). Most comics include text and usually rely in part on the interplay between the image and the text, which are physically integrated or juxtaposed. Critics generally agree that the panel is the basic unit of comics, and it is com-

---

12. Pascal Lefèvre also explains this in "Recovering Sensuality in Comics Theory."

13. Arguably, the gutter has always been an essential part of the comics form, particularly if one considers *comics* and *sequential art* as mostly synonymous categories. Prior to the work of William Hogarth, the progenitor of what we commonly understand as graphic narrative, sequential art of many kinds employed negative space that perceptually both divided and linked discrete iconic content. Friezes, for example, often employ gutter-like spaces that indicate a temporal or spatial change, while Aztec codices contain gutters within a larger single-page narrative. Hogarth's *A Harlot's Progress* and *A Rake's Progress* rely upon the space between each individual engraving to imply both temporal and perspectival transitions, as well as implying a space for personal reflection on the connections between the static images (especially in regard to their moral content). Throughout the history of the form, comics have employed gutters in part for clarity and to guide the reading process. Gutters sometimes marked shifts in perspective or transitions through time or space, but artists often also divide components of actions into parts or behave as visual synecdoche. Stan Lee (1978), Will Eisner (1985), and Scott McCloud (1993) have all insisted on the importance of the gutter as a part of comics grammar. Moreover, Chute argues that "while all media do the work of framing, comics manifests material frames—and the absences between them. It thereby literalizes on the page the work of framing and making, and also what framing excludes" (*Disaster Drawn* 17). The emphasis on limitation defined by Chute gestures toward one of the functions that is literalized by the presence of the gutter but is in effect always there in comics whether or not a gutter is visually present.

posed of the interior (where the action occurs), a frame (which may or may not be distinct from the content), and the surrounding gutters (the spaces between panels). In addition to basic physical properties, comics also rely on several concepts. Will Eisner's 1985 *Comics and Sequential Art* established the comic artists' manipulation of point of view in the panel as an essential component of the art form. "Functioning as a stage, the panel controls the viewpoint of the reader; the panel's outline becomes the perimeter of the reader's vision and establishes the perspective from which the site of the action is viewed. This manipulation enables the artist to clarify activity, orient the reader and *stimulate emotion,*" according to Eisner (88, emphasis mine). The stimulation of emotion occurs in concert with reader orientation and illustration of the situation, that is, the point of view represented. What is depicted is part of what creates an emotional register for the reader. Scott McCloud's 1993 *Understanding Comics* introduced the term "closure," which refers to the process by which the "human imagination takes two separate images and transforms them into a single idea" in the gutter (66). The gutter is a space that cues the reader to imaginatively connect two or more panels, but there is not a direct projection of that connection into the space of the gutter. The representations within the panels show the reader a scene, but the gutter figuratively prompts readers to engage with what is depicted, creating connections between images and ideas as a part of the reading process.

Furthermore, this imaginative engagement has repercussions for our emotional engagement. McCloud also introduces the concept of icons, "any image used to represent a person, place, thing, or idea" (27), which he says can prompt the reader to identify with characters. "When you look at a photo or realistic drawing of a face—you see it as the face of another. But when you enter the world of the cartoon—you see yourself," argues McCloud (36). The perspectival structure gives access to a range of vantage points within the narrative, which has implications for how graphic narratives can be read as affectively productive. The affective dimension of graphic narratives suggests ways that the form produces an ethical framework for the reader. Reader's feelings, their level of identification and affective attitude, are critical in terms of reception but are also essential to the political project of the text. Eisner's and McCloud's concepts are foundational but are not without revision and elaboration, which I will explore further in a discussion of the consequences of the form.

Readers' awareness of the graphic narrative as something *produced* is embedded in the form, which gives comics the possibility of engaging in commentary on the production of history and its violences. In particular, the constructedness of the page, highlighted by the gutter, creates a space of imaginative possibility. The concept of embodied simulation works at the imagistic level and curiously taps into the structure of graphic narratives. While in studies on cognition in psychology and neuroscience embodied simulation refers to humans' capacity to mentally visualize language as they read or hear it, graphic narratives tap into this capability by using the gutter as the space of collaboration. If the reader projects a connection between the two static images on either side, then, according to McCloud, "Every act committed to paper by the comics artist is aided and abetted by a silent accomplice" (68). In his 1999 *Système de la bande dessinée,* published as *The System of Comics* in English in 2007, Thierry Groensteen concedes that "the gutter, insignificant in itself, is invested with an arthrologic function [the task of joining together] that can only be deciphered in light of the singular images that it separates and unites" (114). This distinction, that the gutter is invested with meaning through the images that stand on either side of it, is important to the reader's affective engagement in that those images shape a range of imaginative possibilities, and, ultimately, those possibilities are shaped by the perspective from which the panel is rendered. However, he rejects the idea that the gutter "is the interior screen on which every reader projects the missing image (or images)" (113), which is in line with his assertion of "the primacy of the image" (3). Similarly, Neil Cohn insists that "the gutter does not provide any meaning—the content of the panels and their union does" (136), conceding only that "readers definitely make inferences for information that is not depicted, this inference does not occur 'in the gutter'" (1).

It's true that we don't automatically project a new connecting image into the space between the panel we just read and the panel we are about to read. What we instead do is use the gutter as a cue to employ our imagination in connecting the images. It is not so much that the collaboration occurs "in" the gutter in the initial reading process but that the gutter provides an essential space whereby we are cued to a creative investment. In Groensteen's view, it is the image to be deciphered that must be the emphasis, but this negates comics' reliance on the tension "between reading-as-experience and the text as material object" outlined by Hatfield (36). I hold to the view that the physical form of comics and the action of producing meaning are mutually enriching. That there is a "relationship between narrative content and physical medium" is paramount (63), and, moreover, this relationship stresses "the distance between text and reader, and foreground[s] the reader's creative intervention in meaning-making" (63). Indeed, if the gutter was as minimally functional as Cohn and Groensteen assert, why has it remained such an essential part of comics? The (normal) physical features of graphic narratives generally serve some function, and while McCloud's initial explanation of closure is insufficient, it is nonetheless the space that—I argue—allows the reader to invest in rapport with the content in the panels.

There are a number collaborative relationships outlined above. The first is embedded in Eisner's discussion, in which the artist's choice about point of view encourages the reader to see the scene not only from a particular perspective but also to have a certain affective relationship with that content. McCloud's definition of the icon also relates to this because—like point of view—it refers to a specific characteristic in a panel. In this case, the reader may be prompted to identify with a particular character or may invest another icon with their own sense of its symbolic meaning. Closure occurs across panels and involves the imaginative reconciliation of different iconic content in the panel and often different points of view. This takes place partly through the cognitive process of embodied simulation because—like Hatfield and others—I understand comics as a form in their own right wherein text and image cannot be easily separated into distinct functions. The reader's perception of the comic as a created artifact—and not simply a window through which they can view a scene—is embedded in the relationship between the narrative content and the formal aspects of the page, creating several levels of awareness of how the content is being delivered.

This metacognitive level is significant also to the relationship between text and image alluded to above. Both Groensteen and, as Hatfield rightly notes, McCloud downplay the importance of the verbal in this development, arguing that "the process of transitioning, or closure, depends not only on the interplay between successive images but also on the interplay of different codes of signification: the verbal as well as the visual" (Hatfield 44). The reader interacts with text and image simultaneously, and rather than employing two distinct types of literacy—the traditional literacy of reading and visual literacy—they are instead employing a literacy that combines elements of both. Comics are, to a certain extent, their own language.[14] He explains that "in comics word and image approach each

14. The argument about whether or not the comics form constitutes its own language is beyond the scope of this project. However, this has been written about extensively. Robin Varnum and Christina T. Gibbons's 2002 *The Language of Comics* collects a number of early essays on the subject, including works about visual grammar, graphic enunciation, and the ways in which textual and visual content can both undermine and reinscribe one another in the form. More recently, Barbara Postema's *Narrative*

other [. . .] the written text can function like images, and images like the written text" (36). Insisting that comics destabilize the distinctions between word and image, between perceived and received information, Hatfield notes that "pictures are not simply to be received; they must be decoded" (37). When we are confronted with an image—much like when we are confronted with a word or phrase—we bring our own experiences and ideas to bear upon that image in order to make sense of it. Rather than projecting ourselves simply into the cartoony face of a character, we are also recognizing that face and other symbols, as well as words, and bringing our own experiences of these depictions into conversation with the narrative content. As Kukkonen remarks, "the textual elements in comics can signify different things in different contexts" (23), and between our own associative leaps and the varying contexts informing a graphic narrative, a complex network of possibilities for reception emerges.

These collaborative relationships recall the tensions I outlined in my discussion of representations of atrocity. When we seek out literatures on historical disaster, we are often inspired by an admirable desire to "feel with" the victims, as well as to learn warning signs so as to heed the call of "Never again!" However, while reading accounts of violence from those who experienced it firsthand, we *don't* actually experience what they did. Graphic narratives, because of the createdness of the page and the interplay of text and image, draw our attention to that distance. But to what end? If we want to "feel with" victims, are graphic narratives a poor choice of form? On the contrary, because the very constructedness that makes the reader aware of the gulf between his own experience and that which is depicted also cues the reader into an engagement more ethically nuanced than he might have had otherwise. The relative "truth" of a particular account of genocide, for example, is not something most caring, compassionate human beings are inclined to question. Discussions of audience or stylistic choices can, in the case of survivor testimony, feel positively sacrilegious. The comics form, however, frees the reader to discuss *choices* made

---

Structure in Comics (2013) and Neil Cohn's *The Visual Language of Comics* (2014) argue persuasively for two very different views. Cohn contends that there is indeed a "grammar" of comics that can be understood in light of studies of cognition, while Postema focuses on the ways in which the narrative structure of comics creates meaning. While Cohn sets his own and Postema's arguments in opposition in his short article "Building a Better 'Comic Theory,'" instead, these two scholars can be understood in terms of offering alternative approaches (one scientific and one narratological) that provide different outcomes.

about representation and thus engage more deeply in the ethical project of cultural memory.

Furthermore, closure as I see it automatically has an ethical dimension; who you are and who you are prompted to identify with, how you are prompted to make inferences about what is and isn't depicted, how you make sense of your own imagination in relation to what is depicted, these are only a few areas in which comics create a *different* ethical universe for the reader. For example, identifying with a perpetrator and identifying with a victim are two very different ethical relationships with a text. Prompting the former may be the author's way of asking us to think of the ways we benefit from historical atrocity, while prompting the latter may be an author's plea to alleviate suffering. The author may place different demands on the reader in different places in the text to help the reader understand history in a more nuanced way and to better connect with how people make complicated decisions even in the context of moral extremes. Our representations of history have consequences, and those representations have the possibility of deploying empathy and identification in a variety of ways that make us see a situation through different points of view. However, too often the voices of the victims, the marginalized, and those subject to extreme oppression and violence are not included in the historical record. This is sometimes because no one asks, sometimes because we can't understand, but also, sometimes, because those who would speak have been destroyed. Fictional representations of historical atrocity open the possibility of reincorporating victims' voices, but that is not all they offer. As I mentioned above, prompting a connection with a perpetrator, choices about employing emotionally charged iconography (like Confederate flags) or situations (like the gruesome murder of favorite characters), can also be ethical choices made by the author. Perhaps what I find more important about this is—in graphic narratives—because of how the reader is situated in relationship to the characters and the content, our own complex ethical position (very often, as beneficiaries of the suffering we are consuming) becomes more legible. This, I think, creates an important metacommentary within comics about the insufficiency of emotional response, in which the reader's initial connections may be questioned or subverted, or their affective relationship to the text is illustrated as only the first step of a longer journey.

The "gutter" in *Ethics in the Gutter* encapsulates not only the literal gutter—the blank space between panels—but also the range of perspectives embedded in the work and the choices made by artists and writers to not say and not show. The gutter is not only the physical space between two discrete depicted moments in the panel but is also what it implies: not everything is shown.[15] When two panels are conjoined by a gutter, the gutter represents a space not merely of "imaginative possibility," as termed by McCloud, but also of material evidence of how the gaze of the reader is situated in specific ways in relation to what is shown. Matthew Sutherlin used the metaphor of the brain to emphasize the importance of the gutter. He writes that "the brain itself is a self-organizing system that creates a narrative from a semiotic network [. . .] the space between panels is a metaphor for the space between neurons" (10). In this formulation, the narrative is created along a certain trajectory, the "blank space" representing a pathway. The gutter is simultaneously many things: pathway, imaginative space, and consolidator of the gaze as it is represented in the panel.

Furthermore, the "gutter" is also the space of arbitration in regards to the narratives that we create that constitute both our individual and cultural memories. Fernyhough notes that "as a society, we are 'remembering' all the time, falling silent on cue for Armistice Day, 9/11, and other momentous dates" (243), but it is worth reminding ourselves that those memories are arbitrated, and, moreover, it is worth questioning which events are memorialized and subject to a communal recollection and which events (and people) are resituated as marginalia. That "such acts [of memory by a community] come with ethical and moral responsibilities, too" gestures toward the problems of cultural amnesia (243), which fixates on one tragedy at the expense of another, which can create screen memories by which a people avoid a difficult truth because it sits behind an image that is more palatable.

THE ETHICAL SITUATION

The term *ethics* has been subject to countless definitions, many growing out of Aristotelian notions of ethical behavior as a good habit of mind that is then enacted in the world. The emphasis here should be on the active assertion of ethical behavior in the world, rather than the passive state of

---

15. It is also important to mention that some comics do not feature literal, physical gutters, per say. In spite of the lack of a clearly defined space between panels, the comics form always implies what the gutter literalizes: the conjoining of two discrete images by both the artist and the reader. Furthermore, because the gutter generally denotes a change in perspective, changes in perspective even without the literal gutter imply the type of imaginative work needed for the form. Comics without gutters do not illustrate that shifts in perspective or imaginative closure are the property of gutters alone but rather that the gutter is not merely a representation of negative space.

being ethical. Ethics must be understood as actions in the world, as opposed to those conflating *ethics* and *morals,* an elision that serves to cast ethics in the same Manichean, passive framework often associated with morality in which one "is" good rather than one "does" good. Ethics can be understood in the sense of action in what Andrew Gibson—relying on Levinas—calls "the excess that cannot be known positively within any system of morality" (16). Here, morality is understood as a set of guidelines for good behavior, but its limitation is partly in its resistance to our affective and imaginative engagement with the world. How do we appropriately feel? Sympathize? Empathize? Articulate a better future? Memorialize the "truth" of the past?

Ethics in Gibson's definition grow out of imaginative processes and are rooted in the same imaginative negotiation we undergo when we seek to understand another's perspective or experience. We commonly call such imaginative engagement *empathy,* although this is in itself as fraught a term as *ethics. Empathy* is often defined in terms of the old adage exhorting us to "walk a mile in another's shoes," but this adage is usually half quoted and half remembered. The full proverb commands that we "do not *judge* until we have walked a mile in another's shoes." The primary clause is all but forgotten in contemporary repetitions of the phrase, so a demand to withhold judgment until one has experienced a near impossibility—living as another person for a time—has become instead a catchy way of co-opting others' experiences. Empathy is, however, a more difficult process. Peter Goldie defines empathy in *The Emotions* as "a process or procedure by which a person *centrally imagines the narrative* (the thoughts, feelings, and emotions) of another person" (195, emphasis in original). To empathize, Goldie argues, one must "be aware of the other as a centre of consciousness distinct from [one]self [. . .] the other should be someone of whom [one has] *substantial characterization* [and one] must have a grasp of the narrative which [one] can imaginatively enact, with the other as narrator" (195, emphasis in original).

Ethics and empathy are rooted in processes of remembering,[16] simulating,[17] and narrating. Historiographic metafictional graphic narra-

---

16. Henry Giroux, in *The Violence of Organized Forgetting,* argues that "America—a country in which forms of historical, political, and moral forgetting are not only willfully practiced, but celebrated—has become amnesiac" (25). While I do not believe Giroux's "disimagination machine," "a set of cultural apparatuses [. . .] and a public pedagogy that functions primarily to short-circuit the ability of individuals to think critically, imagine the unimaginable, and engage in thoughtful and critical dialogue" (27), is limited to America, I think that his emphasis on the connection between memory and imagination in relation to ethics is essential to arguments about how texts can create a collaborative space in which an ethical imaginary is possible.

17. Recent cognitive studies, including those of and cited by Benjamin Bergen in *Louder Than Words* and the work of Zwaan consider "immersed experience," i.e., "read-

tives also interrogate authenticity and memory but from the vantage point of an author/artist who is explicitly different from the victims he represents. The added layer of distance between author and experience serves several functions in these works as a metacommentary on the reader's distance from the victim's experience. In the deployment of extreme experiences on fictional characters, it makes an argument that it is allowable to mimic real-world atrocity in fiction. Furthermore, it demonstrates that, when rendering atrocity in a fictional context, there are specific parameters that must be adhered to in order to foster an ethical interaction between reader and text. These interactions have an overt ethical dimension, as described by James Phelan in his introduction to *Living to Tell about It.* He describes the reader's ethical positioning in fiction as "result[ing] from the dynamic interaction of four ethical situations:

1. that of the characters within the story world; how they behave—and judge others [. . .]

2. that of the narrator in relation to the telling, to the told, and to the audience [. . .]

3. that of the implied author in relation to the telling, the told, and the authorial audience; the implied author's choices to adopt one narrative strategy rather than another will affect the audience's ethical response to the characters; each choice will also convey the author's attitudes toward the audience;

4. that of the flesh-and-blood reader in relation to the set of values, beliefs, and locations operating in situations 1–3. (23)

Phelan's excellent delineation of the categories of ethical positioning are useful for both fiction (his focus) and graphic narratives. However, because comics are a distinct form, it is useful to consider how these categories are modified based on the interaction between image and text, panel and panel, and panel and gutter. The first level refers to what is explicitly said and rendered within the panels, and an emphasis must be placed here on the interplay between word and image, as the text may communicate a different message to the reader than what is rendered. For example, a character may show physical discomfort while claiming delight. The relationship of the narrator to audience and narration, at the second level, is compli-

---

ing or hearing a word activates experiential representations of words [. . .] as well as associated referents" (6). Essentially, words prompt us to embody a simulation in addition to simply intaking information.

cated in graphic narratives by the fact that there is frequently no narrator elaborated as a specific figure, whether first or third person, limited or omniscient. Instead, readers contend with characters narrating in dialogue and thought bubbles, while text boxes narrating other information may or may not intervene. The images instead are the closest thing comics have to narration, as there is clearly a hand shaping what is seen, but this is closer to an implied author than a narratorial figure. At the third level, the implied author is both author and artist and is communicating along at least two distinct pathways.

Embedded in these complicating elements of the form are several other considerations I'll be working with in close readings, including the relationship between what the image depicts and what the text relates, as these levels may either support or undercut one another; what is said is often betrayed by what is shown, because graphic narratives do not merely illustrate the text. Furthermore, the relationship between the point of view and what is shown will be a major concern, as it implicates all of the ethical levels outlined by Phelan. Graphic narratives generally do not have traditional narrators but rather are focalized through one or more characters, with whom the reader may (or may not) occasionally share perspective. For example, a scene may show a character inflicting violence from a third-person viewpoint, as though the reader is a bystander witnessing the act. Alternatively, it may show the scene from a second- or first-person viewpoint, in which the reader occupies the perspective of a character (I include second person here because the panel that shows violence first-hand, as if this is what the reader sees, necessarily addresses the reader as "you" — "you" are inside the character's head, doing this/seeing this). The choices that the implied author and artist make about showing a scene from a particular character's point of view or from a third-person point of view imply an ethical relationship between the reader and the story. Finally, I will be considering the ethics of the gutter. As discussed above, the gutter is the space between the panels that has been variously theorized as a pause, as a place in which the reader imaginatively connects the two separate panels, and as a space in which the reader is actively involved in constructing the text. At the ethical level, McCloud's discussion of complicity in imagining actions between panels is certainly important, but it is also important to question how gutters mark a change in the reader's position in the text. Hatfield's concept of the tension between both various panels and between the image and the text also implies a transition in the tensions within a relationship at these varying levels of signification. Rather than simply communicating two separate events for which the reader must provide "closure," the gutter also represents the shift from one point of view to another, signaling a transition in the ethical relationship between reader and character and reader and implied author. The reader, Phelan's fourth ethical component, is at the core of my project because historio-metagraphics, I will attempt to show, leverage a complex ethical and empathetic relationship with the reader in order to prompt metacognitive reflection in the process of consuming their historical fictional content.

Comics contain a metacognitive aspect of representation, emotion, and personal ethical positioning wherein the reading process itself causes us to reflect on the representation itself, our imaginative engagement with that representation, and our relationship to the content. The added layer of distance between author and experience serves several functions in these works, including as a metacommentary on the author's distance from the situation, the reader's distance from the victim's experience, and the distance between the experience and the representation. In the deployment of extreme experiences on fictional characters, it makes an argument that it is *allowable* to mimic real-world atrocity in fiction. Furthermore, it demonstrates that, when rendering atrocity in a fictional context, there are specific *parameters* that must be adhered to in order to foster an ethical interaction between reader and text. To demonstrate how these types of ethical positioning operate, I turn to a short reading of a scene from Denise Mina et al.'s *Hellblazer: The Red Right Hand*, which will be taken up again in the conclusion. This story arc provides a nuanced critique of the dangers of idealistic approaches to empathy and emphasizes the extent to which one must risk oneself to feel *with* and *as* another.

EMPATHY IS THE ENEMY

Mina et al.'s run of *Hellblazer* is a meditation on the problems associated with empathy, rather than an encomium. *Empathy is the Enemy* begins when the main character, John Constantine, encounters Chris Cole, who is overwhelmed by his empathetic feelings. In order to save his life (Cole is on the verge of suicide), Constantine erases his memory, and the two attempt to piece together how Cole came to this point. As the story unfolds, Constantine discovers that Cole was involved with a religious cult intent upon discovering the "Third Place," an alternative afterlife to Heaven or Hell. To find the Third Place, they crafted an empathy engine. The empathy engine is a building constructed in a sacred symbol that is designed to infect all of those in the vicinity with the ability to feel nearby people's emotions and to see their memories. When it is activated, people in the area are ill-prepared for the sudden flood of feelings and images it generates, particularly because in an average population, many individuals have committed terrible acts. The unsuspecting people in the engine's district are suddenly confronted with the memories of their neighbors and friends of when they beat their wives, raped their dates, molested their children, and murdered their loved ones. They are also forced to feel what victims in their social group have felt, abruptly flooded with traumatic memories of survivors of violence. While the group's goal is to inoculate the world with empathy for everyone they encounter in order to create lasting peace on earth, instead mass suicides ensue because people are unable to deal with the reality of feeling as perpetrators and victims felt. The city of Glasgow, Scotland, quickly devolves into a hot zone in which the empathy contagion invokes self-harm in the shock of feeling what others feel *as they feel it.*

The Red Right Hand begins with Constantine's explicit cultural positioning (see fig. I.1). The average *Hellblazer* reader is already aware that he is a rakish antihero from England with a penchant for accidentally getting friends killed. He has been trapped in Glasgow along with Steve Evans, another man involved in the construction of the empathy engine. In the opening panels in *The Red Right Hand,* Constantine's eyes are first framed in a thin panel, with a wider view following, as the text boxes relate his thoughts: "Glasgow . . . highest murder rate in Western Europe. Lowest life expectancy. Home of the knife-wielding twelve-year-old. But that was the good old days" (30). Here, Constantine is both narrator and actor, filling the reader in on the information they need to know to follow the narrative but also performing within the context of that world. In addition, it gives the reader context for the city in which the tragedy is occurring.

The relationship between point of view and what is shown is drawn out in the opening pages. The first two panels show Constantine looking directly at the reader. The third panel, a third-person/bystander panel, shows Constantine relaxing on a bench as Evans looks out toward the reader in horror, pleading for Constantine's help. The first five panels are marked by their outward directedness; rather than acting within the panel, both Constantine and Evans are looking directly out, into the reader's eyes. The reader is placed in the uncomfortable position of being the object of a gaze filled with terror on the part of Evans and anger on the part of Constantine. The fourth panel on the page shows a Praexis demon looking directly at the reader as well. Briefly, the Praexis demons are scavenger demons that move in packs, devouring the souls of the dead in the wake of large-scale massacres. The name (a misspelling of "praxis," the active

FIGURE I.1. John Constantine and other characters' points of view in *The Red Right Hand*. Mina, Denise, Leonardo Manco, Lee Loughridge, and Jared K. Fletcher. *Hellblazer: The Red Right Hand*. New York: DC Vertigo, 2007.

implementation of a theoretical idea) implies that they are the practice of the theoretical extermination, since they consume even the spirit. The final panel shows a close-up of the splay-eyed, crying, sweating Evans.

These shifts of points of view emphasize the relationship between the reader, the point of view, and what is shown. By positioning the reader as the object of alternately stern and horrified gazes, as well as the object of a predatory gaze, the reader is primed for a scene of destruction, but, furthermore, they are embedded within that scene. As Constantine narrates through these panels, he explains the way in which the history of Glasgow is less shocking than the scene for which we are primed, but as he narrates, he is also simultaneously ignoring Evans' pleas for help. At first glance, this appears callous but also functions to remind the reader of Evans's complicity in creating the empathy engine. The only panel without text is the fourth, in which the reader is directly confronted with a Praexis demon, which suggests that the demon represents something outside of what can be told about the event. In being confronted with three sets of eyes that portray anger, horror, and hunger, the reader is encompassed in the dread surrounding the scene, but through rapid shifts in point of view marked by gutters, there is no stable emotional vantage point.

The next page depicts the demons swarming around dead bodies, grabbing and biting spirits flying through the air. Constantine narrates in text boxes, describing the scene as "Rwanda all over again [. . .] Center of an empathy epidemic" (31). In this panel, the reader is viewing the scene that Constantine and Evans were observing on the previous page, but the reader's placement is flipped. Constantine is both narrator and focus of this panel, as we see through his eyes and are also given context through his narration. The average *Hellblazer* reader relies on Constantine for these explanatory moments, but he is also not the center of the moral universe in the series; he is reliable in his ability to accurately relate what is happening, but he is deeply unreliable in regard to his own ethical position in relation to what he tells. His sarcasm about the "good old days" of Glasgow betrays a callousness that stands in stark contrast to the unmitigated terror of Evans, who while weeping is difficult to identify with because his sniveling is contrasted with his collusion in creating the gory scene.

The Praexis demons swarm over bloodied corpses, fangs closing around the spirits as they flee the bodies. The rendering of the spirits is disturbing; rather than depicting them as transparent versions of the bodies they once occupied, they are instead depicted as cartoonish ghosts, barely resembling anyone in particular but, because of their iconic faces, resembling everyone generally, as McCloud describes in his discussion of the cartoony face outlined above. These, however, are not the smiley face used as a point of identification by McCloud but rather are twisted icons, screaming as the demons lift them out of realistically rendered bodies and bite into them.

On the following pages, Constantine remarks that "the contented Glaswegians suffered the most. The people happily dozing through their lives. Hurrying home after work and school to a warm tea and their favorite soap" (32). His account continues in this panel, showing that the city has been turned into a war zone. The soldiers loitering outside of the city are depicted in gas masks that obscure their individual features, again recalling McCloud's smiley face as that iconic image onto which we project ourselves. However, the gas masks do not invite any identification, nor does Constantine's narration of the cynical remainders of the population. In fact, the gas masks, because of their generality, inhibit affective connection, although, as will be discussed in the conclusion, it is on them that the fate of the world ultimately depends. Their specific identities hold the key to the empathy epidemic.

These pages demarcate a world in which Constantine is the arbiter of all we see. He remarks on the ways in which we are meant to read the deaths but nonetheless expresses confusion over why he and Evans are being avoided by the scavenger demons. The implied author represents Constantine during these pages as a filtering consciousness through which we interpret what we are given, but the average *Hellblazer* reader, already familiar with the character, would recognize that the characters surrounding Constantine are always in more immediate danger than he is himself. The character with whom the reader is most primed to identify is ironically the one in least danger throughout, a fact that at every moment shadows the ethical relationship between the reader and the work.

However, the reader is also in conversation with Constantine's narration, which recounts the way in which happiness renders individuals more vulnerable to the effects of the engine. Understanding empathy in this regard as something that is *life-threatening* suggests an ethical quandary. One identifies with Constantine in the work, a component of the construction of empathy, and thus is at risk in the world elaborated in the text. However, simultaneously, it critiques the level of empathy *normal* people show in the course of their daily lives as Constantine remarks that most "lazily assum[e] everyone else was as happy as they were" (33). Here, through Constantine, Mina critiques the reader's level of identification with Constantine by pointing out that this empathy does not go beyond the (fictional) character. Instead, those who feel the most when affected by the empathy engine are in fact those who feel the least in the day to day.

Empathy, in this work, is an *imagined* state: the theory of feeling what other people feel as they would feel it. In practice, empathy is an active engagement with a complex set of circumstances that must be negotiated with care and analysis. Empathy is the enemy insofar as it has become a passive, lazy theory rather than an active affective connection that is practiced.

The Praexis demons' position, when read against this interpretation, becomes more complicated. Rather than the practice of a theory of atrocity, they are instead representative of the relationship between the reader and the work. In the initial five panels, the reader sees Constantine and Evans from a vantage point within the carnage, a viewpoint briefly marked as that of a Praexis demon. In this, the normal *Hellblazer* readership is invoked, as the average reader does not buy the comic in spite of its depictions of violence but at least partially *because* of storylines that meditate on atrocity. In using the point of view of the Praexis demon as an opening to the graphic narrative, the implication is that the demons' *consumption* of the spirits bears a relationship with the reader's consumption of the story—and of comics as a whole. However, this is more complicated than a one-to-one correlation between reader and spirit-consuming demon. Because the pathway for identification runs toward Constantine, and the reader is shoehorned into the vantage point of the demon, the ethical dimension of the gutter is a space of ambivalence.

FOCALIZATION

Identification with characters is complicated considerably by Phelan's ethical situations, so that the reader—a site of her own attitudes, values, and expectations—is negotiating between the desires and attitudes expressed by characters within the story as well as how they are positioned by the implied author/artist. The reader's engagement with the text and ethical assessments about it are framed by how they imaginatively collaborate with the comic. Bergen notes that

> people are creating scenes in their minds from the perspective of an immersed experiencer. Motor simulation is intrinsically about projecting oneself into a body, often someone else's, and when you simulate what it would be like to do things someone is described as doing, you're taking their perspective not merely in a visual way, but in terms of what it would be like to control their actions. Understanding language in multimodal ways is a lot like being there. (92)

At the cognitive level, we mentally embody what we're reading or hearing, and so are invested at both mental and physical levels with the text. With comics, however, we are simultaneously presented with images that we have to decode alongside of the text, which on one hand presents a "window" through which we can "see" the scene but on the other hand, reminds us—through the frame and our imaginative closure—that we are *not* "there" in any real sense. This complicated arrangement prompts engagements that simultaneously feel close and are recognized as distant. Narrators in traditional textual fiction can close this gap, immersing the reader into the perspective they provide, but as I mentioned above, graphic narratives do not always have a narrator as such, and when they do, it is usually a character who is rendered within the panel as well. Following Silke Horstkotte and Nancy Pedri, I prefer the term *focalizor* for use in comics. They define *focalization* as "the filtering of a story through a consciousness prior to and/or embedded within its narratorial mediation" (330). Focalization, they argue, is a useful tool in the examination of the graphic narrative because it distinguishes between the "narrating-I" and the "experiencing-I." This distinction offers a way of articulating how the reader is invited to imaginatively project into the narrative, which has implications for the way tension and violence are perceived, understood, and felt.

Initially defined by narratologist Gerard Genette, the concept of focalization was later refined by Mieke Bal in *Narratology: An Introduction to the Theory of Narrative*. "Focalization is the relationship between the 'vision,' the agent that sees, and that which is seen [. . .] Because the definition of focalization refers to a relationship, each pole of that relationship, the subject and the object of focalization, must be studied separately. The subject of focalization, the focalizor, is the point from which the elements are viewed," Bal argues (149). Bal's definition emphasizes how focalization occurs within a network of objects and consciousnesses, which can be further elaborated (in comics especially) to include the reader's relationship to the focalizing character. While Genette developed the term in part to avoid visual metaphor—and in comics, *point of view, field,* or *vision* would seem to be equally useful terms, given the pictorial dimension of the text—*focalization* is preferable because it preserves the multiple layers of the narrative articulated by Bal, as well as the visual-verbal interplay that characterizes the form. These layers of narrative line up with Phelan's ethical situations, so that focalization refers necessarily to a relationship, and, according to Phelan, those relationships have distinct ethical characteristics and questions.

Characters and their behavior relate to the focalizor and through identification or investment to the audience, in various ways, and this crafts a legible ethical arrangement prompting questions about how characters act out their attitudes. Horstkotte and Pedri use Genette's distinctions between relative levels of access to information to demonstrate how the narrative conveys perspective, wherein "zero focalization [provides] the narrator with unrestricted access to information, internal focalization [restricts] the narrator's access to information provided by one or more focal characters, and external focalization [restricts] the narrator's access to the external information available to an uninvolved bystander" (332–33). These various levels of focalization, I argue, imply different roles and different affective states for the reader. In the case of zero focalization, the reader perceives the graphic narrative in the third person omniscient, while internal focalization develops the narrative through a character or set of characters whose perceptions frame the action. In the case of external focalization, the reader's access to the narrative most closely mirrors their access to what appears on a television news segment—viewing elements of the narrative at greater or lesser proximity to self. These levels have an affective context that influences how the reader perceives not only characters but their own position in relation to the narrative. For clarity's sake and because adding these terms risks clunky prose, instead of employing them throughout the work I will be pointing toward the specific ethical relationships that develop in relation to focalization.

Focalization offers a powerful distinction between how a panel is *framed* (i.e., what point of view it depicts) and how it is *positioned* (i.e., through which character's memory the scene is filtered or, alternatively, how the reader is connected to the characters in the scene). For example, a panel may depict the point of view of a nonfocalizing character, so the reader may see through the eyes of a relatively minor character in the story. Furthermore, it offers a pathway to empathetic engagement in which the reader fully immerses his consciousness in that of another. This empathy, rather than clarifying the ethical relationships at stake, instead complicates it. Kai Mikkonen effectively discussed the tension between these modes of delivery in "Presenting Minds in Graphic Narratives," remarking that the "spatially determined perspective of the graphic image is usually marked, as in images in narrative film, by a relative independence from the center of perception, e.g. from the character whom the story follows, and from the verbal narrative information that accompanies the image" (309–10). While the focalization of a graphic narrative is often bound to several characters, these characters generally appear within panels. On rare occasions, however, the scene is focalized through the character as a perception, in order "to see, as it were, through this character's eyes" (310). The subjective viewpoint is an important intervention in regard to empathy, as the reader is not only occupying the perspective of a character but is also meant to provide closure between the panels, imagining even what the focalizing consciousness does not show.

Furthermore, as Goldie asserts, empathy is not necessarily tied to ethical action because it is "consistent with indifference: you can imagine the other's suffering, yet simply disregard it; or you might empathize with a person who has committed a terrible crime yet feel no normative demands to help him" (*The Emotions* 215), or, at the extreme, one may use her empathic understanding of another to increase their suffering.[18] Indeed, the term *focalizor* also preserves the ambivalent ethics surrounding the reader's empathetic engagement with characters, which also opens other pathways for understanding his own ethical relationship to a text. In order to feel what another is feeling, as mentioned above, one must have a clear characterization of that person or character as well as a sense of their situation, surroundings, and culture.

Empathy and focalization as defined above both align with contemporary cognitive understandings of how our minds make meaning. Bergen argues that available evidence points to the likelihood that when people encounter language, they immerse themselves in mental simulations. This immersion, the adoption of another's perspective, is key to the form of comics. But how does this relate to the historical element? Awareness of perspective and point of view has redefined historical writing, discussed above, so that while historians are still crafting narratives about what happened in the past and how it came to be, they are also increasingly aware of the framing of their writing, particularly in relation to subjects that demand an ethical stance. In 1989, Joseph Witek argued persuasively in *Comic Books as History* that comics should be taken seriously as historical artifacts that could impart knowledge about the past or about the realities of peoples' lives. The term *historio-metagraphics* is meant to add another dimension beyond the discussion of autographics and other fact-based comics to encapsulate works that deal with real-world events in fictional ways so as to comment on the way in which we shape narratives, receive them, and reframe them.

---

18. E. Ann Kaplan defines the term *empty empathy* in *Trauma Culture* to refer to "empathy elicited by images of suffering provided without any context or background knowledge" (93), but expanding this definition to what qualifies as empathy isn't a useful critical apparatus.

Graphic narratives use the historiographic metafictional layer of mediation to suggest several ideas. First, they use point of view and focalization as methods of drawing attention to the textual mediation between reader and event. While the events that are depicted are often "true," the reader is aware of the fictional nature of the piece as well, and these dual elements suggest to the reader that the story at issue is not the "whole" story, instead highlighting elements that have been obscured through focus on the "real" story. Furthermore, it highlights the role perspective plays in mediating any historical event, and graphic novelists' careful manipulation of point of view demonstrates how the way we are positioned in relation to the story inflects how we read. Second, the fictional dimension combined with the graphic narrative form situates the reader within a space of self-reflexive ethical and affective negotiation. Because of the play on perspective, readers are more conscious of their own vantage point in relation to the action of the text as well. Third, this strategy draws attention to the ethical and aesthetic dimensions of framing an event for the reader and how these registers work together.

Graphic narrative life-writing is certainly a worthy interest, and the quality and popularity of, and scholarly attention to autographics by Spiegelman, Satrapi, Bechdel, and many others clearly shows this. These were the works on the vanguard of burgeoning interest in comics, although equally well regarded in some circles are the "spandex" titles that deal with superheroes, as well as independent comics and fabulism. The eclectic mix of focal texts in volumes dealing with graphic narratives suggests that scholars are readily embracing the variety available in the form. However, scholarship on how historio-metagraphics engage the reader in different ways than autographics has been relatively sparse and, in general, focuses primarily on a historicist approach. Autographics are explicitly interested in the perspective and experiences of the author, an author who often renders herself within the context of the work. This maneuver has proven enormously popular both with the public and with critics, which has resulted in other types of works being frequently overlooked by comics scholars and others. The exclusion of other types of texts is partly due to autographics' claims to veracity (no matter their conscientious self-reflexive questioning). Historiographic metafictional graphic narratives, on the other hand, present a disconnected creating hand, and the characters that are manipulated within the pages of a work are more clearly at the whim of the tides of history. They are not recreating and framing their own story but rather are subjects even within their own story. The creator is unmistakably *outside* of the text as compared to autographics, a distance which points to a further level of mediation from the "real."

The author's relative distance from these sites of violence frees them up to reintegrate forgotten or marginalized atrocities that exist outside of our normal network of cultural memory and associations, to make visible the source of traumas still dealt with in many communities today. Michael Rothberg's *Multidirectional Memory* comments on the connection between memory and identity but importantly connects this to the shared memories in collectives. Historio-metagraphics seek to reincorporate what is left out of sanctioned cultural memory but nonetheless has persistent effects on the cultural consciousness. Multidirectional memory "highlights the displacements and contingencies that mark all remembrance" (15–16), he claims, and historio-metagraphics function similarly, to emphasize in both form and content the *collective* negotiation of what will be remembered and how and to critique the marginalization of important histories that continue to affect citizens today. Rothberg insists that "questions about recognition and representation are crucial for establishing and contesting *what* form justice will take, *who* gets to count as a subject of justice, and *how* or under what jurisdiction justice will be adjudicated" (310, emphasis in original), centering the collective remembrance and the representational memorialization of history at the center of the ethical project of justice in the present. Taking up these questions, to my mind, also means that it is necessary to engage with the affective relationships we develop with those representations, because we feel our way through both memory and ethical interaction. We do not necessarily make decisions about those emotions, but we are more likely to question how we came to a strong emotion when we are confronted with a narrative that allows us access to these questions about representation as well.

MOVING FORWARD

Charles Fernyhough's contention that "much of how we navigate relationships must be about negotiating memories. [People] negotiate an agreed representation of events in their shared past" (105) highlights the way in which memory is arbitrated through multiple perspectives, but it is important to emphasize that this representation may deviate considerably by group. When groups whose memories are left out of a broader cultural narrative, our shared history is impoverished. This "agreed representation" is a small, key part of the broader category of cultural memories, in which certain events are remembered and memorialized in a particular way by the population at large. Included in this category are the difficult histories—massacres, atrocities, genocide—and as with other forms of memory, these agreed-upon representations sometimes err on the side of convenient cultural amnesia. This book seeks to make central how these events can be retold to make marginalized experiences and events more central to cultural memory. By using the form of comics, the authors and artists surveyed in this text are employing a form that already insists the reader participate in the narrative process through imaginative collaboration as well as affective investment. By using historiographic metafictional techniques, they seek to expose the extent to which—in successive retellings—history often leaves out voices that change the meaning of our historical narratives. The case studies are ordered such that they begin with temporal contexts that will be relatively familiar to readers, the Rwandan Genocide of 1994 and then an alternate America in the 1980s, and move backwards in time to illustrate how historio-metagraphics negotiate a variety of social, cultural, and historical contexts.

J. P. Stassen's *Deogratias* is the focus of the first chapter, in which I study Stassen's choice to limit textual explication of the Rwanda genocide as an ethical decision. As a short graphic novel that relies more heavily on images than text, *Deogratias* is ideal for laying out the concerns for the rest of the book. *Deogratias* follows the title character through the post-genocide landscape of Rwanda as he begs for alcohol to dull his memories of the time before the genocide. The text vacillates back and forth between the present and the past, weaving a complex story of love, guilt, and traumatic memory. In the present, Deogratias is a sick alcoholic who, when he cannot find Urwagwa (a banana beer), turns into a dog as a consequence of his persistent memories of the time before the genocide. Stassen adopts the bystander as a focalizing figure, present throughout the recollections and Deogratias' experiences after the genocide. Unlike most autographics, *Deogratias* self-consciously avoids elucidating how what is depicted may be interpreted, and instead relies on point of view and gutter placement to direct the reader's engagement. Through these means, Stassen gestures at the silence surrounding the genocide in the era following it, and deploying memory, anthropomorphism, and point of view to destabilize the reader's allegiance.

The second chapter focuses on an examination of an often-overlooked scene in *Watchmen*: the attempted rape of Sally Jupiter by the Comedian. *Watchmen* is the most prominent text of those I adopt for my case studies, and furthermore, depicts a context familiar to readers: white characters in

America in the 1980s provides representations that are relatively familiar on the level of identity, geography, and temporality. Dr. Manhattan, Ozymandias, Rorschach, and other characters have been the subject of scholarship, but the attempted rape, and Sally Jupiter's subsequent decision to have consensual sex with the Comedian resulting in the birth of her daughter Laurie, is often bracketed as a dramatic side note. I argue instead that this scene constitutes an important counterpoint to the Rorschach narrative, and moreover, is among the most considered commentaries on perspective in graphic narratives today. The historiographic metafictional elements of *Watchmen* serve to underscore how point of view is arbitrated through a network of power. While Sally is a relatively minor character, the attempted rape she endures and the child she later conceives by her assailant represent the center of the two main plot arcs in *Watchmen*. I contend that this episode constitutes an important intervention into how point of view adjusts a narrative, and explicitly uses Sally as an argument for the way in which women's experiences of sexual violence are co-opted by grander narratives. I am also interested in the manner in which Moore and Gibbon's use point of view to make a metacommentary about the relative proximity of the reader to various characters' experiences. By offering specific points of view from male characters, they appeal to the assumed male reader's emotional engagement, but simultaneously de-center the victim narrative, commenting on how women become minor characters in their own stories. This central scene offers a legible commentary on the erasure of women in relation to atrocity, as well as an argument for the centrality of private experiences of sexual violence even in relation to large-scale public atrocities.

While remaining within a contemporary American context, the third chapter moves to examine Jason Aaron and R. M. Guera's *Scalped,* which follows a constellation of American Indian characters as they negotiate life on the Prairie Rose Reservation, a fictional version of the real world Lakota Pine Ridge Reservation in South Dakota. Adding the element of a less familiar set of characters with whom to empathize complicates the way in which readers engage with historical atrocities depicted in its pages, and while its present-day representation of America is familiar, *Scalped* seeks to interrogate the selectivity of cultural memory that continues to marginalize Native concerns today. Pine Ridge is the site of some of the most famous conflicts between whites and American Indians in history, including the Wounded Knee massacre. Pine Ridge became a hotbed of American Indian Movement activism in the 1960s and 70s, and in 1975, two FBI agents were shot and killed. Leonard Peltier was convicted of the crime, although many suspected that he was in fact innocent. The case came to stand in for the more generalized mistreatment of American Indians, and raised significant awareness of the traumatic elements of reservation life, including low life expectancy. By examining the subplot of how memory of the fictionalized version of the shootout is altered and negotiated by those who were involved, I seek to demonstrate the ways in which American cultural memory has ignored the historical circumstance by which American Indians came to suffer from the difficult conditions of reservation life today. Furthermore, I explore how claims to "authentic" American Indian identity involve a relationship to shared cultural memory, and clarify how these identity claims are connected to a history of repression that is often not acknowledged in the popular consciousness. Aaron and Guera use both textual and imagistic historical artifacts as inspiration for this tale of contemporary reservation life, in order to explore how historical trauma results in intergenerational cycles of poverty and violence. Over the course of the series, the writer and the artist manipulate point of view in individual comic panels in order to transfer readers' allegiances, and more importantly, in this process, cause the reader to acknowledge their own distance from these events.

In the fourth chapter, I add a more complicated temporal element, wherein the historio-metagraphic depicts the American landscape, but is concerned with exploring the experiences of marginalized African Americans in the past. This added temporal complication demonstrates the flexibility of historio-metagraphics in recouping and reframing history, particularly in *Bayou,* a two volume graphic narrative series that follows Lee Wagstaff, a young African American girl in Mississippi in 1933. The first volume opens with Lee diving down into the bayou to retrieve the body of a young African American boy named Billy Glass, who had been lynched for allegedly whistling at a white woman—a clear historical allusion to Emmett Till. *Bayou* becomes a journey of resilience even in the face of intractable, individually unsolvable problems. Lee's father is arrested for Lily's kidnapping, and she sets out to find Lily in order to exonerate him. In a "through the looking glass" moment, she steps into the bayou, and swims through into an alternate world. Immediately upon her arrival, she stumbles into one of Cotton-Eyed Joe's traps, and is speared through her chest. Although the character named Bayou stitches her up, the ghost of Billy Glass informs her that she is dying. She nonetheless journeys out to find Lily, braving a series of characters that stand in for different manifestations of racism in the U.S., including a monstrous Golliwog that tries to drown her in the bayou, roving bands of thugs with white sheets thrown over their heads, Jim Crows that descend on their victims and peck them to death, and various animals from African and African American folktales work on chain gangs.

The final chapter presents the most difficult context for the reader in terms of identification and ethical consideration, focusing on a single issue of the *Hellblazer* series, from Mike Carey's run, entitled "Third Worlds: The Pit." By using a work that concentrates on unfamiliar identity and historical markers, as well as a geographically distant place and a temporally distant atrocity, I seek to illustrate how historio-metagraphics can mobilize readers to question the ways in which they traditionally emotionally engage with graphic narratives. This short installment follows Constantine and his girlfriend Angie to Tasmania, where he attempts to gain information about the Shadow Dog, a creature reputed to be a harbinger of the apocalypse. He goes on a dream walk in an attempt to ask the spirits of the Tasmanian Aborigines, who were wiped out in a genocide during the 19th century. Constantine is instead deposited into the dream of the British soldiers who massacred the Aborigines, while Angie, in the "real" world, encounters the ghost of an Aboriginal woman who seeks to tell stories with her. This comic provides a powerful discussion on what accessing traumatic memories means, what can and cannot be said, and how point of view inflects one's understanding of history. By focusing on Carey and Frusin's use of the gutter in a comic devoted to consideration of the crossing of boundaries, I demonstrate how formal choices suggest an ethics of viewership. The comic, focalized through the white, Western characters, suggests a level of distance between the "whole" story of the genocide and what may be communicated, and furthermore, explicates the complexity of ethical situatedness in contesting narratives of pain.

I have also chosen texts that dwell on experiences that are distant from the author's life as well. *Deogratias* focuses on the life of a Hutu man, but the author, J. P. Stassen, is a white Belgian émigré who moved to Rwanda after the genocide. The passages in *Watchmen* that I examine are preoccupied with the marginalized experiences of women and the poor, distinct from Moore and Gibbons' lives. Jason Aaron's *Scalped* explores American Indian Plains reservation life while Aaron grew up in Alabama. *Bayou*, written by Jeremy Love (an African American man), focuses on an African American girl in 1930s Mississippi. The issue of *Hellblazer* explored in the final chapter focuses in part on the genocide of the Tasmanian Aborigines, but was penned by British author Mike Carey. I chose authors whose experiences were dissimilar from those of their characters in part to emphasize what historio-metagraphics can offer, but this was also a method of drawing a firm line between historio-metagraphics and autographics. Many autographics are relentlessly introspective, meditating on questions of authenticity, facticity, and memory. The authors of graphic memoirs take pains to analyze how they are telling the story, even in the process of rendering it, and often pointedly ask questions about the reliability of their memories in the pages of their completed works. Historiographic metafictional graphic narratives also interrogate authenticity and memory, but from the vantage point of an author/artist who is explicitly *different* from the victims he represents.

Each chapter draws from a different geographical and historical context as a method of highlighting how historio-metagraphics work across national and temporal boundaries to create spaces for identification and ethical reflection. These boundaries are—like the gutter—their own spaces of imaginative possibility, and while they are often seen as horizons or limitations, through the comics form, historio-metagraphics seek also to illustrate how reflection on those gulfs between experience can be productive at both the historical and ethical level. Rather than windows into the past, each of the chapters interrogates a work that insists on reader's presence and engagement in negotiating how depictions relate, what different points of view offer, and how their placement in relation to the content makes certain demands.

This study will provide a basis for understanding how point of view in historio-metagraphics operates as a powerful tool for creating more complicated ethical responses in readers through pathways to and obstructions of empathetic identification. *Ethics in the Gutter* is meant to supplement the growing critical literature devoted to the formal qualities of comics, particularly by focusing on an underrepresented genre that puts forward arguments about the ethics of engaging with extreme experiences. I have purposefully chosen texts that represent very different historical time periods and cultural situations to better foreground how the *form* of graphic narratives offers distinct ways of looking at both history and fiction. I have avoided conflating the Rwandan Genocide, sexual violence, mass violence committed against American Indians, the Lynching Era, and the genocide of the Tasmanian Aborigines as *historical periods* and as representations within literature, instead treating each text as an example of the historio-metagraphic *phenomenon* rather than as interchangeable atrocities. I seek to retain the ambivalence offered by this juxtaposition because it underscores the promiscuity with which readers render their empathy, which in turn foregrounds how the formal qualities of graphic narratives may be manipulated for ethical self-reflection.

Ultimately, graphic narratives that fictionalize dark episodes in history expose the fault lines between what we think we know about violence and what we fail to understand about the complicated circumstances of atrocity in the real world. The characters in the works I examine in this volume are often motivated by a desire for justice, or knowledge, or control over their destinies, but are often simultaneously unable to grasp their own failures. Moreover, the ways in which the characters and scenes of violence are staged in relation to the reader suggest that the representation of the divide between what we think we know and what we fail to recognize is less about making the historical realities transparently accessible and more about visualizing the way these failures can't be papered over by the pat lessons too often attached to actual horrors.

CHAPTER 1

BEING A DOG

Transformation, Focalization, and Memory in
Deogratias

We are preaching hope, standing on the bones of the past.
—John Ruchyahana

If the pictures of tens of thousands of human bodies being gnawed on
by dogs do not wake us out of our apathy, I do not know what will.
—Kofi Annan

DURING APRIL of 1994, much of the world was confused and horrified by
the images pouring out of Rwanda, images that prompted both sympathy
and a certain helplessness as they were rarely explained, making the audience unsure about what they were seeing. Refugee camps flashed on the
screen, along with occasional interviews with people bearing stark wounds
and scars across their faces and heads. While those on the screen were positioned as sympathetic victims, little was said about who they were and
how it had come to this (aside from the unbearably paternalistic and vague
phrase "ancient tribal enmities"). These stories and images were embedded
in no recognizable narrative, which on one hand enhanced the horror while
on the other depersonalized those experiencing the atrocity. The images
were ambivalent, and the mobilization of ambivalent images was part of
what allowed the slaughter to continue relatively unabated, because there
was no coherent narrative that would make sense of *how* to understand this
conflict.

The Rwandan Genocide suffered not from a dearth of images but rather
from a surplus of images that failed to capture the realities on the ground.
These images and snippets failed to differentiate between African nations

and to distinguish between perpetrators and victims, who were often living alongside one another in the refugee camps in Zaire and Uganda. Edgar Roskis, in "A Genocide Without Images: White Film Noirs" describes how journalists attempting to document and invoke international outcry in fact documented a more ambivalent space. "It was there, in Zaire, that most of the images of 'Rwanda' that are imprinted on our memory were photographed," he writes (240), a replication of the phenomenon by which all of Africa is seen as an undifferentiated mass rather than a continent of many distinct nations, cultures, ethnic groups, and histories. The Western vision of Africa as "large, anonymous groups of people floating through ethereal clouds of dust; the beautiful bodies of the ill and injured; the wide, imploring eyes of children" is meant to serve an ethical purpose (240): those at home watching these images are supposed to be mobilized to give aid to those suffering. However, in the very process of appealing to the better angels of our nature, the humanity of those in need is undercut. In fact, media attention to Africa often only comes when atrocity calls, profoundly distorting the Western viewer's perspective of African nations.

Western media has historically had little use for Africa, particularly nations like Rwanda that lack natural resources and significant tourism. Rwanda is the smallest African nation, its population composed of three ethnic groups: Hutu, Tutsi, and Twa. Prior to colonization, there were some ethnic tensions, but these were significantly heightened by Belgian colonizers who encoded the ethnic divisions as core identity markers. Hutus were predominantly relegated to the lower class, often living through subsistence farming, while Tutsis were favored for their lighter complexions and frequently exerted some control over the Hutus. Twa, comprising only a small portion of the population, were largely mocked and ignored. In the early 1990s, Rwanda was embroiled in a civil war between the Rwandan Patriotic Front (RPF) and the Rwandan Governmental Forces. UN peacekeepers were sent in to monitor the situation as the Arusha Accords were signed. Tutsi and Hutu ethnic tensions had risen during this period, particularly after the rarely discussed genocide of Hutu citizens in neighboring Burundi. The death of Rwandan President Habyarimana, whose plane was shot down in Rwandan airspace, marked the beginning of the genocide. An ethnic cleansing of the Tutsi population had been under discussion in the highest ranks of the Rwandan government for years, and while the Arusha Peace Accords between the governmental forces (RGF) and the Rwandan Patriotic Front were faltering, the government had been arming *interahamwe* militias, semitrained Hutus who could be rapidly mobilized to slaughter their neighbors. Since the genocide, numerous books have been written that explore precisely how genocide on such a massive scale was carried out virtually in full view of television cameras, reporters, UN peace-keepers, and the world by proxy. The history of Rwanda was vaguely for-mulated by Western media, which noted "long-standing atavistic hatreds" and "tribal enmities" as reasons behind the violence. By failing to note the differences during this period, the media painted Rwanda as a primitive state always on the verge of lapsing into war. In spite of the gloss of Rwan-da's historic ethnic divisions, it is worth noting that the groundwork for the genocide was laid during the colonial period; Tutsi and Hutu ethnic groups preexisted colonial occupation, but Belgian colonial rule codified differ-ence through identity cards that marked the ethnic group of the holder.[1] However, while these tensions existed, the period leading up to genocide was remarkable because of the inflamed rhetoric, the level of organiza-tion behind the violence, and other factors that contributed to the violence, including radio broadcasts by the RTLM, a militant Hutu Power station, persistent policies of disenfranchisement that were exploited to increase tensions, fear produced by the recent genocide of Hutus in neighboring Burundi, and so on.

The Rwanda Genocide has the distinction of being documented as it was occurring, making it an important event for inquiries into narrative strate-gies that resist an uncomplicated assertion of empathy. The real-time docu-

---

1. Prior to German colonization in the nineteenth century, Rwanda had repelled intruders because of a centralized power structure that allowed militias to be quickly called in case of invasion. Germany's claim was established at the Berlin Conference in 1884–85, which laid out the major goals for colonialism as "'effective occupation' and the 'civilizing mission'" (Taylor 38), goals that were continued when Belgium took colonial power from Germany after World War I. Belgian colonial rule also continued the practice of favoring the Tutsi based on the "Hamitic hypothesis," which theorized Tutsi ethnic superiority on the principle that Tutsi were "the remnants of the lost tribe of Israel, the descendants of Ham—Noah's son, banished to the south of the Promised Land" (39). Taylor describes the way in which the Belgians did, however, intervene in the Rwandan economic system so that "instead of a complex system of interlocking authorities who owed their allegiance to the Rwandan king but were locally in compe-tition with one another, the Belgians instituted a system where the powers and respon-sibilities of local authorities were clearly delineated both vertically and horizontally" (43). The annihilation of this redundancy, wherein a number of people in a region fulfilled the same role in terms of patronage, gave individual Rwandans little recourse aside from submitting to unfair patronages, and the hierarchical system that formerly protected the politically fragile through redundancy now inhibited the ability to move outside of that system, building tension that finally erupted into violence in the late 1950s. In spite of these contributions to a toxic environment, Hutu and Tutsi tensions long predated colonial rule, but the colonial apparatus created a system in which inter-ethnic divisions were relentlessly exploited.

mentation gave the illusion of access. "Everyone knows" what happened in Rwanda because it was one of the most accessible genocides in history in terms of the general availability of images and video recorded during the violence. However, much, if not most, of this access was limited to refugee camps, giving only a partial, incomplete picture of what was occurring.[2] After the extent of the violence was brought to light, media focused primarily on the viciousness of the massacres, ignoring the precise organization of the killings. The genocide was depicted as riotous and primitive brutality on a massive scale and was inflected by Western cultural expectations about Africa: namely, that Africans were simply cruelly slaughtering each other in an example of tribal warfare at a substantially swifter rate "than usual."[3] With the combination of expectations about African violence and the perceived accessibility of images from the field, not to mention a largely uninformed audience that knew nothing of Rwanda before the genocide, it is little wonder that the violence was so widely misunderstood.[4]

The Rwandan Genocide, while in some ways distant from the United States—the geographical center of the next three chapters—has also been represented primarily with a framework of Western media, which often

---

2. The fact that the genocide was largely not recognized as such during most of the major violence was problematic, to say the least. Like Roskis discussed above, Lindsey Hilsum writes of the often-uncontextualized documentation of refugees fleeing Rwanda in "Reporting Rwanda: The Media and the Aid Agencies" that "the story was not simple—were these people fleeing war or retribution? Were they victims or perpetrators? But the images were simple and recognizable: Africans on the move, living in camps, at the mercy of the generosity of the outside world" (173). This comment addresses one of the most problematic aspects of awareness-raising campaigns operating during the genocide. Because the images were relatively clichéd, and because they concealed the events from which this stream of refugees fled, their impact was mitigated by the idea that this was "Africa as usual," condensing a complicated situation into a regional archetype.

3. This hegemonic understanding of African violence has inflected reporting and U.S. policy in African countries, although the genocide in Rwanda was one of the events that most raised questions in the popular American consciousness about this framework.

4. The level of mediation between the viewer and the violence is not immediately apparent, however, because it operates at both conscious and unconscious levels. At the level of consciousness, we are aware that we are watching these events unfold on television, from the safety of our living rooms, but nonetheless, the events appear before us in full color—we can see the tears streaming down human faces. We try to imagine ourselves in this situation. At the level of the unconscious, we have certain cultural expectations of Africa and Africans—colonialism evacuated the specific histories of African ethnic groups, leaving only hallmarks of "primitivism" for Western culture to attach to the continent as a whole. The essential component is the ease with which free-floating signifiers of primitivism are converted into representations without specified sources.

misrepresented the violence and the historical circumstances that led to it. I open my study with this graphic novel in order to show the way that historio-metagraphics can work cross-culturally and transnationally as objects that may confront the Western viewer with an alternative perspective, representation, and method of memorialization.

First published in 2000, only six years after the genocide, J. P. Stassen's *Deogratias: A Tale of Rwanda* attempts to offer insights into the period leading up to the genocide and to show some of the results. Stassen uses *Deogratias* to critique the way images of the Rwandan genocide are consumed in the West, and the Western reception of genocide in general. Stassen is a Belgian comics writer and artist who has travelled extensively in Africa and presently lives and works in Rwanda. Though Stassen has a number of previous works, *Deogratias* was his first large-scale success. The graphic novel won the Goscinny Prize in 2000, after its French publication, and was translated into English by Alexis Siegel in 2006 for First Second Books, an American publisher of graphic novels. In spite of its auspicious beginnings, readers regularly take issue with Stassen's artistic style, his decision to shift time, and, occasionally, his renderings of graphic brutality. Perhaps most importantly, readers have regularly complained about the lack of a sympathetic central character with whom to connect when reading the story. These criticisms, I believe, demonstrate why *Deogratias* is an essential text to consider when exploring graphic novels that deal with atrocity. *Maus* has at its heart a desire to understand a distant experience and to connect with a remote father, while *Persepolis* develops a sympathetic protagonist who exhibits the familiar confusion of children at unfamiliar events, and the oeuvre of Joe Sacco is often a plea for understanding. Stassen's graphic novel has a different aim. Rather than creating an environment that encourages understanding, empathetic identification, and political action in the present, *Deogratias* is a warning about the problems posed by these practices. By focusing on the life of a perpetrator before, during, and after the genocide, Stassen forestalls the empathetic projective fantasy of the reader in favor of an ethical anticatharsis: the reader does not experience a surge of hope for the characters at the conclusion and instead is left to engage with what hope could mean in such a context. Furthermore, this choice satirizes the assumed Western reader's approach to texts that deal with marginalization and extremity.

The question of the representation of atrocity in a recent genocide is necessarily to engage with the photographs from that genocide because the present day provides images that seek to make suffering transparent. As Sontag asserts, "Photographs objectify: they turn an event or a person into something that can be possessed. And photographs are a species of alchemy, for all that they are prized as a transparent account of reality [. . .] Indeed, it is one of the functions of photography to improve the normal appearance of things" (81). The aestheticizing function of photography can be viewed as dangerous ("some things *should* be ugly") or as necessary ("beautiful things draw more attention"). Thus, the aesthetics of the representation of atrocity always have a political motivation. However, "There is no straightforward road from the fact of looking at a spectacle to the fact of understanding the state of the world," Rancière stresses in *The Emancipated Spectator* (75). This is reminiscent of Goldie's discussion of the ambivalence of empathy explored in the introduction, in which he describes empathy as not necessarily involving motivation to end suffering (*The Emotions* 215). The graphic narrative form can leverage this ambivalence in relation to images of atrocity by deploying point of view as a device for metacognitive reflection on acts of looking in relation to what Rancière calls "the intolerable image" (*The Emancipated Spectator* 83).

When Raphael Lemkin coined the term *genocide* in response to what was then known as the Shoah—the Holocaust—he sought to name a collective action against a collective whose end was to annihilate the latter's existence. This is not the naming of a single action but rather the naming of a collection of actions that in concert constitute the crime of genocide. Genocide is popularly understood in terms of the perpetrators and the victims and, when relevant, an outside force that seeks to protect the victims. However, the presence of the bystander complicates the neat perpetrator–victim dichotomy, and as Arne Josef Vetlesen notes in "Genocide: A Case for the Responsibility of the Bystander," the vast majority of those who come into contact with a genocide neither fall neatly into the group of perpetrators nor the group of victims. Those in geographic proximity *and* those spatially distant form the group of those who occupy "a passive role, that of onlookers, although what starts out as a passive stance may, upon decision, convert into active engagement" (520). In fact, in some cases of spectatorship, Rancière argues that "the mere fact of viewing images that denounce the reality of a system already emerges as complicity with this system" (*The Emancipated Spectator* 85). Vetlesen further points out that both genocide and "bystanding" are collective actions that diffuse moral responsibility. To be a bystander is to be aware of but be neither victim to nor perpetrator of a genocide, which is a painfully broad category. However, given the vast network of people who may witness (and act to alleviate suffering in) a time of atrocity at this period in human history, is it worthwhile to preserve the broadness of the term. By preserving a variety of meanings, this term can be used in relation to Stassen's method of commenting on the act of looking, which he returns to in a variety of ways throughout *Deogratias*, including characters looking at images, characters looking at one another, characters looking outward toward the assumed reader, and other formations that draw attention to the demands placed on the spectator.

Following the title character as he alternately recalls the times before and during the genocide and awakens in the present, in post-genocide Rwanda, the past and present storylines are juxtaposed, the temporal shifts marked in part by Deogratias's clean or dirty attire (from before and after the genocide, respectively) and the black frames or lack thereof bounding the panels. He encounters other characters, including a French sergeant who was complicit in the genocide; Bosco, an officer of the Rwandan Patriotic Front that helped stop the genocide; Julius, a leader of the genocidal *interahamwe*; and others. He remembers scenes from before the genocide, including his friendship and romance with two Tutsi sisters, Apollinaria and Benina. Periodically, when his memories grow too vivid, he attempts to drink away the images. If he is unable to find enough alcohol, he turns into a dog. *Deogratias* does not articulate how one is meant to read memories, self-reflection, or narrative instances.

By complicating empathetic response by placing a perpetrator at the center of the moral world of the text, *Deogratias* asks us to negotiate our own moral imaginations without the safety of a narrator describing an appropriate response. Lacking the conventional narrative strategies familiar in literatures of violence, it provides an example of how graphic narratives seek to comment on the ethics of consuming narratives of genocide. The careful manipulation of empathetic identification in J. P. Stassen's *Deogratias* illuminates the situation of the bystander. The bystander is the most frequently overlooked character type in narratives of genocide, an uncomfortable, liminal figure that cannot be as easily indicted as the perpetrator nor as easily made an object of empathy, as the victim. Stassen emphasizes how readers who are distant from the atrocities that occurred during the Rwanda genocide are also implicated by their spectatorship in reading the graphic novel.

In *When Victims Become Killers*, Mahmood Mamdani articulates the relationship between the Holocaust and the Rwanda genocide in part through the similarity in political and racial groupings. He writes that "whereas the Hutu were killed as individuals, the Tutsi were killed as a group, recalling German designs to extinguish the country's Jewish population" (8). Mamdani ignores the larger implications of the Holocaust as an attempt to produce a global extinction-level event, but the similarity remains, given the general goals. He draws an important distinction, however, when he argues that "the Rwanda genocide was very much an intimate affair" (6), wherein direct involvement in the killing was common, as it is estimated that hundreds of thousands of Rwandans assisted in the slaughter of their neighbors. This provides a pointed distinction between the historio-metagraphic *Deogratias* and the autographic *Maus*: rather than focusing purely on survivor reflections, because of the vast level of personal involvement, *Deogratias* must address perpetrator experience. Furthermore, because it is not the author's direct account of his own experiences or that of a family member, the reader is expressly aware of the complexity of telling.

Deogratias is particularly important in terms of the relationship between the author, the characters, and the audience because it is situated at a problematic postcolonial nexus. Stassen is a white Belgian, a member of a nation that was complicit in the historical subjugation of Rwandans, but he is also devoted to rendering the unconscionable behavior of some whites during this period. The implied Stassen renders Deogratias's story with a great deal of compassion, in spite of the grotesque nature of portions of the story. However, in spite of the consideration shown in crafting round, dynamic characters, the implied Stassen also does not shy away from indicting his creations, and the reader, for their compromises. As a historical primer, *Deogratias* is incomplete but functions instead as an affective map of the pre- to postgenocide transition of a nation.

Prior to the genocide, the title character is romantically involved with two sisters, Benina and Apollinaria. During the genocide, he is a member of the *interahamwe*, a Hutu militia responsible for the bulk of the massacres. After the genocide, he is only a madman, wandering the streets begging for alcohol and occasionally believing that he is turning into a dog when his memories become too strong. His individual life is set against the backdrop of one of the most sprawling horrors of the twentieth century, which is also one of the most widely misunderstood. The text resists identification not only through the use of a perpetrator as the protagonist but also through the use of formal qualities that foreclose identification. In ways that will be discussed in this chapter, the reader is offered a character's point of view, sometimes discovering that this window into another's viewpoint is not what it seems. In addition, the text incorporates historical realities alongside of mythemes present in Rwandan culture prior to the genocide, implicitly questioning the extent to which genocide is an object that is "knowable" and how a reader should negotiate the ethical relationships between the implied author, the main character, the victims, and the historical context.

Deogratias has to be understood in the context of Rwandan history, as its introduction outlines many of the basic historical events before and during the genocide, but it also must be understood as an artifact of Western intervention, as the introduction also emphasizes. Written and illustrated by a Belgian émigré who arrived in Rwanda after the genocide, it is qualitatively different from graphic memoirs, which deal with experiences of proximity, namely works like *Maus*, *Persepolis*, *Fun Home*, and others. The distance of the author himself from "the experience" of the Rwanda genocide articulates an alternative ethical and aesthetic paradigm by which we may read texts of genocide: readership not as a project of identification—and not as a call to empathy as the be-all-end-all of action—but readership as a project of articulating how resistance formulates an ethical reaction to atrocity. While a work of fiction, *Deogratias* adopts the flashbacks of memoir, which relate minor incidents in daily life that have become magnified by Deogratias's memory in the wake of the recent genocide.

In *Deogratias*, it is the bystander that focuses the narrative through a network of shared experiences to show how that communal knowledge may be disrupted in individual experience. The book switches between flashbacks and the present day, vacillating between the eponymous protagonist's experiences in postgenocide Rwanda and his memories of the time before the genocide. Prior to the genocide, he is depicted as an average young man trying to win the affections of two sisters. Apollinaria works at the local church, where Father Prior ministers to the local population. Father Prior and Brother Philip are committed Catholics attempting to do ministry work in the region, while another white character, a French sergeant, is immediately depicted as a crude, racist neocolonialist. In general, the panels are from various third-person points of view, wherein the audience is not watching a scene unfold as a particular character but rather as an outsider. In pregenocide panels, Deogratias becomes a bystander in his own memories, viewing himself from a distance. Pregenocide panels are also unframed, while postgenocide panels have a thick, black frame, a clear division between present and past. Before the genocide, the French sergeant was in the country, but at this stage in the narrative, it is unclear where he was during the genocide. After the genocide, the French sergeant has returned to Rwanda and retains his negative characteristics. Several other characters stand in for the larger political factions, including Bosco, a former RPF officer, and Julius, a former leader of the *interahamwe*. Bosco and Julius provide context for the political realities and cultural myths present in the period surrounding the genocide. Benina and Deogratias briefly date, and at the beginning of the genocide, he attempts to hide her in his room until she escapes to find her sister and her mother. He ultimately joins the Hutu militia and assists in the rape and slaughter of his neighbors, and at the end, tells Brother Philip, who has also returned to Rwanda following the violence, that he has murdered all of the other complicit parties, from other Hutu to corrupt RPF officers, through the use of poison. As with Deogratias's memories, the postgenocide panels have few moments in which the reader occupies a character point of view, effectively placing the audience in the same position as Deogratias during his memories, in which we watch the plot unfold but rarely participate in it.

Unlike many depictions of genocide, *Deogratias* does not end on a note of redemption, expressing hope for the future and the survivors' mission to educate and enlighten others. Instead, it takes place in the postgenocide landscape of Rwanda, where most of those who have survived were complicit in the slaughter, and so is permeated with a sense of irrecoverability and disruption. The text is structured to experientially mimic posttraumatic stress disorder. The protagonist of the title operates both in the present and the past, the past repeatedly disrupting his present-day life through a series of flashbacks that cause him to regress both physically and mentally. This regression is portrayed through Deogratias's literal transformation into a dog at those points when memories from his pregenocide life intrude on the present and he cannot find enough alcohol to dull his senses.

While the flashbacks in the narrative develop a fairly familiar coming-of-age story, this bildungsroman is interrupted by the genocide and Deogratias's participation in it. Like many adolescents, Deogratias is concerned with girls and drinking, making him quite recognizable to the average Western reader. However, at the cusp of his adulthood, rather than becoming a man, he becomes a dog. His involvement in the genocide, both what he has witnessed and what he has done, damage his self-image and ultimately turn him into something bestial, nonhuman. His transformation is important not only in its subversion of the coming-of-age narrative but also in its allusion to *Maus* and other graphic narratives in the zoomorphic tradition. In *Maus*, the characters have animal faces throughout the graphic novel, while in *Deogratias* only one character transforms into an animal and only during the incursion of traumatic memories. The zoomorphic tradition is traditionally applied using familiar animal symbolism. Works like *Maus* tend to use animal features to denote certain traits or to comment upon how the elision between human and animal has particular consequences, given the animal. Dogs are generally seen as companions and protectors, but the genocide introduced an alternative symbolic role for dogs: scavengers. In *We Wish to Inform You that Tomorrow We Will Be Killed Along with Our Families,* Philip Gourevitch discusses how

> the nights were eerily quiet in Rwanda. After the birds fell silent, there were hardly any animal sounds. I couldn't understand it. Then I noticed the absence of dogs. What kind of country has no dogs? I started to keep watch in the markets, in the streets, in the countryside, in churchyards, schoolyards, farmyards, graveyards, junkyards, and the flowering yards of fine villas [. . .] I made inquiries, and I learned that right through the geno-cide dogs had been plentiful in Rwanda [. . .] But as the RPF fighters had advanced through the country, moving down from the northeast, they had shot all the dogs. What did the RPF have against dogs? Everyone I asked gave the same answer: the dogs were eating the dead. (147–48)

Throughout the literature on postgenocide Rwanda, authors remark upon the absence of dogs, an absence that stands in stark contrast to most other areas in the world, where dogs are as abundant as humans. The transition between the time before the genocide and the time after the genocide is divided in part by the presence and absence of dogs, which stands together with the absence of up to a million Rwandan citizens. While coming-of-age stories are often marked by a nostalgic longing for a simpler past, in *Deogratias* this absence is emphasized through the dog metamorphosis, to remind the reader of all that is missing.

THE IMAGE WITHIN THE PANEL

Through embedded panels, Stassen comments on the reader's act of look-ing and the need to distinguish between the acts of reading about an event and actually experiencing it. He is deeply concerned throughout *Deogratias* that the reader recognizes the mediation of Rwandan histories and stories that his work represents, particularly at the moments of closest proximity in terms of point of view. Character point of view, for Stassen, is not some-thing easily adopted, but rather, the prospect of looking through a char-acter's eyes is complicated. By appearing to offer us a character's point of view and then showing unexpected consequences, his work undermines our assumptions about perspective when panels are taken in sequence. We see this, for example, in the scene that opens the graphic novel (see fig. 1.1). Deogratias and the French sergeant, who has returned to Rwanda follow-ing the genocide, meet in Hotel Umusambi at the opening of the graphic

FIGURE 1.1. Deogratias, point of view and vacation photographs. Stassen, J. P. *Deogratias*. Trans. Alexis Siegel. New York: First Second, 2006.

novel. The sergeant is excited to see Deogratias and eager to show him the pictures he has taken of gorillas on his recent trip to a wildlife reserve. A close-up image of these pictures, held by the fingers of the sergeant, occupies a full panel, along with the sergeant's remark that "I had them developed in Kigali—in just a day, like in Europe!" (2). While the reader has not yet seen the sergeant in the context of pregenocide Rwanda, the sergeant's shock at finding any of the "comforts of home" in the country is telling, as is his decision to come back to Rwanda, not long after the genocide, as a tourist. The next panel shows Deogratias turned from the pictures, intent on the beer he is pouring, as the sergeant looks on in surprise, eyebrows raised. While we appear to be looking through Deogratias's eyes when the sergeant is showing the images, the following panel reveals that there is a more complicated relationship between character point of view and reader point of view at stake.

This scene sets the tone for the graphic narrative: the sergeant, a representative of the West, is blithely unaware that his friend from before the violence no longer exists as he once did, and, instead of asking how he has fared in the months since the genocide, excitedly shows him images of the gorillas that are the primary tourist draw of the country. Under what circumstances would anyone assume a tourist's pictures would interest a native Rwandan? Given that the safaris available to tourists are unaffordable for individuals living in many African nations, this scene could be a commentary on monetary rather than geographical accessibility. In any case, Deogratias is uninterested in the images. The single panel that would have the reader share his perspective—the image of the sergeant's photographs—is immediately followed by a panel that shows us that he is not in fact looking at the pictures. We find in the following panel that, instead of looking through Deogratias's eyes, we were the only ones looking at some tourist's pictures. By sharing a perspective then withdrawing that perspective, Stassen emphasizes the extent of the distance between the tourist experience of Rwanda and the experience of being Rwandan after the genocide. Ultimately, the gorillas are disconnected from the reality of postgenocide Rwanda. The idyllic scenes of the forest and wildlife are framed by stark white borders, much like the panel itself. A gutter marks a panel as a discrete unit, and embedded within this panel, another set of borders marking discrete units are encountered by the reader. Stassen's reiterative method of framing increases our awareness that our own point of view is separate and outside that of Deogratias in this scene. The reader may, at the outset, identify more strongly with the Western character, who offers the ragged Deogratias a drink and is enthusiastic about seeing him again. This identification may take place in part because the sergeant is willing to share an experience, while Deogratias neither speaks nor shows.

A panel appears within a panel more literally in another scene, in which Deogratias attempts to woo Apollinaria, showing her a romance comic (see fig. 1.2). In one panel, they are shown sitting next to one another, and in the following panel, the reader shares either Apollinaria's or Deogratias's perspective, looking down at the panels in the comic. The panel shows a woman sitting alone on a couch, looking downward, and part of another panel that depicts a man rubbing his face, perhaps in frustration. The textual marker framing Deogratias's portion of the dialogue does not have an arrow, so one could contend that the reader looks through his eyes as he attempts to impress Apollinaria with this gift. However, the reader sees Apollinaria's hand holding the comic, and the angle at which the comic is set suggests that we are looking through Apollinaria's eyes. Keen asserts that these panels correspond to the way in which "the transaction between representation of romantic love and acquiescence to his advances is not so straightforward" ("Fast Tracks to Narrative Empathy" 136), positing that representation is not equivalent to experience. However, in this case, it is taken as such; the representation that we see through Apollinaria's gaze is not an attractive one. While she is upset that Deogratias has stolen money to buy the comic for her, her eyes are drawn back to the page, and she only rejects him when he asks "don't you ever wonder if we could do the same things as in those stories?" (Stassen 13). Given the content of the romance comic panels, which hint at the loneliness and misunderstandings in love, perhaps it is not surprising that she rebuffs his advance. The tension is not only between representation and acquiescence but also between what Deogratias thinks he is showing her and what she actually sees. Because we are seeing the comic through Apollinaria's eyes, we have access to the images that inform her decision to reject him. Deogratias, however, believes that he has shown her something entirely different, as a subsequent scene makes clear.

The scene is repeated almost word-for-word on the following page, except now Deogratias is paired with Benina. As Benina approaches him, Deogratias is turned away from her, but the reader is shown his face; he has been crying, but he tells her that nothing is wrong and wipes away his tears before she sees them. He turns to her with a smile and re-gifts the comic. As Benina gazes at it, Deogratias repeats the question he posed to Apollinaria, asking "Did you ever think that we could do the same things as in those stories?" (15). This question is in a text box in the panel showing another romance comic panel, but this panel depicts a white man and

FIGURE 1.2. Deogratias and Apollinaria read a romance comic. Stassen, J. P. Deogratias. Trans. Alexis Siegel. New York: First Second, 2006.

white woman kissing passionately beneath a starry sky. Here, Deogratias is showing Benina what he *thought* he was showing Apollinaria: an attractive representation of sexuality. In this case, Benina accepts him, not knowing that he has just used the same ploy with her sister and in fact prefers her sister over her. Additionally, she has not seen the page in the comic that Apollinaria read and so sees only a partial representation of love as well. This repetition indicates that representations and affective identifications *can* be tied together. Benina identifies with the characters in the comic and wants what they are represented as having: passion and love. However, identification comes at the expense of not having the whole story. On both the level of the panels and on the level of the graphic novel as a whole, Deogratias's gift of the comic and *Deogratias* the graphic novel have goals in mind, but the representations are also dependent on what the readers look at most closely.

At the metafictional level, the implied Stassen is critiquing unreflective and uninformed consumption of art, which is expressly dangerous: Benina's lack of knowledge about Deogratias's character, her uninformed mimicry of the affective response he attempts to elicit through the comic, allows a relationship to begin between them. While she is not simply "consuming" the relationship as she consumes the comic, the partial viewing of the gift allows for the possibility of the relationship. Benina does not know that she is the recipient only because the first choice rejected it, and she sees only the part of the story that Deogratias had hoped she would. The comic, rather than being a representation of a reality, is only shown in parts. The individual panels are removed from the larger story, and each panel only tells a part of the story.

By showing how the individual panels of his own work must be situated in relation to the others to be adequately understood, Stassen is also demonstrating how even these representations are provisional. While Keen contends that this scene demonstrates that "Stassen acknowledges within his text that the uses of graphic narration are not as predictable as the naïve boy imagines" ("Fast Tracks to Narrative Empathy" 136), neither are the uses predictable for the readers. In these panels, the reader occupies the perspective of a character, and the panels are also re-creations of photographs and magazines, which foregrounds their constructedness as representations of representations. In the scene depicting the sergeant and Deogratias and in the scenes showing Deogratias's interactions with the two sisters, the character offering a representation has specific aims in offering the images. In the cases of both the sergeant and Apollinaria, the reality falls short of the goal: Deogratias is uninterested in the pictures; Apollinaria is uninterested in a romantic relationship. Stassen could be demonstrating how decontextualized images may not be received in the ways expected by those who proffer them, but it is also important to note *how* these images are disconnected from reality. In the case of the sergeant, the disconnect is partly at a cultural level: he does not understand Deogratias's disinterest and cannot conceive of what Deogratias has recently endured. The photographs of the gorillas obscure what had recently taken place in Rwanda, and are disingenuous representations of only a small facet of the nation. Apollinaria, for her part, sees the comic as being a disingenuous gift with an accurate representation. She sees the isolation and dissatisfaction depicted in the panels as being closer to the truth than perhaps the cover of the romance comic would lead one to believe. Benina is the only character who sees what the person offering the image wants her to see, to her detriment. Benina is an object lesson in the careful consumption of visual texts, but in spite of the difference in her reaction, the lesson is similar in the other two cases: these images must be recognized as representations, necessarily partial and provisional.

TIME AND MEMORY

While the image within the panel demonstrates the extent to which decontextualized images can mislead or emphasize only certain elements, Stassen also insists that the reader recognize how perspective can inflect information that is offered. Graphic narratives represent time as space, and *Deogratias* is a work fixated on the irrecoverability of time.[5] By imbricating multiple different times and places on a single page while keeping each time separate via the frame and the gutter, Stassen flirts with the idea that memory constitutes a way to return to another time. Most of these individual scenes could occupy a one- or two-page spread, but Stassen carries the scene onto a following page to connect it more clearly with another separate scene. Stassen's choice to place panels depicting different times on the same page stresses how the time after the genocide is ruptured by memories of the time before.

Stassen juxtaposes memory and present alongside representations of many of the contradictory reasons offered by commentators for the genocide, including long-standing ethnic enmity and colonial heritage. Over the course of several pages, the scenes change rapidly to reveal these alternate interpretations, which appear to be hollow when set in contrast with

5. See Charles Hatfield's *Graphic Interventions: Form and Argument in Contemporary Comics.*

one another. The first example begins with a panel depicting Deogratias's hands holding a jar of Urwagwa in the present, while the following panel shows him in a schoolroom alongside a much-younger Benina and Apollinaria, listening to a lecture by the teacher, who asks which students are Hutus. The first panel is cropped so that the reader cannot see Deogratias's current visage, his face covered by Bosco's remark that Deogratias will not go to jail because there is "certainly no room for dogs" (17). By cropping his head, Stassen may be playing with the idea of closure, in which the reader projects her own image into this space.[6] Alternatively, Deogratias's head is effaced because he is drinking Urwagwa, and his mind has "gone elsewhere": no longer properly present in the hut, drinking with Bosco, he has returned to the past. The first image of the schoolroom, however, is not depicted from Deogratias's perspective; instead, the reader shares the perspective of the teacher, who looks at the three characters in the front row. This is reversed in the second panel, which shows the teacher from the students' perspectives. After these panels, the page break is jarring, as the reader has barely been introduced to the narrative. On the following page, in a slightly aerial panel, the teacher praises the students who have identified as Hutu, while Benina and Apollinaria look off to either side with their arms folded. The teacher explains that "the Hutu are the majority people. These proud and honest farmers, of Bantu stock, are the ones who cleared the country for cultivation. With courage and care, they turned it into the wonderful garden that feeds us all. You can say that they are the true Rwandans" (18). This clearly polemical narrative, ascribing positive qualities to the Hutus as a people and characterizing them in terms of nationalism, is counterpointed by the teacher's assessment of Tutsis. While the scene is externally focalized, the use of facial expressions and gestures to communicate the interiority of the characters suggests that there are other dimensions. As the teacher asks which students are Tutsis, an exchange of worried looks between sisters and the sympathetic expression of Deogratias gesture to the familiarity of this strategy of villianization and othering. That the sisters are already visibly uncomfortable at the beginning of the Hutu Power narrative that reformulates the history of Rwanda as one of evil conquest suggests that they have already encountered the ambient rehistoricization floating around in the culture. Their introduction to the history of Rwanda is simply a recapitulation of the shame they have already been taught to feel about their heritage by the wider culture.

---

6. As explained in the introduction, *closure* refers to McCloud's theory that the reader imaginatively projects action occurring between two panels, "closing" the space of the gutter.

The exact center of the page is occupied by a panel that depicts an over-the-shoulder view of Apollinaria and Benina reluctantly raising their hands as the teacher lectures on the "history" of Rwandan ethnic groups. This panel offers the reader the perspective of one of the students sitting behind them, essentially distancing the reader from the discomfort of the girls. Because Benina and Apollinaria's faces are obscured in this panel, the reader cannot see the affective content: the emotions that can be read on their faces. Instead, the reader sees the scene through the eyes of one of the dozen or so nameless Hutu students. By offering only this perspective, Stassen gestures toward the way that the cultural narrative of Tutsi manipulativeness has overtaken the dominant discourse, even at the level of grade school. In the following scene, we look over the shoulder of the teacher as he repeats the canard that Tutsis were invaders from the North who, using "their cows and their weapons [. . .] took advantage of the natural integrity of the poor Hutu peasants, and treacherously enslaved them" (18). The teacher asserts a historically questionable interpretation as fact for a classroom largely filled with young Hutu students. Over his shoulder, Apollinaria looks abashed, ashamed at being grouped into this narrative, while Benina angrily looks into the teacher's eyes. This over-the-shoulder view at the center of the page interrupts our access to the facial expressions of the characters, which are the primary clue we have to the character's internal experience.

Unlike many graphic narratives, *Deogratias* does not feature a narrator, either a character in the text or an omniscient narrator, to explain scenes in text boxes, to give the reader the context of the character's past experiences, or to remark on Rwandan history, to better understand this scene. Stassen's use of shifting perspectives and depiction of only the reactions invokes doubt about history as it is presented. Perhaps more importantly, by showing multiple scenes of partial or false history, Stassen emphasizes that misunderstandings imbued everyday life leading up to the genocide. The partiality of these historical accounts is highlighted in another panel, in which the teacher is shown turned away, briefly noting the existence of the Twa ethnic group. The Twa, in spite of being the longest historical inhabitants of Rwanda, are largely effaced in this history lesson. Readers have already been introduced to a minor character named Augustine, a Twa man bitter that he is highly educated yet is paid better to serve white people than to do intellectual work. His worries about his daughter, Marie, prompt him to propose to Venetia, the mother of Apollinaria and Benina, which she laughs about because he is short.

The following panel depicts Deogratias with the sisters after school. He tries to convince them that "the teacher is a fool" (18), the three characters set against the backdrop of the schoolhouse, clutching their books in hand. The first panel reiterates Apollinaria's ashamed facial expression, while Benina's has changed from angry to traumatized: she stares outward at the reader in something akin to shock. The next panel pulls back significantly from the group, so the reader is once again set at a remove and can only guess at the characters' emotional state based on their physical position.

The transition between scenes is marked only by the white space of the gutter and black frames: no other context is given to mark the shift from memory to present. Situated across this brief divide is Deogratias in his present appearance, seated next to Bosco, who complains about ". . . Hutu, Tutsi. . . . The whites made up those differences between us! They wrote those words on our ID cards!" (19). By immediately following the teacher's "history lesson" with the pseudo-postcolonial interpretation of the causes of the genocide, Stassen is developing a genealogy of historical misreadings and cultural myths that were persistent at the time of the genocide and after. These misreadings are not counterpointed by a narration of the historical accounts accepted by scholars. Bosco lectures Deogratias that "before they [the whites] came, before they sowed the seeds of division, before they enslaved us, we lived peacefully here. . . ." (19), a statement that Deogratias finishes with ". . . in the land of milk and honey" (19). This panel represents one of the rare moments in which the postgenocide Deogratias speaks about anything other than dogs and Urwagwa. This scene simply depicts Bosco and Deogratias sitting in a darkened hut, and while the reader is not offered the perspective of any particular character, these panels interestingly mimic the scenes from the classroom in their lack of external information about the interiority of the characters. By framing this scene with the panel that shows Deogratias telling Benina and Apollinaria that the teacher is a fool, Stassen hopes to draw parallels between the classroom scene and the scene with Bosco. Deogratias maintains the same facial expression in this scene that we saw in the panels in the school yard, but this recontextualization of that expression points toward the futility Deogratias feels that arguing with such statements represents in this time and place. The reification of two alternate interpretations of the historical record demonstrate the indeterminacy of identity in the face of powerful cultural narratives. As Phelan notes in his discussion of narratives and contestation,

> To say that every narrative is contestable is not [. . .] to say that the contest among alternatives will always be carried out on a level playing field.

Some narratives acquire a sacred status in a given culture or subculture (religions are often founded on such narratives), and some narratives, while clearly not sacred, have the strong endorsement of culturally powerful groups. Contesting such narratives is not only very difficult but, in many cases, also extremely dangerous. (169)

The scenes used as examples of the cultural scripts in place in Rwanda surrounding the time of the genocide are situated in relation to one another to illuminate how perspective and memory are also contested spaces. Phelan's discussion of relative difficulties in contesting narratives is important in regard to the methods Stassen uses to illuminate how these misrepresentations of history can be doubted partly through their juxtaposition.

The reality of how these narratives affect the everyday lives of Rwandans is embodied in a scene depicting Venetia dressing after an intimate encounter with a governmental official. She remarks, "It's the last time I'm asking a favor of you" (19), immediately informing the reader that this is not a match of passion. The slightly aerial viewpoint shows the thin, curvy Venetia foregrounded against a large man reclining on the bed, his military uniform discarded over a chair to the side. Another over-the-shoulder perspective shows the officer remarking "Venetia, you know it can't be done. There are ethnic quotas, and your daughter . . ." (19). This explanation refers to the policy in place before the genocide that limited Tutsi access to positions in colleges and in civil service jobs, ostensibly to make up for years of discrimination against Hutu applicants. Venetia cuts him off, saying, "And I tell you, my daughter is at least as able as the next kid to take college classes!" (19). Her insistence underscores how myths about Tutsi intellectual superiority, the effects of colonization, and precolonial history have been replaced by a system that seeks to legitimize these histories. These panels also reveal a scene for which Deogratias was not present; while the preceding panels with Bosco frame the passage as another foray into Deogratias's memory, this scene is decidedly not something that Deogratias witnessed. While *Deogratias* purportedly follows the title character and his memories, Deogratias often "remembers" moments that he was not a part of, which suggests that, in spite of Deogratias's status as a focal point, the narrative is not wholly focalized through his consciousness.

By representing three distinct scenes, linked only by gutters, Stassen insists that the reader work to connect how they function as a whole. Rather than confine each scene to an individual page, which would have been a simple matter of an additional single panel on one end or the other, he relies on the top-down, left-right reading process to ensure that the reader will work to produce closure between the panels. This closure does not happen automatically, as in sequences in which the same characters are depicted over the course of an action or conversation. Instead, the gaps must be filled by material mined in the context of the panels, imaginatively connected. The smooth flow of narrative is destabilized by the jumps between various temporalities. The resulting disorientation has two important effects. The first is that it encourages the reader to work to provide a stronger element of closure between these narratives than they might if they were separated by a full-page break or a change in chapter. Second, it enhances the chaos of the temporalities at stake in the narrative, given the way that graphic narratives are read. Groensteen notes that

> a panel is not presented as isolated. It participates in a series (most often sequential or narrative) offered to the reader. Now, in Western culture reading respects an unchanging direction, which moves from left to right. When the comics page respects the classic division of generally watertight horizontal bands ("strips"), it imposes on the panels an alignment that facilitates the sweep of the gaze. Every comics reader knows from experience that, in practice, even when the gaze functions like an 'irremovable beam,' the eye's movements on the surface of the page are relatively erratic and do not respect any precise protocol. (47)

Pages in *Deogratias* that illustrate both the present and the past seem to lend a sense of recoverability, or of coexistence, but Deogratias himself seems to be aware of this as fiction, seeking out Urwagwa as a way to tame his memories. These scenes are a profusion of interaction, depicting Deogratias surrounded by people in the past and barely interacting with people in the present. In addition, some scenes show events for which Deogratias was not present, disrupting the narrative consciousness and introducing perhaps an alternative external focalizor. While the narrative nominally follows Deogratias, the repeated disruption of scenes from his memory by scenes for which he was not present disembodies his experience.

These scenes conduct the tension between the narrating-I and the experiencing-I to the reader through the network of shifting perspectives in the panels. The reification of abstract cultural referents into the actual embodied practices of Rwandans living before the genocide can be taken as a commentary on how scenes "coded for transparency," as Mikkonen puts it, become less transparent in juxtaposition. The reader cannot take both the teacher's statement and Bosco's assertion as fact, and, given the scene with Venetia, these panels show how both have effects yet are both insufficient to understanding the experience of these conflicting cultural scripts. Just as the experiencing-I and the narrating-I are collapsed into one another in these scenes, the temporalities of past and present are a pastiche, paying homage to the actual embodied living of Rwandans prior to the genocide while referencing the evacuation of actual historical context in favor of sound bites. The juxtaposition of these scenes functions to preserve the ambivalence of the focalizing consciousness. The reader receives the story from a problematic character who is not in control of the story himself, an uneasy readerly position because it highlights Stassen's choice to deny the reader the familiar stance in receiving a survivor's story about atrocity. Because there is no narrative explication of these scenes, the reader is left without the normal architecture for a testimony and so is faced with the problems that are usually at play but are occluded in nonfictional genres. Nonfictional genres, like testimony, tend to obscure the distance between the experience and the recounting of that experience, as if listening to a witness makes the listener a witness as well. In *Deogratias,* however, the lack of narrative explication denies the reader the constructed account and interpretations that may be received. The reader is not receiving testimony from a witness, which puts them outside of the redemptive narrative of witness.

THE BYSTANDER AND THE SCAVENGER

Deogratias is not only a book "about" a perpetrator of genocide. It is a book about the constellation of experiences that contribute to memory and how those memories fare in the wake of disaster. The realistic story about a boy in Rwanda is disrupted by his transformation into a dog. Deogratias's transformations always initially appear externally focalized, as if the reader is viewing him change as an uninvolved bystander. In the first such instance, Deogratias asks an older woman for Urwagwa (banana beer) and she says she has none. As he walks back to his shack, each panel shows a stage in his disfigurement. In the first panel, he merely appears dejected that he could not acquire alcohol, but the second panel shows him on all fours, wherein his transformation is also marked by verbal changes. During the day, he generally only speaks to ask whether the Urwagwa is good; in this nighttime scene, he begins to rave about the dogs and the bellies, saying, "They devour the bellies and the bellies spill open" (Stassen 26). This panel depicts Deogratias from an aerial vantage point, which sets the reader at a distance, looking down on him as he talks wildly. This raving represents a rift in the focalizing consciousness of the narrative, as the book is nominally focused on Deogratias's experiences and memories, but at the point at which he begins to speak about his memories (as confusing and disjointed as it is), the actual memories are not offered. This is remarkable because in most scenes that depict the present, scenes from Deogratias's memory appear intermittently. Throughout most of the graphic novel, the absence of narrative voice is important because the reader does not receive any description of how to contextualize what he is seeing. The aerial viewpoints that litter the work enhance the sensation of being set at a remove, as an uninvolved observer (see fig. 1.3).

A panel that depicts him partly transformed into a dog, gazing upward at the reader, also contains his internal monologue, asserting that "from up there, they are watching them fight. You are watching me" (27). This assertion includes pronouns of indeterminate reference, the "they" and "them" not referring to a clear subject. However, the "you," when taken in context with the following panel, seems to refer to the reader—"You are watching me." The reader's aerial vantage point in relation to the character creates a position of superiority, as if we are looking down on a humbled beast, but it is also important to note that, in this scene, Deogratias has not fully transformed into a dog. He still bears a recognizably human nose, and some of his hair remains. By retaining some human characteristics, Deogratias blurs the line between human and animal. This blurring of boundaries is a preoccupation in his speech as well. The next panel offers the reader Deogratias's perspective, which is simply a nighttime horizon filled with stars, emphasizing his loneliness after the flood of memories in the pages leading up to this scene. Beneath the image reads, "The dogs, and my head that's evaporating, spilling out into the night. I am afraid of the night. The stars are dissolved by the bellies, and my head is all filled with cold" (27). That the text is placed as a caption explaining the image, rather than as a remark inside of the image, points toward a moment of interior focalization. Most of *Deogratias* does not give the reader access to the internal thoughts and emotions of characters or does so only through facial expressions. Text is largely limited to word bubbles. However, in this case, the panel is structured to more closely mimic an editorial cartoon, in which an image is accompanied by a humorous caption, rather than having the verbal physically integrated into the visual.

These lines are the only point at which Deogratias expresses an emotion: fear. This expression of fear is placed between one line that references evaporation and another line that references dissolution. Evaporation constitutes the process of vaporization of surface matter, a gesture toward his physical transformation, which blurs the boundary between his body and

FIGURE 1.3. Deogratias becomes a dog. Stassen, J. P. *Deogratias*. Trans. Alexis Siegel. New York: First Second, 2006.

the night. Dissolution is the breakdown of one material in a solution of another material, and when "The stars are dissolved by the bellies" (27), the reader is left to wonder briefly what this seemingly flowery phrase communicates. His surroundings are clearly deprived. His hut is nothing more than a few bricks and beams with a sheet of tin lain over the top. The transformation is recontextualized by another scene, in which Apollinaria is acting as a tour guide for Brother Philip's parents and is taking them through a museum devoted to Rwandan history. In one panel, the reader seems to share the perspective of the group being led on the tour, as Apollinaria narrates, "At that time divinatory and magical practices were very important for Rwandans. You have to realize that back then these poor people thought the world was a flat disk covered by a layer of air, with the blue rock of the sky resting on pillars" (44). The reader shares the perspective of those on the tour in this panel, one of the only moments where we are given a broader historical context for the genocide. By placing the reader as a tourist, Stassen suggests that the reader needs a museum excursion to better understand the events in the narrative. Museums order artifacts and place them in context for the visitor, and the museum guide interprets this placement for the visitor, without drawing heavily upon their interpretive faculties. In spite of what the characters (and the readers) are told, however, in the following panel Apollinaria tells them that "because they did not yet know our Lord Jesus Christ and the greatness of His love, they believed the spirits of the dead filled the underworld, where they schemed spitefully against the living; and at night they lit up the sky over Rwanda" (44). This panel calls on the reader to connect it to the night sky panels that come both before and after. The mythology behind the night sky is essential in the context of Deogratias's guilty memory and his present transformation.

In the following sky panels, the reader is placed squarely within Deogratias's point of view, looking at the night sky, which in the context provided by Apollinaria takes on an accusatory cast. The population of stars is no longer simply a sky under which Deogratias is too traumatized to sleep but is instead the angry dead accusing him. This particular scene shows Deogratias finding Urwagwa, and while dogs trail him through the night as he guzzles the alcohol, he manages to forestall his transformation. However, the transformation cannot be forestalled forever, and Deogratias wakes to find that daylight no longer preserves his humanity. As he transforms and raves about stars in the daylight, the reader briefly shares his perspective in two panels that show a daytime sky spangled with stars. In the first, he says, "My head is spilling out in the day!" (52), reiterating the mechanism of blurring discussed in the first sequence, and the daytime sky is set against lush foliage at the bottom of the frame. The next panel, however, depicts him as a dog: the transformation is complete. He paces around, shown from an aerial vantage point, saying, "The sun isn't watching over me anymore. There are no dogs . . . But the stars are melting . . . Like nails on the skulls . . . There are no bellies" (52). His preoccupation with the absence of dogs and bellies is reflected in the panel, which shows only a mangy dog pacing on a flat patch of parched dirt. The use of cues from the landscape to accentuate the absence contrasts with the way in which Deogratias argues that his head is spilling out, is blurring with the sky.

While in Western conceptualizations dogs are seen as companions, protectors, and members of the family, in postgenocide Rwanda dogs are almost nonexistent. There was a relatively large population of dogs in pregenocide Rwanda, but during Operation Turquoise and after the genocide, most of the dogs in the country were killed by soldiers to prevent them from continuing to eat the corpses. In Rwanda, the pregenocide roles of dogs were irrecoverable. While dogs could again be imported, their cultural role was no longer marked by loyalty but rather became that of a threatening scavenger.[7] The scavenging dog is a role absent from many Western stories of dogs, wherein dogs generally symbolize faithfulness and have long represented a means of finding one's way. However, dogs' scavenging instincts are distinctly absent from these symbolic interpretations. Stassen's depiction of Deogratias as a dog, rather than imbricating nature and symbolic content, stresses their instinctual tendencies. What repercussions does this have for Deogratias as a man? Keen argues that

> Stassen shows that human nature includes its capacity to violate natural law, but also insists that these actions deform inner human nature [. . .] When his character turns into a dog, Stassen sets against the conventions of man's best friend stark imagery of the guilty self as man's worst enemy. ("Fast Tracks to Narrative Empathy" 140)

Stassen does not depict a loveable pup: Deogratias becomes a disgusting, mutated, cringing cur. Prior to the genocide, he did not change into an animal. It was only afterward that this transformation took place. While his

---

7. The scavenging in itself was a problem for several reasons. First, evidence of the atrocities needed to be preserved. Second, the United Nations Assistance Mission for Rwanda (UNAMIR) argues, because the dogs were eating the corpses, they now posed a health hazard. Third, and most importantly, the further desecration of corpses must have been intolerable for RPF soldiers and others.

transformation into a dog fits the image of guilt posited by Keen, prior to the genocide he is depicted as a manipulative (if earnest) young drunk; he is not the stuff of heroes to begin with, although his behavior is clearly meant to approximate that of the assumed Western postadolescent reader. Deogratias the dog is a distinctly ugly creature, inflected by the context in which he/it is placed. The moments at which he "becomes" a dog are irruptions of memory but also signify a shift in the cultural consciousness, which in the postgenocide era has been forced to redefine the symbolic content of formerly "everyday" elements of social life. In addition, Deogratias, through memory, is defined by those entities that are now missing from the landscape. His alienation from the landscape he helped create takes the form of a scavenging dog. While *Deogratias* at certain points appears teleological in thrust, the events unfold instead as a recursive weaving of individual, and sometimes seemingly unrelated incidents in the past erupting into Deogratias's present, which has only visual indices: drunken madman and dog. Deogratias's state of madness calls into question the affective content of the work and the affective engagement of the reader, as Deogratias's paranoia and shame render him animalistic. While even in his animalistic state, he clearly shows emotion, this emotion is disorienting and often disconnected from his personal experience.

FOCALIZING GUILT AND SHAME

One of the most frequent objections readers have to *Deogratias* is that the character best situated for reader identification is a perpetrator. Identification is meant to promote understanding, to create bridges between experiences, and to gird against the incursion of our baser instincts by reminding us of shared humanity. But the emotional construction of this identification is repeatedly called into question by Stassen's choice of focus: focalization through the consciousness of an unsympathetic character, offering his perspective only at intermittent moments. By focusing on, yet not entirely focalizing through, a character such as this one, is the reader meant to resist full identification? What does it mean to retroactively withdraw identification once the extent of Deogratias's crimes becomes clear? What is the ethical stance behind prompting readers to identify with a character revealed to be a *genocidaire*?

After Deogratias has abruptly changed back into a human when children throw rocks at him, he goes off to find Urwagwa again, and comes to the same house depicted earlier, where an old woman gave him enough

Urwagwa to forestall his transformation. There he finds Julius, a violent Hutu *interahamwe* leader, who welcomes him and argues that they have to continue their "work." Deogratias tells him that he doesn't want to, and Julius grows angry about Deogratias's "betrayal." This scene frames a sequence of scenes from the genocide, opening with Deogratias and Benina in his room, listening to the radio. A knock at his door prompts him to hide her under the bed, and upon opening the door, the reader shares the perspective of a group of Hutus as Deogratias asks what they want. The panels on the following page play with this perspective sharing, the first of which offers the reader Deogratias's point of view as Julius tells him to help the armed group with a roadblock. There is no reason given for setting up the roadblock: Julius assumes that Deogratias will know why. In the next panel, this viewpoint pulls back to Benina's perspective beneath the bed, although the reader is looking over her shoulder at Deogratias and the group of *interahamwe* standing at the door, as Deogratias asserts, "I don't take orders from you, Julius" (59). In spite of this stand that he seems to take, the reader once again shares the perspectives of the Hutus at Deogratias's door, as Julius warns Deogratias, "Everyone knows you like Tutsi pussy. Show the true color of your blood" (59). The changes in perspective in these panels create an unstable experience for the reader. While we see the scene unfolding from various angles—from the point of view of various characters—we have no access to their interiority. These swift changes in perspective serve to underscore the problems of point of view at stake in all texts that deal with genocide. The reader is denied a stable perspective from which to vicariously "witness" the events unfold, which foregrounds how these stories are narrativized. The reader—the receiver of testimony—does not have unmediated access to the "story" of the genocide but is given an account that follows literary conventions in order to produce a "hearable" story for the receiver. *Deogratias,* on the other hand, resists conventions like the individualized narrative, stable perspective, and linear progression to emphasize the lack of scaffolding inherent in the experience.

The next few pages reiterate the instability, offering the reader various scenes from the genocide, rapidly moving from one scene to the next, which heightens the confusion marking this time. By first depicting Brother Prior and Brother Philip attempting to hide a church full of women and children, then, immediately, the two Brothers in flight, along a road out of Rwanda, the reader is denied the violence that clearly follows and instead is given an example of cowardice as the two men argue with Venetia against her going back to find her daughters. The final panel on the page depicts the door of the church, half open, seemingly abandoned, with just a bit of blood pooling in the corner, and the next page shows Apollinaria crawling from beneath a bloody pile of bodies to go and hide in the latrines. These two panels seem to offer the perspective of an uninvolved bystander, looking at the outside of the church and then wandering in and looking down upon Apollinaria as she struggles from under the remains of the massacre.[8] The reader cannot reach through the panel to help her to her feet.

Stassen focuses on Rwandans' limited freedom of movement over the next few pages, which show Apollinaria hiding in the latrines, Augustine being brutalized by roving *interahamwe*, and a fight between Benina and Deogratias that prompts her to escape. During the fight, Deogratias remarks that he is doing all he can for Benina "and [her] brethren," a phrasing that suggests that the divisions have crystallized for Deogratias. Furthermore, in this panel, his eyes are rendered exactly the same as Benina's were in the earlier scene outside of the school: traumatized and distant.

Preoccupied with claustrophobia, one panel shows a close-up of Apollinaria hiding in the latrines, while another set of panels depict Benina's fear and frustration at being locked in Deogratias's small shack. After Benina unscrews the hinges of the door, another panel shows her creeping past a group of men holding another man's identity card, a machete against his face. By using close-ups, Stassen emphasizes the confined movements, which is reiterated in the encroachment of the gutter. When Apollinaria and Benina find one another, Apollinaria brings Benina back to the confinement of the latrines. Benina's facial expression shows disgust and worry as Apollinaria asks, "Where were you? At his place? With Deogratias?" (65), to which Benina responds, half-truthfully, "Yes, but I was worried for Mom and you" (65). The following panel, however, shows Apollinaria eagerly asking, "Where is he? What is Deogratias doing now?" Apollinaria is clearly excited, briefly hopeful, her eyes wide and her mouth a near smile as her sister glances away. Benina's gaze is directed over her shoulder, at the reader, as she responds that he is "With the others . . . Doing what he can to help people" (65). At this moment, the reader shares something with Benina that Apollinaria does not know: Deogratias's reference to her "brethren." Benina's over-the-shoulder glance expresses doubts and worry over whether or not Deogratias is helping. In those moments that we share the perspective of a character, we "see through their eyes," but in this moment, the gaze is reversed upon us. At this point, the reader has

---

8. The first of these panels is based off of a familiar image from the genocide: the Nyarubuye Church was the site of one of the most horrific massacres, where approximately 20,000 men, women, and children were slaughtered over a two-day period in 1994.

little information beyond what we are shown in the argument about what Deogratias is doing, but Benina's immediate suspicions, and escape, clue us in to activities more sinister than the vague term "helping" would suggest. She also does not explain who "the others" are and seems intent upon protecting Apollinaria from what Benina herself has seen, in spite of the fact that Apollinaria is obviously aware of the precariousness of their positions, given that she is hiding in the latrines. However, these assumptions about awareness are complicated by the reader becoming the object of the gaze, as well as the fact that these panels are not bounded by the black frame that usually denotes the line between the pre- and postgenocide worlds. By Benina looking out of the panel at us, we are made aware of our own gaze as one looking into a world to which we do not belong. This panel's text plays a game of awareness, where some information is hidden to avoid destroying Apollinaria's hope, suggested by her eagerness to know about Deogratias's whereabouts. Meeting the gaze of the reader, in this context, would seem to indicate that we are privy to special knowledge, knowledge not shared by all of the participants in the story. However, if we look back only a couple of pages, we see Apollinaria crawling from beneath a pile of corpses, sneaking by the *interahamwe*, and finding a disgusting place to hide. Can it be that she is unaware of the danger? That the gaze is directed outward at the reader instead suggests that *we* do not have all of the information, that there are things that *we* have failed to recognize. The scene immediately following the latrines depicts a Western suburban neighborhood with Brother Philip, his parents, and little Marie, Augustine's daughter, sitting inside a large house with a well-manicured yard (see fig. 1.4).

The difference in location is reinforced by a full-page break between the scenes. In the corner of the panel showing the exterior of the house, a caption reads, ". . . All we can say is that the situation remains very unclear . . ." (66), giving very little information, and again, emphasizing that the reader is closed off from the events of the genocide as they are unfolding. The captions in these panels are attributed to a television reporter, the only moment in the graphic novel when there is a narratorial voice overlaying the panels. However, the narratorial voice offers no actual information, suggesting that any verbal claim to authority is compromised. However, these panels cue the reader to a transition because they are bounded by the black frames.

The next panel transitions into an interior view of Brother Philip in front of the television, nearly half of the panel taken up with a text box relating a news report: "From the capital Kigali, where the evacuation of Europeans has now been completed, come reports that small arms fire has been heard

FIGURE 1.4. Brother Philip watches Rwanda through the television. Stassen, J. P. *Deogratias.* Trans. Alexis Siegel. New York: First Second, 2006.

all night and that many lynchings were witnessed" (66). While this news is reported, the frame is occupied only by the character. Throughout this scene, the reader is shown nothing from the actual genocide. Instead, the reader is shown only a white Westerner, a representative of those who were allowed to flee, rather than those who were forced to remain behind. The reader has, to this point, seen very little violence as it is occurring, through several panels that have shown the remnants (as with the corpses in the church) or the potential for violence (as in panels showing *interahamwe*). After focusing on Brother Philip watching the television, the perspective shifts, and the reader is placed within the point of view of Brother Philip in a panel depicting the television, on which appears a map of Rwanda, and next to the television are a few Rwandan drinking jars, grouped together for display. The map on the television has an abstract quality in juxtaposition with the scene of Apollinaria and Benina: their embodied experiences are effaced by the national demarcations. Additionally, the map suggests that, in spite of the fact that readers have previously encountered Rwandans throughout the pages of the graphic novel, Rwanda is conceptually remote. The reader does not necessarily know even where the country is located. While Brother Philip was recently in Rwanda, he was evacuated along with most of the other whites in the country and thus is only able to access news about the region through the same means as other Westerners: through the television.[9] The voiceover for the depiction of the map reads, "We must warn you about the following footage. Our editorial team debated long and hard . . . about whether to air it or not" (66). Of course, the bulk of the footage available to Westerners at the time were of refugees, not the actual acts of genocide,[10] but more importantly, in the context of *Deogratias*, even these images are not communicated by Stassen. Brother Philip's mother tells him to turn off the television, arguing that Marie, as a child, shouldn't see any of the images. In this scene, Stassen metonymically displaces the actual events with the television to evoke a recognition in the

9. Aside from UNAMIR, led by Romeo Dallaire, and several others.

10. Edgar Roskis argues that this focus on the refugee population served to obscure the careful orchestration and brutality of the genocide, fixating instead on "the humanitarian melodrama, 'the endless lines of refugees, sacks of rice, the orphans and field hospitals, the images of downtrodden humanity and resolute volunteers'" (239). Additionally, Roskis notes that, in the use of images of atrocity, "this idea—that pictures must shock to serve a purpose, including one's own—has been fully embraced by the NGOs, who apply it skillfully and somewhat cold-bloodedly in their communication campaigns, responding to the laws of the new marketplace" in which the consumer must be bombarded with the appearance of suffering to adequately respond to actual suffering (241).

reader of what is actually shared in *Deogratias*: the ability to turn off the television, to close the book. The large, blank white gutter that follows this scene is an aporia, the space in which the violence "should" be depicted, at least through the mediation of a television screen, but readers are instead left to imagine the footage for themselves.

When Brother Philip returns to Rwanda following the genocide, he finds a traumatized Deogratias and takes him to a bar for a drink, where Deogratias relates the final days of the violence. In a large panel, the reader shares an indeterminate perspective at the end of a short column of *interahamwe*, the shadows of other refugees further in the distance. In the following panels, Augustine hails Deogratias, who is in the column of marching men, and Julius reveals that Deogratias has taken part in the rape and murder of the girls that he professed to love. The fact that the actual rapes and murders are denied visual representation reinforces the gulf between victim experience and the reader's development of insight into the genocide. By having the reader, even in the context of the *interahamwe*'s retreat into the Turquoise Zone, hear only about the slaughter second hand, the only actual violence takes place in the reader's imagination. As McCloud notes, "I may have drawn an axe being raised in this example, but I'm not the one who let it drop or decided how hard the blow, or who screamed, or why. That, dear reader, was your special crime" (68). By denying the reader a stable, static image of the violence *as it was inflicted*, the implied Stassen demonstrates that the choice not to represent death, even fictional deaths, can more effectively communicate the position of the Western "bystander" than a gory action scene. Furthermore, as Augustine is killed, Stassen shows Julius raising the machete and shows his corpse, but his decision not to render the stroke implies, on one hand, the reader's complicity in imagining the stroke as it falls and, on the other hand, suggests that the reader is always displaced from the events.

When Deogratias returns from the Turquoise Zone, the reader is shown the result of what took place in the gutters: dogs chewing on the corpses of Benina and Apollinaria and Deogratias's blank stare. There is no verbal component to interrupt or explain, and the dogs are squarely framed within Deogratias's point of view (see fig. 1.5).

This in part signifies Deogratias's inability, throughout the graphic novel, to articulate what he saw and what he did. This noncathartic approach, in which the shame of his actions cannot be narrated, can only be shown and develops an argument for shame in the reader as well. Shame over the actions of another or, moreover, over the inaction of another is among the essential components of ethical empathy. Graphic narratives like

FIGURE 1.5. Deogratias's point of view. Stassen, J. P. *Deogratias.* Trans. Alexis Siegel. New York: First Second, 2006.

Deogratias are powerful partly because they remind us of our own shame, and they help us envision the shame of another. The filtering consciousness, normally set at a slight remove in *Deogratias,* insists on identification during the night sky panels and when Deogratias looks at the remains of what he has done. This gesture toward a universal complicity is further complicated by the lack of explication. Unlike other graphic narratives that deal with atrocity, *Deogratias* does not textually communicate the interiority of the title character, who is a cipher within his own story.

This tale of a traumatized young man attempting to mete out his own justice in the wake of an atrocity points outward at the reader more than inward at the stories of the victims. Much of the present-day plot revolves around his efforts to poison complicit parties, to use his knowledge of how Rwandan culture works, and to capitalize on their lack of knowledge and their trust in the idea that he is nothing more than a madman. This would seem to support the idea that context is the only way in which one can adequately empathize with the victims, but his actions are not, in fact, directed at victims—he poisons perpetrators, collaborators, and bystanders indiscriminately. But are we meant to take Deogratias as a moral example? Is it instead, perhaps, that we *are* meant to feel something he is feeling, but that emotion is not empathy for the victims?

In the context of postgenocide reconstruction, Rwanda was faced with the insurmountable task of punishing an enormous proportion of the surviving population who fell under the rubric of perpetrators: those who drove and inflicted the violence. Collaboration during the genocide was extremely widespread, and individuals who were nominally opposed to the slaughter were frequently forced to kill Tutsis to get through roadblocks. How does one grapple with crime on so massive a scale and so complex a rubric of complicity? How does a country that should be, and is, ashamed of the actions of so many of its population come to some sort of psychological equilibrium?[11] Stassen's graphic novel poses this question in the context of relative guilt. Julius, who "forced" Deogratias to commit atrocities, is slain along with Bosco, an RPF officer whose only apparent crime during the genocide was ordering his soldiers to kill the dogs who were consuming the corpses and, possibly, for failing to prosecute Deogratias himself. The French sergeant is poisoned. Deogratias also tries to kill Brother Philip, who simply fled and was able to flee only by virtue of his skin color.

This seems to be an attempt by a truly guilty party to diffuse guilt among others. But perhaps it is a dimension of what Rancière referred to as "emancipation," "the blurring of the boundary between those who act and those who look" (*The Emancipated Spectator* 19). While Rancière is attempting to preserve the positive connotations of such a definition, emancipation also necessitates the converse; this blurring is a regular feature of life in the media age and creates ethical quandaries in terms of spectatorship,

---

11. Of course, between 1996 and 2003, a countergenocide was carried out against Hutus in the Democratic Republic of the Congo, which has been largely unremarked upon in the Western media.

in terms of who counts as a bystander. It is interesting in this context that "etymologically *shame* comes from the Goth word *Scham,* which refers to covering the face" (Gregg and Seigworth 72). Shame becomes the point at which spectatorship and the guilty perpetrator come together in *Deogratias.*

As a historio-metagraphic, *Deogratias* highlights the importance of recognizing mediation and positionality in our consumption of texts that deal with atrocity. In order to avoid a full denial of identification, which would make the work difficult to read, Stassen instead uses Deogratias's perspective at his least empathetic moments: when he is no longer human, either because he has turned into a dog or because he is surveying the damage done by the monstrous crimes he committed. The perspective of the dog, and the other points at which the reader is invited to enter the text, are *perceived* as metonymic: the fragmented nature of the graphic narrative genre, the partial memories, the lack of confession, and the shame that fills the aporia of the present stand for the thousands of other stories in the gutter, just as the bystander stands for a more complex problem than simply perceiving and failing to act.

Shame becomes the point at which spectatorship and the guilty perpetrator come together in *Deogratias.* To reach his political ends, which are ultimately more affective than exhortative, Stassen uses the "natural" drive to feel empathy for characters within a fictional work to work against readers' complacency. Lawrence Langer, in *The Holocaust and the Literary Imagination,* paraphrases Ortega y Gasset's assertion that "metaphor [is] the most radical instrument of dehumanization in modern art" (166), and here, the dehumanization occurs not as a tool of propaganda but rather as a visual metonym for a range of problematic acts, of looking and of doing.

Deogratias also thwarts the reader's desire to have the circumstances surrounding atrocity reflexively analyzed and explained. In addition to its lack of explanation to undergird reader response, *Deogratias* furthermore denies interiority beyond point of view. While the story is focalized through the title character's consciousness, it does not articulate what he *thinks* about what he has done. He offers no explanations or excuses, posits no lessons or morals that can be taken away from the work. Deeply nihilistic though that may seem, *Deogratias* proposes an alternative way of viewing the spectatorship of genocide: one in which the individual consuming the text is denied the provisional answers, or even the posing of questions, offered by texts like *Maus.* Its very lack of these popular features makes *Deogratias* an absolutely essential text in the study of graphic narratives that address atrocity.

Romeo Dallaire ends his account of the Rwanda genocide with an observation and a question. He notes that "although often couched in the empathetic phrases of humanitarian aid and of supporting the right of persons to be free from tyranny, ephemeral interventions and relief efforts tend to dry up as soon as CNN puts yet another disaster on prime time" (520). The suggestion here is that empathetic engagement with geographically distant human beings is an unsustainable model because we cannot necessarily rely upon our hearts to remain involved in protracted suffering. *Deogratias* interjects at precisely the point apathy begins, because it reminds us that the explanatory mechanisms of both fiction and history are insufficient. In postgenocide Rwanda, Mamdani writes that "neither the identity of the perpetrator nor that of the survivor is as transparent in Rwanda as [differences between beneficiaries and perpetrators] would lead us to think. This is because the identification of both the perpetrator and survivor is contingent on one's historical perspective" (267). *Deogratias* traces this ambivalence of perspective to promote a more nuanced view of how violence occurs within a complex network of social relations, and our reception of images of and stories about that violence is similarly complicated by positionality.

Dallaire's final question in *Shake Hands with the Devil* asks "'Are we all human, or are some more human than others?'" (522), the lingering suggestion of course being that cost-benefit analyses of troop involvement in protecting foreign lives becomes progressively more fraught the further away from our sociopolitical sphere they are. While Dallaire positions himself as an idealist who can see a global sea change in which human life is increasingly recognized as universally human, *Deogratias* takes an opposing position. For the main character, some *are* more human than others. Even in the postgenocide environment of reconciliation, memory is Deogratias's only access to a once-embodied humanity, and explaining his dwindling humanity would be pointless. *Deogratias* undermines the pedagogical impulse, what the reader *can* and *should* learn from genocide, at every turn, down to the recognition of a perpetrator as both a human (like us) and a monster (inhuman). Deogratias is clearly not a monster, but neither is he clearly human. Instead, he is a cringing animal, which is how the crisis in Rwanda was treated at the time: as an animalistic spasm.

The transformation of Deogratias is more than morphing into an animal. He is, in fact, being consumed by the dog. When he becomes a dog, we see the conversion occur slowly, over the space of several panels, but once it is complete, his human visage, that to which we would normally attach our ideas about identity, is utterly annihilated. He is shown as being literally devoured alive by his past and converted into exactly the creature that was wiped out in Rwanda during the waning days of the genocide. The dogs were exterminated as a public health hazard, which is precisely what Deogratias has become. He has purposefully poisoned those he knows or believes to be complicit, participated in the genocide, and is a public drunk. He physically transforms into the animal most emblematic of the genocide, or at least hallucinates such a transformation. This change only comes, though, when his memories threaten to eat him whole.

Stassen's careful work to undercut the identification he promotes in the reader creates a commentary on our ethical relationship with the "intolerable image." Ranciére's contention that "If horror is banalized, it is not because we see too many images of it [. . .] we do see too many nameless bodies, too many bodies incapable of returning the gaze we direct at them, too many bodies that are an object of speech without themselves having the chance to speak" (*The Emancipated Spectator* 96) highlights that we are not ethically bound by the image alone but rather by the narrative. When Deogratias or Benina or the television screen return our gaze in this historio-metagraphic, it is to remind us that "not just anyone is capable of seeing and speaking" (96), but they should be. It is also a reminder that to watch without action is to be complicit.

CHAPTER 2

JUST LIKE SALLY

Rape and Reflexivity in *Watchmen*

"We're not real to them," she said. "We're just characters in a story they're reading. That's why they think it doesn't matter what they say to us."

—quoted in Mary Elizabeth Williams's discussion of the misogynistic comments leveled at negative reviews of *The Dark Knight Rises*

These sorts of images are the norm. We have access to them, they exist, and so we view them—duh. Carry this view a little further and it isn't hard to understand how even a nonsociopathic teenager might opt to view a photo of a girl's rape, or even send it along to a friend [. . .] it hasn't even occurred to many of the kids—the ones who are not, you know, patently evil—that they are violating this girl themselves.

—Tracy Clark-Flory

GRAPHIC NARRATIVES have not always been kind in their depictions of women, with female characters frequently enduring horrific violence in the name of advancing the development of a male protagonist. Gail Simon's *Women in Refrigerators* site documents many of these instances, which in spite of objections about the "erasure" of violence done to male characters, illustrates at minimum the problematic way in which sexual violence may be depicted. However, graphic narratives have been used by women to tell their own stories as well, and female characters in popular titles are increasingly more well developed and have been in the past decade granted unprecedented attention, a trend concurrent with increasing media and public attention to the sexual assault epidemic. While progress has been made, men are still often not prompted to fully identify with female characters (or flesh-and-blood women). Without a measure of identification, can men have empathy for what women endure in terms of sexual violence? Film theorist Laura Mulvey's concept of the "male gaze," wherein the point of view is staged for an assumed male viewer and so genders the viewer male regardless of her identity, that the man is the looker, the woman is the "to-be-looked-at" (837), is useful to consider in relation to comics studies in regard to these questions. While too deterministic to be applied uncritically, the male gaze can be understood under the rubric of Phelan's ethical situations, particularly in the relationship between the implied author and the reader. The implied author may make choices about point of view that appear to uphold a gaze that objectifies female characters while simultaneously undermining that objectification. Similarly, the reader in graphic narratives is presented with a series of points of view and must negotiate those according to his or her own biography, desires, and expectations. Our ideas about gender play such a powerful role in our psyche that reflecting on the extent to which our attitudes are culturally constructed—rather than natural—can be daunting. Historio-metagraphics, however, may play with existing, recognizable gender roles and stereotypes in order to expose the problems, or the violence, at their core.

Rape often acts as a spur for a male main character to avenge the violation of a woman in his life.[1] On its surface, this may appear to be a plot structure predicated on cross gender identification: because the man cares for and empathizes with the woman, he seeks vengeance on the one who violated her. Scratch the surface of this generous reading, however, and one finds instead rage over property damage. Male characters infrequently ask female characters who survive their ordeal what she would like to do to recover, and more often, the woman is raped and murdered, and in silencing the victim, that space can be filled by the drive for revenge. When is rape simply a gratuitous example of sexual violence in comics? To what extent do mostly male comics writers and artists consider their own position in relation to mostly female rape victims' experiences? When is the representation of rape in comics used as a metonymic device that stands in for an overall dysfunctional attitude toward women?

These questions can be addressed through the examination of authors' manipulation of point of view, the way in which various points of view and other content prompt both identification with characters and imaginative closure between images, and the tensions between codes of signification.[2] Rape is a particularly fraught subject in relation to ethical positioning, as it

---

1. *Hellblazer, The Boys,* and *Preacher* are only a few titles in which this formulation occurs.

2. See Hatfield's introduction to *Alternative Comics.*

is a traumatic event primarily (although not solely) experienced by women at the hands of men.[3] Because identification across gender lines for men is strongly discouraged,[4] recognizing rape as a traumatic crime, and empathizing with victims, is often difficult for men. Given that men are by far the most frequent perpetrators of sexual violence, it would make sense that promoting identification with women's experiences would be a positive way to reduce incidents of sexual violence, but by the time such empathy is encouraged, it is often difficult. Furthermore, as one of very few crimes in which it is acceptable to question ways in which the victim might have "collaborated" in their victimization, rape is shrouded in an array of "myths" that not only stigmatize victims but seek to exonerate perpetrators.[5]

The stigma attached to rape has historically made it difficult for victims to discuss their experiences, and while graphic narratives have often relegated sexual violence to a form of inspiration for the male protagonist, other graphic narratives have sought to integrate or showcase women's voices. Hillary Chute, in her *Graphic Women*, critiques the way in which women have largely been left out of "the rise of comics as a literary form" and examines a number of comics produced by women about their lives. She argues that

> the stories to which women's graphic narrative is today dedicated are often traumatic: the cross-discursive form of comics is apt for expressing that difficult register, which is central to its importance as an innovative genre of life-writing. However, the authors do not project an identity that is defined by trauma: they work to erase the inscription of women in that space. (2)

Chute's work is predominantly concerned with revealing how comics intervene differently in questions of ethics in narrative, particularly in terms of women's life writing. Her essential work opens up a range of questions about the autographics that she covers, like Alison Bechdel's *Fun Home*

---

3. Statistics bear out this generalization. While one in six women experience attempted or completed rape in their lifetimes, one in thirty-three men do ("Scope of the Problem"); 9 percent of victims of rape are male (Planty et al.). It is not my intention to erase the traumatic experience of men who have been victims of sexual violence. Instead, in this chapter, I am focusing on female victims because of the way in which the gaze is staged for an assumed male audience.

4. The journal *Gender and Society* frequently publishes work on gender policing that includes discussions of ways in which males are discouraged from viewing females as human like them.

5. Joanna Bourke's *Rape: Sex Violence History* provides an excellent primer on "rape myths."

and Phoebe Gloeckner's *Diary of a Teenage Girl* and *A Child's Life*. Historiographic metafictional graphic narratives dealing with violence and trauma offer alternative insights into understanding the history of atrocity on both public and private scales. Chute's work is explicitly concerned with authors' choices about the representations of their *own* memories, noting that "images in comics appear in fragments, just as they do in actual recollection; this fragmentation, in particular, is a prominent feature of traumatic memory" (4). Autographics often structurally mimic traumatic memory, but how do historio-metagraphics utilize this construct? I contend that historiographic metafictional graphic narratives that deal with rape and the trauma associated with it disrupt readers' sense of a shared history and open up the possibility of complicity in violence, partly through choices made by the implied author about how point of view and the gutter are utilized. While the autographics Chute and others examine seek to structurally communicate and immerse the reader in the experience of trauma in various ways, historio-metagraphics may attempt to implicate the reader in the violence in order to prompt reflection on the audience's abetment of rape culture.

The leveraging of readerly complicity is not a simple, direct statement of guilt, however, and in fact wouldn't be effective if it were. Instead, graphic narrative authors employ a variety of strategies to create a complex ethical document that simultaneously humanizes both the victim and the perpetrator without inviting identification with the former. Alan Moore and Dave Gibbons's *Watchmen* is a particularly masterful example of this phenomenon, as it weaves together large-scale historical disasters and fictionalized versions of atrocities at the level of public violence, while keeping a private, and to some extent unspoken, act of sexual violence at the center of the plot. In this chapter, I will explore how the imaginative work of the reader is manipulated by author and artist to produce certain affective interactions with characters. In particular, I am interested in the way identification with the emotional states of characters can be promoted or withheld by the way in which the reader is positioned in relation to the scene depicted within the panel. The reader may adopt a first- or third-person point of view in relation to the scene, but perspective also shifts between panels, which prompts the reader to connect different points of view. *Watchmen* is the natural choice for this exploration as the relatively stable panel size and arrangement allow for a closer analysis of how point of view varies from panel to panel. Focusing on three instances of memory within *Watchmen*, I will discuss how point of view operates within and between panels to produce or inhibit empathy in the reader. In addition, I will explore how memory and affect are intertwined in the graphic narrative and what cultural attitudes *Watchmen* reveals about sexual violence, empathy, and memory. Departing from the bulk of the literature on *Watchmen*, I will argue that The Comedian's attempted rape of Sally Jupiter constitutes a central plot point, one that has been underexplored in part because of the way in which it is depicted and in part because of what this depiction says about our culture.

WATCHMEN AND HISTORIOGRAPHIC METAFICTION

The publication of Moore and Gibbons's *Watchmen* was a watershed moment in the development of adult-oriented graphic narratives. Set in an alternate America in 1985, as Nixon is re-elected, it follows a collection of "adventurers" who donned masks to fight crime but were either forcibly retired or brought under government control after the Keene Act, which sought to limit acts of vigilantism. *Watchmen* follows a constellation of characters, opening with the murder of Edward Blake, who was also The Comedian, a brutal man who chose to work for the government after the Keene Act. Rorschach, formerly Walter Kovacs, discovers Blake's secret identity when surveying his apartment after the detectives have departed. Rorschach communicates through his diary at the outset, a sort of internal monologue cataloguing his unhinged ramblings. He comes to the conclusion that a "mask killer" may be on the loose and goes to warn Dan Dreiberg, formerly Nite Owl, an unassuming and genteel man who abandoned adventuring many years before. Nite Owl and Rorschach had acted as partners prior to Dan's retirement. Rorschach additionally goes to warn Dr. Manhattan and Laurie Juspeczyk, formerly the Silk Specter. Laurie was pushed into a life of adventuring by her mother, Sally Jupiter, and is now the dissatisfied paramour of Dr. Manhattan. Dr. Manhattan is the only character in *Watchmen* who legitimately qualifies as a "superhero," with abilities including teleportation and the alteration of matter at will, which resulted from an accident in an intrinsic field chamber. Additionally, Adrien Veidt, also known as Ozymandias, appears early as Rorschach races to warn all former adventurers. Veidt retired even before the passage of the Keene Act and is a wealthy entrepreneur widely hailed as "the smartest man on earth."[6]

---

6. In the interest of limiting the scope of this study, I will exclude several major subplots from the bulk of my discussion. The newspaperman, the metacomic *Tales of the Black Freighter*, most textual passages, and press clippings will be left out of the discussion.

Rorschach's journal introduces the murder of Edward Blake in the context of his disgust over the excesses he sees as inherent to the city. As the plot unfolds, the narrative shifts between the past and the present and also shifts between historical realities and fiction. For example, Dr. Manhattan has been used by the United States as a nuclear deterrent for many years; his mere presence and the potential he represents keep the world from catastrophe. Additionally, his god-like control over matter has led to a series of foreign policy successes for the United States in stopping the spread of communism, including a victory in Vietnam. While Dr. Manhattan supports U.S. foreign policy, his personal life has slowly crumbled, and after he is accused of inadvertently giving cancer to his ex-wife and a number of former friends, he leaves Earth for Mars to remember and regret.

Other characters in *Watchmen* also have to face their personal histories as they are set against the potential for nuclear holocaust. Private tragedies, such as Rorschach's abusive childhood in the care of his prostitute mother, Nite Owl's feelings of impotence, and Laurie's despair over her devaluation next to the power of her consort, are all contextualized within rising tensions between the United States and the Soviet Union, as scientists advance the doomsday clock and people talk of the imminence of war on the street. While this graphic novel has received significant attention because of its metacommentary on superheroes and the comic genre, less attention has been paid to the way in which *Watchmen* is preoccupied with perspective. While its nine-panel grid form appears restrictive at first glance, the contents of each uniform panel constitute a meditation on the infinite variations available in point of view. The tagline "Who Watches the Watchmen?" appears in the context of a protest against masked vigilantism but also gestures toward the wandering perspectives on the page. Many flashbacks in the novel rely on first person point of view, in part to mask the identity of The Comedian's killer, as in the first pages of the comic, which depict an aerial viewpoint of a smiley face button in blood that is running into the gutter, overlaid by the bile-laden narration of Rorschach's journal. While Rorschach's journal focalizes the scene, the point of view is distinct from that of Rorschach's, as we see him (without his mask) passing by the building carrying a doomsday sign.

Watchmen is, to a certain extent, a graphic novel about history and memory in postmodernity. It has been mined as a representation of trauma, particularly in the context of the twentieth century, which saw a rise in conflict on a global scale. Critics have discussed Moore's preoccupation with how history is configured in a contemporary context and have also attempted to address the more specific traumas related in the graphic novel, mapping it as a symptom profile for PTSD (Erika Szabo, "An Analysis of *Watchmen*"; Sean Carney, "The Tides of History"; Brandy Ball Blake, "*Watchmen* as Trauma Fiction"). Many of these critiques, however, subsume the smaller traumas, like Sally's, into the overarching narrative of the superhuman Dr. Manhattan and the encroaching nuclear war. In spite of this tradition of criticism dealing with the major issues at stake in *Watchmen*, the elevated narratives of heroism and the salvation of mankind hinge on The Comedian's attempted rape of Sally Jupiter and her subsequent forgiveness of him, resulting in the eventual birth of their daughter, Laurie. Though the attempted rape is the central binding mechanism of the plot, it has remained peripheral in the scholarship on *Watchmen*.

What does it mean to have rape, and the forgiveness thereof, as a central plot point in a graphic novel that largely excludes female point of view and is dominated by underdeveloped female caricatures? Main male characters in *Watchmen* are granted interior monologues, through a journal in the case of Rorschach and through a meditative multitemporal musing in the case of Dr. Manhattan. This extra-linguistic dimension exists for only one female character, Laurie, and her point of view is strongly marked by an inability to listen as well as look. That there are only two major female characters, and one serves only as an object of the gaze, is significant in a work that seeks to put the public into conversation with the private.

This also begs the question, in terms of the overall structure of *Watchmen*, of what it means to have a metafictional confrontation with history in which the god-like character reasserts both linearity and simultaneity. The extra-linguistic female presence exists largely to be viewed, and while women's memories are depicted, the most traumatic memory is focalized through a consciousness outside of the woman experiencing the trauma and outside of her memory of the experience. How does temporality figure into our reflections of the rape that functions as a hinge for the plot? We see the attempted rape in a flashback, in which Sally is remembering the scene. At least, it is ostensibly framed as her memory, but the scene itself only once approximates her point of view. This connection with point of view in which the memory is deployed as not hers but rather from a different perspective is important to understanding how *Watchmen* deals with the individualized, private experiences of women in contrast to the overarching plot, which is distinctly masculine, preoccupied with male characters, and concerned with large-scale public expressions of violence.

RAPE JOKES

The scene depicting The Comedian's attempted rape of Sally Jupiter begins with an approach showing her from behind in an empty room as she removes her dress. In spite of the semierotic nature of the scene, Sally is positioned awkwardly, her arm at an odd angle as she pulls off her costume, indicating that this—instead of the refined and marketed sexuality she adopts when crime fighting—is a private moment. The following panel moves off to the side, a word bubble simply saying, "Hi," without revealing the source of the greeting, and surprise shows on Sally's face. The page break would draw out the mystery of the identity of the intruder, but previous portions have already revealed that it is The Comedian. Why not simply depict him, then? This panel constitutes the only moment in this scene at which we have some access to Sally's interiority: she does not know who is approaching, and by withholding The Comedian as the source of the greeting, we are momentarily held in suspense.

The following page begins with three panels showing Sally and The Comedian in dialogue. The first depicts The Comedian at a distance, asserting that Sally's anger over his intrusion is unwarranted because her announcement about changing constituted an invitation. The second shows The Comedian tearing away the dress Sally was using to shield her body. This would normally be a moment for gratuitous nudity, but instead The Comedian shields Sally's body from the reader's eyes. By denying the reader a frontal view of Sally's body, Moore and Gibbons may be suggesting that she is more than the objectified sexual creature her costume indicates, but the reader does not have access to her narration or an interior monologue describing the emotions she feels. Ultimately, the reader has no more access to Sally's interiority than does The Comedian. The Comedian's reading of Sally's decision to change out of her costume as an invitation for, at minimum, voyeurism, is thwarted for the reader by the way he is positioned in the panel. His body is situated to shield her from the reader's gaze when he says "C'mon, baby. I know what you need. You gotta have some reason for wearin' an outfit like this, huh?" (II 6), echoing a common defense for sexual assault, when a woman's attire is attributed the blame. Behavior and attire are both interpreted as enticement, which mirrors real-world experiences of sexual assault, but in addition, the mirroring that takes place between panels emphasizes the manner in which the victim is caught in a "hall of mirrors," in which every active denial is construed as incitement. The tensions between word and image, "whose implications can be played against each other" (Hatfield 37), underscore that

Sally's intensions are erased. Similarly, when she stutters out a "No . . ." replete with ellipses that indicate she would go on, he interrupts "Sure. No. Spelled Y, E . . ." Denying the reader access to the way in which she would articulate her own experience of the event is, I argue, an important aspect of this scene. Rather than have her narrate the specific feeling she had (or has) about the attempted rape in the memory, it is instead depicted as if it is not her memory at all. The reader never sees the actions unfold from her perspective but rather at a slight distance. A perspective that is independent from the characters in the scene is not uncommon in graphic narratives, but *Watchmen* contains a number of moments in which the reader occupies the character's perspective, so this external point of view in such a pivotal scene is curious. The series of panels is framed by Sally in the present day, so it is reasonable to attribute the flashback to her own memory of the experience of the attempted rape. However, in other scenes that depict a character's memory, at least a few panels depict the character's point of view. In this memory, Sally's perspective is excluded, and pointedly so. Not only is her perspective unavailable, but the scene also lacks text boxes that could narrate her internality.

The external point of view is maintained in the following panel, in which Sally scratches The Comedian's face, replying "Spelled ENN OH!" The panel beginning the next row alters the viewpoint, depicting Eddie's blank stare over Sally's shoulder. The over-the-shoulder viewpoint is the closest the reader comes to Sally's perspective in this scene, which begs the question: with which character are we meant to empathize? Creating distance in these panels while The Comedian recycles now-famous justifications for rape is a curious move. Why create this distance from the victim? This is important in part because Sally is a vigilante. In spite of the sexy costume, her major role requires significant strength in order to subdue criminals, and as is indicated elsewhere in *Watchmen,* she does in fact have some impact on crime. So why, in this circumstance, in which her own safety is at stake, is she unable to fend off her attacker by herself?

The panel at the center of the page depicts The Comedian forcefully punching Sally in the stomach, while the following panel shows a close-up of his fist smashing across her face, an approximation of his first-person point of view. Is this panel a commentary on the identity of the assumed reader? Is it meant to be a critique of violence against women, or is it a vehicle by which male readers can vicariously experience this? The tension between the "text as experience vs. text as object" (58) here, as Hatfield notes, "highlight[s] the distance between text and reader, and foreground[s] the reader's creative intervention in meaning-making" (63). Furthermore, this emphasis is meant to recall rape myths and narratives surrounding sexual violence the assumed male reader may feel implicated in.

The final row of panels on this page first shows the continued beating as it is reflected in Moloch's Solar Mirror Weapon, an artifact from a previous battle. The image one would see in the mirror if the reader was in the position of either of the characters. However, neither of the characters' faces are turned toward the mirror. Is this the image The Comedian sees out of the corner of his eye? Is the mirror used as a symbolic representation reflecting the reader's consumption of violence against women back at him, slightly distorted, involving him in the commission of the crime? Or is it meant to show the distortion inherent in such acts?

The next panel simply shows The Comedian on top of Sally, undoing his belt, as she pleads with him. The blood from her mouth and her tears, the fear in her face, are all clearly rendered. While he is not directly facing her, the reader instead is confronted with her face distorted by pain and fear. The final panel on the page shows The Comedian's hand holding Sally's arm to the floor, beside a display of King Mob's Ape Mask, a word bubble from outside of the scene asking "Sally? What's keeping you?" The reader views The Comedian partly pantsless, sitting on top of Sally, through Hooded Justice's leg, and in the ensuing panels, the reader sees a reiteration of the beating Sally just endured, but The Comedian has replaced her. A close-up of Hooded Justice's fist crossing The Comedian's face, his nose spurting blood is followed by the center of the page, occupied by a panel very similar to the panel in the same position on the previous page.

The closest the reader gets to Sally's point of view is over her shoulder, but the reader is placed directly within the point of view of both The Comedian and of Hooded Justice (see fig. 2.1). The reader views The Comedian through Hooded Justice's eyes in one panel, and the reader looks up at Hooded Justice in another as The Comedian says, "This is what you like, huh? This is what gets you hot . . ." (II 7). This movement is questioning both the characters' and the readers' motivations. In spite of The Comedian's status as ostensible villain of the scene, he is also articulating the problem of pleasure in reading about and viewing violence. The panel from The Comedian's viewpoint simply shows the surprise and anger in Hooded Justice's eyes in response to this comment. By using the first-person point of view panels, both from the perspectives of individuals involved in brutality, are Gibbons and Moore commenting on the problematic nature of violence in masculinity? Since these two panels virtually mirror each other, how is the reader reflected in the images?

FIGURE 2.1. Hooded Justice's point of view. Moore, Alan, and Dave Gibbons. *Watchmen.* New York: DC, 1987.

The choice to have these pages mirror one another connects to the overall storyline in which our world is mirrored, with difference, in the world constructed by Moore and Gibbons. Erika Szabo briefly discusses some of the incidences of symmetry in *Watchmen,* arguing that the correspondence between panels in the graphic novel makes for a structure that is balanced. Furthermore, she contends that the occasional instances of irregularity should be used to understand the work as a deconstruction of symmetrical ideas of history. Indeed, the mirroring effect here, which leaves out Sally's point of view, demonstrates that the articulation of "both sides" of any event necessarily effaces other experiences that don't fit into the heroic narrative that pits protector against aggressor.

In one sense, the mirroring between the pages shows how violence is experienced similarly by all humans, whether they are "bad" or "good." However, this equivalency is disrupted within the scene, since the reader does occupy the point of view of Hooded Justice and of The Comedian but does not have access to the viewpoint of Sally, ostensibly the true victim in the scene. The panels that offer the perspective of Hooded Justice and The Comedian are each filled with the other: as Hooded Justice looks down, his gaze is directed at The Comedian's bloodied face. As The Comedian looks upward, he sees the surprised eyes of Hooded Justice. The supposed point—Sally, beaten and scared—of their violent interchange is entirely excluded from their points of view. This exclusion is purposeful, I argue, because it illustrates the way in which even women's personal, private traumas are co-opted by "grander" narratives of vengeance in many comics.

In place of being invited into Sally's perspective, seeing the scene from her eyes, or being encouraged to empathize with her, the reader is offered a retributive beating. Sally appears only in the first and in the final two panels on the page, and only in part in the first and penultimate, which shows that she has been reduced to her parts. In the final panel on the page, her breasts take up the majority of the panel, standing in for the rest of her body. By excluding her point of view and her body from the bulk of the page, Sally is excluded from her own history—and from her own memory.

This mirroring between pages is an implicit nod to the pervasiveness of rape and violence against women in our own world. However, Moore and Gibbons specifically exclude Sally's point of view not to dehumanize her experience but rather to emphasize that this contingency is distant from the existence of the assumed male audience, always already closer to the perpetrator than to the victim. This seems, on one level, to insist that the audience is not capable of empathizing with Sally. On closer inspection, since this scene is staged as her memory, in spite of the dissociative visual elements that never access her perspective, the reader is confronted with the problem of how memory is constituted outside of the subject (in this case, Sally). Sally herself never articulates her memory of the attempted rape, and the reader never sees it from her perspective, so we are denied potential pathways for identification and empathetic reaction to her victimization; rather than a call to action, this disavowal of identification gestures to empathy as a moral tranquilizer. "Feeling with" Sally is an insufficient reaction.

On the following page, the first panel is the final panel of the scene and shows Sally on the floor, still bleeding from the mouth and crying. The reader sees her from behind Hooded Justice's legs as he says, "Get up . . . and, for god's sake, *cover* yourself" (II 8), her large breasts at the center of the panel. The remainder of the page is taken up with an exchange between Sally and Laurie in the present day, in which Laurie is complaining to her mother about an old porno comic one of Sally's old fans had sent her. The center panel is depicted from Laurie's perspective, in which the pornographic comic depicting her mother is the object of her gaze. Much like the first- and third-person points of view in the scene that is framed as if it is Sally's memory, once again, Sally's point of view is explicitly excluded from this passage. That the daughter's perspective frames this particular memory is essential: in Sally's memory, she is dissociated from her actual experience, and the pornographic comic stands in as a continuation of this. In the final panel, she is shown still looking at the photograph of the team as Laurie berates her, saying, "don't you *care* how people see you?" (II 8). This remark once again underscores how Sally is objectified even within the progress of her own memory—she is subject to it—and in the pornographic comic as well. She cannot be the source of her own gaze in either the past or the present.

This scene appears in textual form, severely truncated, in a passage of Hollis Mason's memoir *Under the Hood,* which ostensibly describes his time with the Minutemen as the original Nite Owl. A photograph from the group's 1939 Christmas party shows The Comedian holding Sally by the waist as he holds a sprig of mistletoe over her head. Sally is leaning away from him, her arm lightly pushing his back, as Hooded Justice glares at her from behind them. The following page tells us:

> The worst of these [worms] was The Comedian. I'm aware he's still active today and even respected in some quarters, but I know what I know, and that man is a disgrace to our profession. In 1940 he attempted to sexually assault Sally Jupiter in the Minutemen trophy room after a meeting. He left the group shortly thereafter by mutual consent and with a minimum of publicity. Schexnayder had persuaded Sally not to press charges against The Comedian for the good of the group's image, and she complied. (II 32)

While the scene visually depicting The Comedian's assault on Sally adopted a number of different viewpoints to better evoke the terror and confusion of the moment, the textual relation is stark in its simplicity. Rather than describing the assault in brutal detail, the event itself occupies only one sentence, and the sequence of events following it is described without particularly loaded emotional language.

Bryan D. Dietrich argues in "The Human Stain: Chaos and the Rage for Order in *Watchmen*" that "the text . . . adopts a variegated complex of visual symbols to address the notion that to be human is to be inherently visually impaired" (124). While Dietrich is preoccupied with visual symbolism as it represents the way that character orders the world, this idea of visual impairment is interesting in part because of the perspective that the text does not offer. Dietrich's reading of the rape scene is appealing for its insight about how The Comedian's eye comes under attack and the way in which the smiley face logo of the book is reiterated in Moloch's mirror; it ignores how actual point of view inflects the interpretation of these depictions. Even in this interpretation, Sally is incidental, a sidebar to the "actual" story.

Suzanne Keen argues that *"empathy,* a vicarious, spontaneous sharing of affect, can be provoked by witnessing another's emotional state, by hearing another's condition, or even by reading. Mirroring what a person might be expected to feel in that condition or context, empathy is thought to be a precursor to its semantic close relative, *sympathy"* (*Empathy and the Novel* 208, emphasis in original). Mirroring is, in her terms, an essential component of empathy, so does this mean that it is unnecessary for empathy to have a situation focalized through a character's viewpoint? In the case of *Watchmen,* Sally is largely seen with less concern than characters with which the reader shares a point of view, so although we can see her pain, its sensation is foreclosed. Emotional legibility does not necessarily translate into emotional sharing. Peter Goldie's definition of empathy, that to empathize is an "essentially simulationist approach, and involves *imagining the experience of a narrative* from that other person's point of view" (*The Emotions* 3) is crucial in this distinction, because it emphasizes not only the affective sharing, but also the imaginative closure with a separate consciousness. As a brief note, much has been made of mirror neurons in recent years, neurons that are stimulated both during an experience and during the observation of another's experiencing,[7] and Vitorio Gallese cautiously posited that "it seems we're wired to see other people as similar to us, rather than different" (Winerman 1).[8] However, as another neuroscientist, Marco Iacoboni, asserts in a 2008 interview in *Scientific American,* mirror neurons—like empathy—do not necessarily create positive effects, and he notes that they

---

7. Discovered by Giacomo Rizzolatti and his colleagues, mirror neurons were first named in 1996 in *Brain* 119.2, pages 593–609.

8. Gallese's caution is well founded. J. M. Kilner and R. N. Lemon's "What We Know Currently About Mirror Neurons" reviews the existing literature on mirror neurons, noting that many studies are limited in what they can tell us about human subjects, that "there is difficulty in relating these results to mirror neurons, in that they only employ an action observation condition and have no action execution condition" (4). Additionally, they note that recent studies have effectively broken the one-to-one, "monkey-see-monkey-do" understanding of mirror neurons, because work by Pierre Jacob and Marc Jeannerod has illustrated that "mirror neurons discharge during action observation not because they are driven by the visual input but because they are part of a generative model that is predicting the sensory input" (249). Ultimately, the causative role often associated with mirror neurons is more complex because we can understand actions (or visible emotional states) that we cannot replicate, and the neurons themselves do not control this.

may be responsible for the link between representations of violence and imitative violence.

Empathy is seen in part for its political utility, as an emotion or process that may produce changes in attitudes that, furthermore, may promote altruistic behavior. However, as Keen notes, most studies of empathy show that humans have a limited range of engagement and usually empathically bond with those who already share identity characteristics such as sex, age, and race (*Empathy and the Novel* 214). So what is the utility of empathy in literature if it is limited to those like us? Sally's experience is quite unlike that of the average reader of *Watchmen*; comics have traditionally had a male audience, and in this case, even the women reading *Watchmen* would have a difficult time identifying with Sally. It requires a leap across sexes for many, generations for most, and the idea of masked crime fighting for all. However, I think that the rape scene is at the core of Moore and Gibbons's ethos in *Watchmen*, in part because of the scenes that do offer fully subjective viewpoints to the reader. I will return to this below, after examining several instances in *Watchmen* that use first-person point of view in order to open pathways for identification to the reader. Rorschach and Laurie are the major examples of this, although several other characters periodically have portions of scenes depicted from their perspectives. Rorschach and Laurie, however, stand out in part because they represent two poles of reaction to Sally's experience. In the case of Rorschach, he dismisses Sally's trauma early in the work because he sees it as a sidebar to real historical problems, an attitude familiar in even in the present day, when women's experiences of sexual violence are treated as a minor drama. Laurie, on the other hand, is able to focus only on the ways in which Sally's complex feelings affect Laurie. By beginning with Rorschach, I seek to foreground how Moore and Gibbons's choices about perspective and memory create a complex relationship between the gaze of the reader and the gaze of the character.

SEEING WHAT YOU WANT

Rorschach is the only character aside from Laurie who receives a sustained first-person subjective point of view, although this switches between his own view and that of his therapist after he has been caught in a sting. Chapter 6 is partly taken up with this trading of point of view panels, in which Dr. Malcolm Long attempts to figure out Rorschach through the use of Rorschach tests. Focalized through Dr. Long, his notes provide the narrative text boxes. From Rorschach's point of view, the reader sees Long's face, looking curiously out, with an ink blot card foregrounded, held on either side by Rorschach's hands. However, this panel has Long's narrative overlain, noting, "Physically, he's fascinatingly ugly. I could stare at him for hours . . . except that he stares back, which I find uncomfortable. He never seems to blink" (VI 1). While the reader is ostensibly presented with Rorschach's point of view, Long's narration disrupts this illusion. Long's unflattering description of Rorschach overlays an image of Long himself, a moment of cognitive dissonance that suggests the mirroring strategy developed during the Sally scene. Set in the center of the page, this panel also recalls the title of the chapter, "The Abyss Gazes Also," a part of an often-quoted chiasmus from Nietzsche's *Beyond Good and Evil.*

Nietzsche's original German has been translated as "He who fights with monsters might take care lest he thereby become a monster. And when you gaze long into an abyss the abyss also gazes into you" (52). As a cornerstone of understanding the Rorschach character, it also gestures at his genesis as a masked adventurer. His original identity was Walter Kovacs. When he looks at the card, the reader is shown what he sees: a dog with its head split down the center, a bit of brain matter bulging up through the cleaved cranium. The following panel shows Rorschach looking calmly at Long, telling him that he saw "A pretty butterfly" (VI 1). The final panel on the page shows Long slightly from below, smiling, as the text of his journal reads, "His responses to the Rorschach blot tests were surprisingly bright and positive and healthy. I really think he might be getting better. I just wish he wasn't so intense" (VI 1). This dissonance between what Rorschach saw, what he said he saw, and how readily Long believes his answer indicates in part the difficulty humans have understanding the interiority of another person. While the reader is privy to special information—the revelation of what Rorschach actually saw as opposed to what he said he saw—the reader also accesses Long's perspective, which hints at blindness on the part of the reader as well. This blindness is partly framed through interpretive capacity. As with The Comedian's reinterpretation of Sally's denials, the ink blot becomes the body onto which another's memory is mapped and mirrored.

Mirroring reoccurs at the outset of the chapter, in which the left-hand side of the page has a column of three panels, two of which show the ink blot and the third of which is the image of the dog's head. These panels each reoccur throughout the chapter, arranged differently on the page, but still showing, at least with an approximate subjective point of view (sometimes, over the shoulder) of Rorschach, or Kovacs as he was when he was a child. The next ink blot is followed by the child Kovacs, seeing the shadow cast on the wall by his mother having sexual intercourse with a man. The reader watches young Kovacs walking down the hall, fear clearly showing on his face. It is, however, only the first panel that actually shows the scene from his point of view. The rest follow him, and even in the panel in which he sees his mother and the man pressed against one another, his face is clearly visible just between them. The reader is not exactly seeing what he sees but, rather, is watching him see, and misunderstand. The penultimate panel in this sequence repeats the shadow, only this time it is cast by his mother beating him, abruptly shifting back to the original ink blot.

This portion of the narrative unfolds through the intertwined focalizors Dr. Long and Rorschach, alternating between the therapeutic scenes and scenes that focus on the memories or present-day experiences of one or the other. Perhaps the most pertinent scene is Rorschach's memory of the Kitty Genovese case. At the time, he was working as a dressmaker, and a couple of years prior to her murder, Genovese failed to pick up a dress made of a fabric that mimicked shifting ink blots. When he reads about her murder, he is reminded of the dress, which he has kept over the intervening years. He narrates that she was

> Raped. Tortured. Killed. Here, in New York. Outside her own apartment building. Almost forty neighbors heard screams. Nobody did anything. Nobody called the cops. Some of them even watched. Do you understand? Some of them even watched. I know what people were then, behind all the evasions, all the self-deception. Ashamed for humanity, I went home. I took the remains of her unwanted dress . . . and made a face that I could bear to look at in the mirror. (VI 10)

Rorschach's feelings toward the Kitty Genovese case stand in stark contrast to his attitude toward The Comedian and Sally Jupiter. Interestingly, in this case, it is not the crime itself but rather the fact that so many people allowed it to happen without disruption that so profoundly disturbs Rorschach. His narration overlays three panels. The first two depict a number of people standing by their windows, looking down. The reader shares the point of view that would have been Genovese's or that of her attacker. One of the most important elements of this scene is the mirroring between the third panel and the final panel. In the third panel, Rorschach holds up his new face, and the reader shares his perspective as he admires his handiwork. In the final panel, when he remarks that he "made a face he could bear to look at in the mirror," the mask as a face is shown in the first panel in order

FIGURE 2.2. Rorschach's point of view. Moore, Alan, and Dave Gibbons. *Watchmen*. New York: DC, 1987.

to promote solidarity between the reader and Rorschach. The intertextual references to the Genovese rape and murder are significant in that, within the context of a larger narrative about a culture in which Good Samaritan behavior is perceived as declining, a human face for Rorschach no longer bears the same empathetic content as it once did. Furthermore, the actual Genovese story, an important historical event and media sensation, is appropriated into Rorschach's individual narrative, which calls attention to the curious juxtaposition of Sally's story and Genovese's story. Neither Sally nor Genovese are the arbiters of what their story contains or the way in which it is received. Instead, their stories serve as background elements to the stories of male characters. However, in both cases, Moore and Gibbons are careful to include panels that depict other characters' points of view in order to emphasize that the women's narratives have been subsumed in a larger discourse.

In spite of Long's hopefulness, he eventually realizes the Rorschach has not been telling him the whole truth, and he offers Rorschach the first of the ink blots again. The panel from Rorschach's perspective (see fig. 2.2), showing his hands on either side of the card, is reiterated, but this time the card covers most of his view of Long's face as Long encourages him, "Go on. Tell me what you really see" (VI 17).

The center panel shows Rorschach looking carefully at the card, and the following again shows the dog with its head split open. This time, when the reader once again shares Long's point of view, Rorschach tells the truth:

"Dog. Dog with head split in half" (VI 17). In profile, Long asks, "And, uh, what do you think split the uh, split the dog's head. In half," and also in profile, Rorschach asserts, "I did" (VI 17). The following pages are narrated by Rorschach, illustrating from a mostly outside perspective his memory of the case that caused this particular ink blot interpretation.

While this scene is narrated by Rorschach, the point of view largely includes his actions in each panel, showing each step in the narrative not from his perspective but rather from some external source. This flashback to his past, when he was still Kovacs, shows him searching for a missing child. Rorschach is the underdog of the series, already the focus of sympathy and identification, so the external visual narration of searching the dressmaker's shop is jarring in part because there are no text boxes. The scene remains distinctly inflected by his voice in spite of two full pages without any narration overlaying a panel. The first of these simply shows Rorschach searching a run-down studio. The second, however, shows him in thought, examining a cleaver and a saw, touching a cutting board, and, finally, just gazing out of the window at the dogs fighting for a bone in the yard. At this moment, we realize along with him that the child was murdered, chopped apart at the cutting board, and the dogs are now playing with the child's bones. A three-panel spread suggests the violence that is about to take place. In the first, the dogs look up hopefully from their bone while the second depicts Rorschach's arm raised, the meat cleaver in his hand. Rorschach's narration returns in the third panel, which shows only the original ink blot, as he describes the experience, "Shock of impact ran along my arm. Jet of warmth spattered on chest, like hot faucet. It was Kovacs who said 'mother' then, muffled under latex. It was Kovacs who closed his eyes" (VI 21). This spread occupies the center of the page, and is interesting in part for the closure it insists upon: the reader must imaginatively project the violence that takes place between the panels, collaborating with the images actually shown and extrapolating from these the resulting dog with its head split open. However, the image of the bloody dog's head does not reoccur here, and it is simply replaced with the ink blot. Having the reader collaborate in imagining the violence is essential at this point in the narrative as it emphasizes that ink on paper always stands between the viewer and an experience.

Rorschach continues his story by asserting that "it was Rorschach who opened them [his eyes] again" (VI 21), looking blankly out at the reader as we share Long's point of view. These statements are significant to the way in which the gaze, and the objects thereof, may reframe the identity of the gazer. The violence he inflicts on the murderer and his dogs is not what Rorschach sees as his moment of transition but instead the way in which his character changes between two discrete moments of *looking*. In one panel, he still sees as Kovacs—and in the gutter, which in this case is correlated to a moment when his eyes are shut—and in the next panel, he is Rorschach. He ensures that the man responsible for the murder of the child is dead and, at the end of his narrative, explains to Long that "Existence is random. Has no pattern save what we imagine after staring at it for too long. No meaning save what we choose to impose" (VI 26). Events in all of Rorschach's narratives are frequently replaced with the ink blots being shown in the present. The ink blots operate as substitutions for the faces of characters or the depiction of events, implicitly questioning the reader about his own perception of the narrative. By replacing panels with ink blots rather than showing more parts of the narrative, Moore and Gibbons expand the space available for closure, the imaginative projection of the reader's ideas about how panels fit together. This expansion asks readers to reflect on how we have perceived the events depicted.

Rorschach, arguably the most brutal of the characters featured in *Watchmen*, and certainly the most morally uncompromising, is also the least concerned with The Comedian's attempted rape of Sally Jupiter. In chapter I, after surveying Edward Blake's apartment, Rorschach goes to the secure government facility that houses Dr. Manhattan and Laurie to warn them of a potential mask killer. While he is there, Laurie tartly remarks that the murder "couldn't have happened to a nicer person. Blake was a bastard. He was a monster. Y' know he tried to rape my mother back when they were both Minutemen?" (VII 21). Rorschach asserts, "I'm not here to speculate on the moral lapses of men who died in their country's service. I came to warn . . ." at which point Laurie interrupts, "Moral lapses? Rape is a moral lapse? You know he broke her ribs? You know he almost choked her?" (VII 21). I relate this scene simply to show that, while Rorschach has been labeled as seeing the world in black and white, perhaps his only moment of moral compromise in the book is when sexual violence is involved and the perpetrator is a man whom he respects.

This is problematic at the outset, as the reader develops, if not empathy for Rorschach, perhaps what can be called an affinity or an understanding: Rorschach is the poor, uncompromising underdog of the story and provides an ideal vicarious identification because of how clearly his contextualized experiences have shaped him. This affinity is reinforced through the ink blot test substitution panels, which invite the reader not to look at Rorschach but at their own perceptions. Peter Y. Paik's reading of Rorschach in his essential *From Utopia to Apocalypse* is significantly more nuanced than

simple underdog identification. He interprets Rorschach as undergoing
a transformative journey prior to his ultimate demise at the hands of Dr.
Manhattan, particularly contrasting Rorschach with The Comedian in that
while

> Blake had prided himself on his ability to laugh at the horrors of the
> human condition and the imminent annihilation of all human life—and is
> reduced to a mortified shambles when he is forced to laugh at his own
> joke—the thoroughgoing nature of Rorschach's identification with excre-
> ment renders him immune to the flaw that leaves The Comedian vulner-
> able to such a shattering blow: a predilection for rapacity. (62)

The Comedian's avarice duly acknowledged in contrast with Rorschach's
self-containment, Paik turns to the transformation that occurs when he
refuses to remain silent about Veidt's production of the alien attack, affirming that "What is unbearable for Rorschach, and reckoned worse than the
fate of apocalyptic destruction, is the amnesia that the world will make
compulsory in embracing its salvation" (64). Rather than reading his stub-
bornness as more of the same, Paik argues in favor of a recuperation of this
last act of rigid justice as an article of evidence that Rorschach has evolved
past Manichean notions of good and evil. However, his initial resistance to
the idea of censuring The Comedian, even posthumously, for his actions
toward Sally Jupiter remains a stain at the center of his character that cannot necessarily be whitewashed with the same brush. Rorschach spends
more time on the streets in the filth with "the people" than do any of the
other vigilantes or heroes, but at the same time, he is largely incapable
of assessing individual instances of humanity, particularly in the case of
women. His horror at compulsory forgetting does not extend as far as Sally.

Rorschach, when he returns to collect his things at his former apartment, briefly contemplates killing his landlady for the fact that she told the
media that he had made sexual advances toward her. However, his anger
fades into sympathy as he looks at her cowering children, clearly recognizing his childhood self in their faces. Ultimately, sexuality is a dimension uniformly foreclosed by Rorschach, and the barest suggestion of it
invariably invites his reproach. The silence surrounding Veidt's act of evil
is too much for Rorschach to bear, but does this necessarily suggest that he
repudiates the silence he himself demanded about The Comedian's "moral
lapse" at the beginning of the text? While it was the rape and murder of
Genovese that prompted his transition into a more uncompromising crime
fighter, it wasn't the fact of the murder itself that made him don a new face.

It was the gazes of the people in the apartment building above that made him choose to become a vigilante. Furthermore, it wasn't the murder of the child herself that instigated his transition from Kovacs to Rorschach. It was what he saw while looking for her.

LAURIE ON MARS

The scene in which Laurie discovers her true parentage is, in part, about temporalities erupting into one another, times and places converging and abutting one another as she strains to experience time in the way that Dr. Manhattan does. In contrast to her mother's memory of The Comedian's attempted rape, and in contrast to Rorschach's memories, which seem to be imagined by Dr. Long, one of Laurie's memories is distinctly first-person. When Jon asks her about her earliest memory, the reader is shown two small hands clutching a snow globe, eyes and a mouth reflected in it as if the reader herself were looking at the glass. The entire scene from Laurie's memory is depicted in this way: a first-person point of view. While the first panel is from her memory, the second, which shows her point of view with Jon on Mars, interrupts the memory with her experience of the present while Jon exhorts her to "Let yourself see it" (IX 6). The final panel in this row, also from her memory, has her narrating the scene through text boxes while simultaneously showing her memory of it. She says, "Well, I . . . I was five, something like that. I must have got woken up . . . there was shouting downstairs. . . . My mom and dad. God, I can hear them now" (IX 6). The narration of the memory ends after she asserts that she can hear them now, and her memory of her own viewpoint takes over her present perspective.

The second page of this memory begins not with Laurie's narration of the scene but rather with her memory of the conversation passing between her mother and stepfather. In the first panel, Laurie is shown as a child looking in a hall mirror, as her mother says to Schexnayder ". . . shouted at him, he looked surprised, couldn't imagine why I'd bear a grudge. See, it's different for him, and I just couldn't sustain it, the anger . . ." (IX 7). This passage is Sally discussing, in her own words, her decision to have consensual sex with the man who tried to rape her. But her words are truncated, partial, interrupted by Schexnayder who tells her that "God, you know, really, you need analysis, I'm serious" (IX 7). Sally's explanation is not only cut off but is cut off to argue mental deficiency. Laurie walks down the hall as they continue their exchange, peeking through an open door at Sally and Schexnayder fighting and then continuing further down the hallway.

She opens a door into a room containing a television as Sally says "First off, he was there, right? Plus, he was gentle. You know what gentleness means in a guy like that? Even a glimmer of it?" (XI 7). Sally's account, even when uninterrupted, is partial and intensely subjective as well. While the adults continue to argue, it is unclear whether or not present-day Laurie is narrating the content of their argument to Jon or if she is instead reliving this sequence of events, but it seems as though she is in fact reliving this memory in part because of the persistence of the first-person subjective viewpoint. In addition, when the narration returns in text boxes in the final sequence of panels on the page, she seems to be narrating what we have already witnessed in the first six panels on the page, beginning with "I tiptoed downstairs to the TV room" (XI 7). The panel in which the narrative text box appears does not illustrate Laurie tiptoeing down the stairs—that appeared in the final panel on the previous page and the first panel of the present page—but rather depicts the TV room, the final object of the tiptoeing.

Maintaining a first-person point of view throughout an entire scene is relatively rare in graphic narratives, unlike in fiction, wherein an entire novel may be narrated by a single character. The fictional aspect is important as well, as historiographic metafictional graphic narratives like *Watchmen* include fantastic elements that sidestep common readerly concerns about veracity. Laurie's memory is her own, but, interestingly, she is still in some senses narrating a scene from the outside. She is not involved in the conversation between her mother and Schexnayder, although it is in part about her. The memory is not entirely her own, but the reader sees through her eyes and reads what she heard, rather than having it formulated as a story she relates.

When the final sequence of three panels on the page reverts to Laurie's present-day narration, she tells Jon that "Nobody knew I was there. These moments were just mine and everything felt secret and enchanted" (XI 7). Rather than an enchanted scene that communicates her childish wonder at a room in which she is alone, the viewer simply sees a common living room: a television set, several pictures, and a few knick-knacks. However, the following panel depicts a snow globe sitting on top of the television, shining slightly in the low light, Laurie's child hands reaching out for it as her adult self narrates that "it was like a whole world; a world inside the ball . . . it was like a little glass bubble of somewhere else" (XI 7). The final panel on the page reiterates the panel that introduces the memory, in which her hands hold the ball, and the reader sees a cartoony, undefined face reflected in the glass. It differs only in the narration overlaying it, in which she says that "I lifted it, starting a blizzard. I know it wasn't real snow, but I couldn't understand how it fell so slowly. I figured inside the ball was some different sort of time. Slow time" (XI 7). This remark on the way in which time works is reminiscent of how we experience time as a child as well, wherein time is telescoped and only moves more quickly as one ages.

These panels are remarkable for the sheer consistency of point of view. While *Watchmen* is predominantly composed of panels that depict a variety of viewpoints, this scene in particular is the only time in which the reader consistently occupies a character's point of view through successive panels. Sally's experience of rape is set at a remove, and the reader only occupies the vantage points of The Comedian and Hooded Justice briefly, but Laurie's point of view is followed throughout this scene. The visual and textual elements of her narrative are focalized entirely through her consciousness, offering the reader a subjective viewpoint of her memory.

Laurie's memory is what Freud would have called a "screen memory." Rothberg describes the screen memory as that which "stands in or substitutes for a more disturbing or painful memory that it displaces from consciousness" (13). Rothberg's distinction between screen memories and his own concept of multidirectional memory is important to understanding how Laurie's memory operates in association with the imagined and/ or remembered scene of the attempted rape of her mother. Distinguishing between these types of memory "concerns the question of the affective charge of the memories at issue" (16), and he discusses how certain historical traumas, like the Holocaust, cannot be legitimately described as screen memories because they are not particularly comforting or innocent replacements of a more disturbing reality. He argues that "While screen memory might be understood as involving a conflict of memories, it ultimately more closely resembles a remapping of memory in the conscious and unconscious. To be sure, the truths of memory are often in tension with the truths of history" (14). Rape, unlike the larger historical traumas of the Holocaust and colonialism explored by Rothberg, is believed to be an individual, private trauma. However, its placement within *Watchmen* suggests a different reading: the individual's memory of rape as distinctly important within the historical enterprise. Laurie and Dr. Manhattan's debate about the value of human existence is representative of the debate between the relative importance of individual traumas in the face of more sweeping historical disruptions, and its outcome reveals that rethinking this opposition is essential. Laurie must convince Dr. Manhattan to return to Earth and save the world from increasing hostilities that may result in a nuclear strike. Perspective is crucial to the ways in which we examine both individual and collective memories, and the distinction between them is blurred by the very concept of point of view. In their argument on Mars, Dr. Manhattan tells Laurie that "you complain, perhaps rightly, that I won't see existence in human terms . . . But you yourself refuse to consider my viewpoint, letting your emotions blind you" (XI 23), as if emotions are not a significant part of perspective. The dichotomy between feeling and seeing set up by Dr. Manhattan operates contrary to the way in which point of view serves as an entry point into experience and how it inflects all of the interwoven narratives in *Watchmen*.

As Laurie's memories continue to unfold, she slowly comes to realize that her father is actually The Comedian, Edward Blake, the man she had hated for many years because he attempted to rape her mother, and that she was the product of a consensual encounter. The pages that contain this revelation rapidly change between her current situation, standing on a glass clock gear on Mars, and her memories. In the former, Laurie is depicted from a third-person point of view, while the latter reiterates the approximate subjective viewpoint that marked earlier memories. She shatters the gear structure Dr. Manhattan built upon the revelation, but this realization is what changes Dr. Manhattan's mind about existence. He tells her that

> thermodynamic miracles . . . events with odds against so astronomical they're effectively impossible, like oxygen spontaneously becoming gold. I long to observe such a thing. And yet, in each human coupling, a thousand million sperm vie for a single egg. Multiply those odds by countless generations, against the odds of your ancestors being alive; meeting; siring this precise son; that precise daughter . . . Until your mother loves a man she has every reason to hate, and of that union, of the thousand million children competing for fertilization, it was you, only you, that emerged. (26–27)

As Dr. Manhattan continues to explain what he means, the point of view changes panel to panel, zooming out from a scene just above he and Laurie to a wider view of them standing next to the remains of the glass clockwork ship to reveal that they are standing near the eye of a huge smiley face on the surface of Mars, a reiteration of the smiley face icon that repeats throughout the graphic narrative.

Although it is the recognition of the value and "miracle" represented by each individual human life that ostensibly encourages Dr. Manhattan to return to Earth, the real value of individual human lives and experiences are annihilated in the smiley face. McCloud contends that "when you look at a photo or a realistic drawing of a face—you see it as the face of another. But when you enter the world of the cartoon—you see yourself" (36), and this recognition of the self in the object that is least distinguishable as human has important repercussions in *Watchmen*. In looking into a cartoony face, rather than feeling empathy for the experience of another as it is classically defined, instead, the reader projects her own ideas and emotions onto that screen. This is not empathy as such but instead what Goldie refers to as "Centrally imagining oneself as narrator" (*The Emotions* 200), wherein one does not have sufficient information about a character (or person) to empathize but instead thinks about a situation from his or her own perspective. The cartoon face on a dead planet reminds the reader that people become distinct from the self only through narrative. The simple rendering of a face is nothing more than a mirror or a Rorschach test, telling us more about ourselves than others.

When Dr. Manhattan and Laurie return to the planet, they find the devastation wrought by Adrian Veidt, Ozymandias, who has orchestrated world peace by teleporting an "alien" monster with telepathic abilities into the center of the city, the resulting psychic shockwave killing millions in the vicinity but simultaneously securing a cessation of hostilities between the Soviets and the United States. On its surface, *Watchmen* is preoccupied with this move toward global-scale violence—the standoff between nuclear superpowers, wars, the development of weaponry, and, of course, the super-man Dr. Manhattan—but it is the individual struggles and exigencies that render these grander narratives luminous. For Dr. Manhattan, this is the recognition of the value of human life through the ambivalent circumstances of Laurie's conception. For Laurie, it is the recognition of her history as intelligible through memory.

Perhaps empathy, in the case of *Watchmen*, is not wholly about "feeling with" a character or seeing a situation through his eyes. *Watchmen* is partly a commentary on the inability to see a situation from the perspective of another, but empathy is indeed the ability to adopt another context when feeling with another. Empathetic ability is that which allows us to look at a situation, a condition, from the perspective of someone different. We more readily empathize with Laurie's position—her horror at her true parentage and her confusion about her mother's choices—than we possibly can with Sally. Moore and Gibbons do not give us Sally's point of view because her point of view is not shareable; the trauma of both rape and forgiveness have made it other to such an extent that it becomes a cipher at the center of the text.

WHO WATCHES?

Watchmen was developed into a film that premiered in 2009, a few months after I taught a course examining vigilantes in graphic narratives that included *Watchmen* on the reading list. After the release of the film, and its success at the box office, David Hayter requested that HardcoreNerdity.com publish an open letter to *Watchmen* fans to encourage them to not only watch but also return to view the film multiple times in theaters, arguing that, like the graphic novel, the film could not be adequately understood in one viewing. At the conclusion of his impassioned plea, Hayter asserts that

> You say you don't like it. You say you've got issues. I get it. And yet . . . You'll be thinking about this film, down the road. It'll nag at you. How it was rough and beautiful. How it went where it wanted to go, and you just hung on. How it was thoughtful and hateful and bleak and hilarious. And for Jackie Earle Haley [who played Rorschach]. Trust me. You'll come back, eventually. Just like Sally. Might as well make it count for something.

Dislike of films that are adaptations of comics are a normal part of fan discourse, so normal as to generally go unremarked. Hayter's letter is interesting in part because it seems to dismiss normal fan discourse as essentially not worthwhile. By using the fundamental plot point of The Comedian's attempted rape of Sally, and her subsequent consensual sexual encounter with him, Hayter attempts to feminize the fan community's "hysterical" reaction against the film. However, he inadvertently points out exactly the scene that bears the most complex relationship between emotion and perspective, a scene that has been regularly ignored in discussions of *Watchmen* or treated as subsidiary to the larger plot if it is mentioned at all. This suggests, at its core, that the scene depicting The Comedian's attempted rape of Sally is in fact central to the narrative, a moment of real complexity in the relationships between the reader, the image, the point of view, and the social dimensions of violence against women.

Watchmen is an attempt to formulate an ethical situatedness in relation to disaster, but Moore and Gibbons's efforts reveal a world in which recognizing another's pain is less a vicarious experience than a confrontation with the reader's status as a beneficiary of a system that seeks to exclude the most uncomfortable of perspectives. Sally's experience is not focalized from within her own consciousness, and while we share The Comedian's (and Hooded Justice's) perspectives briefly, we are still set at a remove. The panel frames the action of the plot for the reader. The reader has the illusion of seeing through a character's eyes but, in fact, because of the instability of the point of view, is approached as "you" in the form of second-person address. Rather than maintaining the distance of the third person, which focalizes through an omniscient consciousness, or the first person, which approximates the experiential, perspective-bound subjectivity of a character, the reader is taken as a part of the narrative.

This form of address pervades *Watchmen*. The scene of the attempted rape is framed by Sally's memory and her discussion of "the old days" with Laurie, but it is set at a distance from her consciousness and so becomes a voyeuristic imagining on the part of the creators that addresses the reader *as if we were doing the imagining.* Similarly, Rorschach's therapy sessions are framed as a conversation in which the reader is addressed. His memory of the night he went from being Kovacs to being Rorschach is again contrived in this fashion; while the scene is ostensibly Rorschach's memory, his point of view is only available intermittently. While one of Laurie's memories is focalized entirely through her point of view, here the reader is made ever more aware of the frame and the gutter, that which denotes a viewpoint to be occupied. The division is not between memory and present, or between public and private, but rather between the "I" and the "you."

Paik argues that *Watchmen* shows that "community as such is only possible on the basis of a 'disavowed knowledge' or trauma, an act of collective repudiation that unavoidably relies on a stable distinction between the public and the secret" (65). This argument is made in reference to Veidt's insurance of world peace through the introduction of an outside terror. However, I wonder if this could not also apply to the attitudes toward the attempted rape that rest at the center of the plot. While the attempted rape is certainly not a secret—in fact, it has been published in a widely read book and is seemingly common knowledge among the characters in the story—knowledge of the rape more accurately fits the category of "disavowed knowledge" than Veidt's plot because most of the world is not aware of the plot, while most of the world is well aware that rape is a pervasive problem but few seek to change it. Rape is disavowed in part through victim-blaming rape myths, like Hooded Justice's anger over Sally's partial nudity, and also in part by the victims themselves, who are unsure of how to confront what has happened to them, as Sally awkwardly articulates in an interview included in a later chapter. "Moore and Gibbons confront us directly with the lives that are extinguished," Paik asserts, "for the sake of achieving this perfected and unsurpassable order, whose power to haunt the survivors, it seems, has become defused by the blackmail of universal well-being" (69). Violence on a grand scale extinguished by violence on a grander scale. Yet the attempted rape is violence on an individual scale that, because of Sally's forgiveness and Laurie's parentage, promises redemption. Through Laurie's recognition of her own individual history, Dr. Manhattan returns to Earth to attempt to mitigate against the possibility of nuclear war.

The penultimate scene of *Watchmen* shows the disguised Laurie and Dan Dreiberg arriving at Sally's house. In an externally focalized scene that does not offer shared viewpoints, Laurie tells her mother that she has discovered the identity of her real father. Her mother pauses for a moment in her ranting, and we see only Sally's horrified face as she apologizes, haltingly trying to explain: "Oh, Laurel, I'm so sorry. Wh-what must you think? It . . . it was just an afternoon, in summer. He stopped by [. . .] I tried to be angry, but . . . I mean, I never wanted you to know. I should have told you but . . . I don't know, I just felt ashamed, I felt stupid, and . . ." (XII 29). Sally's attempt to explain is marked by uncertainty about her own emotions and her inability to sustain what from the outside would appear to be the "correct" emotion: anger. Laurie responds that "People's lives take them to strange places. They do strange things, and . . . well, sometimes you can't talk about them. I know how that is" (XII 29). Framed in the ambiguity of ellipses, standing in for things that apparently can't be explained, this exchange textually replicates the gutter.

The conversation is over quickly, and Laurie and Dan depart, leaving Sally alone. She pulls the curtains closed, lifts a framed picture, and kisses it while weeping. The final panel of the scene shows her sitting on the edge of her bed, drying her eyes, while the photograph is foregrounded, a lipstick stain around the face of The Comedian. "Universal well-being" is conspicuously absent from this scene. While Laurie and Dan indicate that they will return to adventuring, Sally is left with the confusion that has haunted her life. The personal, everyday violence(s) of women's lives are, it seems, not extinguished by Veidt's act so much as they are disavowed. The violences that are important enough for memoir but are not worthy of the history books are those that persist in spite of the new world order. Hayter tells us that "You'll come back, eventually. Just like Sally." Confusion in relation to private violence is here conflated with fans' objections to a movie, and similarly, Sally's private experience of violence, and forgiveness, is used in the plot as something that has ceased to be her own.

Whenever Sally is asked to speak about it, she stutters and explains that she was and is confused, that she "tried" to be angry and that she felt that she had played some role in her assault. The ellipses and pauses insist that we must imagine how she came to this on our own terms, much like our imaginative reconciliation of various points of view, because we are not granted a full, clear picture or explanation. Her experience is never laid bare for the reader; her subjective experience of violence and forgiveness are always set at a distance, while other characters' opinions about her experience and other characters' perceptions of her life are examined and are represented in points of view shared with the reader. Why, given the importance of the attempted rape and her subsequent acquiescence, is her viewpoint never offered? Why, when she is exhorted to speak about her experience, does she stutter and repeat problematic myths about a victim's collusion in victimization?

In *Watchmen*, the victims never articulate their experiences outside of the historical, and for Sally's experience, historical contextualization only takes place from outside of the trauma. When Rorschach describes his life, he uses the rape and murder of Kitty Genovese alongside his own experiences to contextualize his worldview. Rape, in *Watchmen*, is indexed alongside the other indignities of life. The fictionalized representation of a constellation of experiences surrounding a moment of large-scale atrocity dwarfs the experience of a woman who barely qualifies as a main character. Sally is only seen through the perceptions and histories of others.

It is no accident that the Genovese murder is set alongside Sally's brief brush with sexualized violence. The Genovese case ushered in a new era of the critique of spectatorship, and while the actual details of the case were much more ambivalent,[9] the idea that the tenants of an apartment building merely looked on as Genovese was attacked has entered the realm of mythology, prompting research into the bystander effect. The diffusion of responsibility among many bystanders decreases the probability of anyone taking action to stop the commission of a crime. While the bystander effect operates in real world circumstances,[10] fictional graphic narratives offer reflexivity. Paik asserts that "when one speaks of fictional atrocities, when the victims belong to imaginary societies or alternate realities, the gaze of the perpetrator, as well as that of the beneficiaries of his or her violence, more easily infiltrates the perspective of the interpreter" (21). Arguing that this positioning short circuits easy morality, Paik's discussion is preoccu-

---

9. A 1995 article in *The New York Times* describes the murder of Kitty Genovese as "first a tragedy, then a symbol, then a bit of durable urban mythology." While it was popularized as a story in which dozens of Genovese's neighbors merely watched as she was raped and murdered, in fact none of the witnesses observed both assaults, the second of which occurred in a sheltered area and resulted in her death.

10. Recent examples include the death of Esmin Green in the waiting room at Kings County Hospital in New York and the death of Wang Yue in China, a two-year-old who was hit by a car; bystanders stepped over and around the girl for seven minutes before someone attempted to help her.

pied with Veidt's plot, but his analysis of the gaze can apply also to the reader's positioning in relation to the memories explored above. *Watchmen* insists upon a reflexive gaze in each instance, and this insistence is the ethical core of the text.

In the case of Sally, the reader never shares her point of view, but it is because the reader is positioned as merely a bystander to the violence that anger is aroused. Something recognizably wrong is occurring, and while we do not identify with Sally, it is nearly impossible to identify in this scene with The Comedian or Hooded Justice because both treat her badly. In spite of this affective disengagement, it is The Comedian's perspective that we briefly share, which immediately calls into question whether the reader can stake out a moral high ground. In addition, we also briefly share the perspective of Hooded Justice, who essentially scolds Sally for her victimization. By viewing the world through these characters' eyes, Moore and Gibbons gesture at the regularity with which we dismiss sexual violence toward women. In fact, while the rest of the plot is haunted by this scene, it is still disavowed.

Rorschach refers to it as a "moral lapse," but it is ostensibly the moral center of *Watchmen*. His morality is indeed viciously skewed, but as Paik contends, "Rorschach switches sides, so to speak, once he recognizes that the true horror comes to reside not in the destruction of the world but rather in the sacrificial massacre that puts an end to violence and enmity" (64). Yet even in this cleansing fire interpreted by Paik, the confusion and self-blame of the victim erupts through the utopic vision. Laurie's experience of the discovery of her parentage causes her to self-reflexively censure her own life as a joke rather than to look beyond her own perspective and her memories as viewed by the readers to see that this is a function of the system. She needs a god, Dr. Manhattan, to assure her that her life has value.

PERSPECTIVE AND OCCUPATION

Women's perspectives in *Watchmen* are relentlessly colonized by guilt and anger, but the structure of the work overall provides a key. The graphic novel as a whole reflects back on itself, particularly book V, which is perfectly symmetrical. The mirroring that takes place throughout *Watchmen* does not only reflect the individual panels and events but reflects back on the reader's attitudes. As with The Comedian's reinterpretation of Sally's denials, the ink blot becomes the body onto which another's memory is mapped, interpreted, and granted or denied credence. However, Moore and Gibbons undercut the potential of an exclusion like this by emphasizing it. Rather than merely glossing over Sally's story, it lingers. The narrative of the attempted rape, and how others feel about it, is returned to again and again, and in each subsequent return, it is made more apparent that Sally's voice is purposefully being excluded. When Sally is allowed to speak, it is focalized through another—through Laurie's memories, through Hollis Mason's biography, through an interview transcript—setting her experience at a remove that makes a powerful commentary on the way in which women's voices are regularly left out of fictional comics. Moore and Gibbons, however, are preoccupied with this exclusion in their incessant return to what many commentators have considered a relatively minor plot point.

The mirroring that takes place in these scenes reflects the assumed readers' attitudes about sexual violence in graphic narratives: that it is indeed a minor plot point that merely creates an origin point for the larger story. Anna Gibbs argues in "After Affect" that "Mimesis is rather like an image in which the figure and ground can always be reversed, so that sometimes subjectivity is in focus, while at other times it recedes into the background, leaving something new to appear in its place" (187). Revisiting this, however, becomes one of the primary indices of the narrative, and the exclusion of her point of view, rather than incidental, is absolutely essential. Sally's point of view isn't accessible because *Watchmen* maintains that private narratives negotiated in public space say more about the onlooker than they do about the character who recounts. The revisiting of the story and the revision of perspective in *Watchmen* challenges interpretations that treat the attempted rape scene as incidental to the larger story arc. Instead of reflecting an individual moment of tragedy and confusion, Sally's story, reinterpreted through multiple perspectives, becomes a commentary on historical minimization of women's shared history of sexual violence. Sally's experience is set not only against the Genovese murder discussed above but also against a horrific, orchestrated disaster that claims millions of lives. We can all agree that Veidt's plot results in a tragedy, whether or not the ensuing world peace holds. We can all agree that the Genovese murder was tragic, whether or not it constitutes a commentary on our social ambivalence. But how can we agree that Sally's experience was an unmitigated private calamity when Sally herself cannot articulate it as such?

Moore and Gibbons include the interview with Sally partly to promote this sense of disorientation in the reader. Sally articulates a sense of responsibility, echoing rape myths that place the woman's behavior at the center of inquisition. Thwarting this paradigm of victim interrogation is difficult, however. For example, The Comedian has been virtually excluded from this discussion. Instead, I have focused on Sally, the victim, her daughter with her attacker, and a man only tangentially related to the drama that unfolded. The Comedian has been interrogated in other works, for other ends, but I would be remiss here to point out how victims are seen as complicit in their victimhood without at least briefly addressing the perpetrator at hand. The Comedian is an archetypal amoral creature, not only because of the scene with Sally but also another scene that shows him murdering his pregnant Vietnamese mistress.

The Comedian, however, has subjective experience that is interrogated by other characters throughout the graphic novel. Rorschach, Laurie, the interviewer, and others all attempt to "make sense" of The Comedian within the story. Sally, on the other hand, remains remote, unable to articulate anything aside from fear, confusion over her own choice and use of her agency, and a vague sense of complicity. Perhaps more to the point, no one truly questions Sally and her actions. While the interviewer poses questions, it is from a space of relative ignorance, and Sally does not offer more information than is asked for. And upon finding out her true parentage, Laurie responds with an aphorism, that "no one knows where their lives will take them." *Watchmen* deals with grand narratives: the rise of the superhuman, the nature of vigilante justice, the question of what it means to be human and what it means to compromise. Sally's story, however, is an aporia at the center that gestures to the extent to which exalted narratives are insufficient reflections of lived experience, particularly for women. When you are the abyss, do you have a choice to stare back at things that do not reflect you? Or do they reflect too well?

The abyss of the Rorschach chapter is in part the danger of a generalized humanity ascribed in totality but relentlessly unspecified. Paik contends that

> the world created by Ozymandias [. . .] would be one in which everyone would be trapped in a state of flight, caught in a perpetual moral retreat, thanks to the all-devouring terror of its foundations. But before the world closes up into a happy and inhuman forgetfulness about the victims of the history from which it has been delivered, Moore and Gibbons confront us directly with the lives that are extinguished for the sake of achieving this perfected and unsurpassable order. (69)

The generalized ends of a comprehensive means of bringing about peace also contains indiscriminate, sacrificial destruction. However, Ozymandias's world will be utopic only in the broadest sense. The lives that are extinguished in order to create peace are not the only victims of history, and Moore and Gibbons emphasize this in the penultimate scene in which Sally weeps as she kisses the photograph of The Comedian. Death, they remind us, is not the only form of victimhood. Marginalization and enforced confusion, living a life over which you feel powerless: these also play a role. Sally herself has lived a life "in perpetual moral retreat," but not from her traumatic experience. Instead, she has fled, afraid of admitting a choice she made in the full flush of agency.

The attempted rape is the moral center of *Watchmen*'s universe. Rather than being a representation of one possible ill of society, it is a representation of the inherent violence of a society turning its hand against itself. The public trauma inflicted by Veidt at the climax of a plot is carefully shown in its private dimensions, particularly those of Dr. Long attempting in vain to express some connection to the world. Just before the creature is teleported into the center of the city, Dr. Long argues with his wife about whether or not to intervene in a scene of domestic violence occurring on the street. He tells her ". . . I'm sorry. It's the world . . . I can't run from it" (XI 20). He and everyone else on the street corner are killed by the creature in the process of trying to intervene into the private drama playing out in public space. Similarly, Sally's experience of private violence stands in for the illness at its heart. This illness is, ostensibly, what Veidt seeks to address through his spectacle of violence.

However, Sally reappears in the final chapter, unreconciled to her past, still ashamed and confused by both her own decisions and the violence that was inflicted upon her. Veidt's utopia has replaced the public fear of massive attack or nuclear war with the perpetual memory of private violence. The accord between nations mentioned on the final pages gestures toward world peace, but world peace has already come at the cost of millions of innocent lives. The reality of Veidt's world is most clearly shown in Sally, in which the private body is ruthlessly and repeatedly offered up as sacrifice for the public good.

Crimes of sexual violence in contemporary society bear an uncanny similarity to this, as one in six women are victims of rape or attempted rape, but few women report to police, and fewer prosecutions go forward. While women are aware of the prevalence of sexual violence, the culture at large minimizes its impact, preferring it stay as a private acknowledgment of confusion rather than a symptom of a larger issue. In this, we see what is really at stake when we share the perspective of The Comedian, of Hooded Justice, and of Rorschach. As Slavoj Žižek argues in *Enjoy Your Symptom,* "the gaze involves the reversal of the relationship between subject and object [. . .] the gaze is on the side of the object" (228). The points of view depicted throughout maintain Sally as outside of the realm of subjectivity, though she clearly has a subjective experience of the scene with The Comedian. That we are given access only to the viewpoints of other subjectivities and third-person point of view asserts how the gaze, the abyss staring back, reveals that Sally's absent subjective viewpoint and absent subjective discussion of her experience point toward forms of violence permanently absent from most popular discussions.

In the next two chapters, I will take up the issue of disavowed knowledge and marginalized perspectives from a different angle. *Watchmen* is a study in the centrality of private violence to large-scale public violence and a study in how point of view shapes emotional legibility. The ethical center of the text insists that we not only acknowledge hidden, persistent violences but that we place them alongside more widely recognized historical traumas. As discussed in the introduction, Hutcheon defines the purpose of historiographic metafiction as "both to enshrine the past and to question it" (6), and the intertextual and historical eruptions in *Watchmen* emphasize that history is a constructed artifact of collective memory that must be brought into conversation with individual experiences. Historiographic metafictional elements in *Watchmen* serve to highlight what is at stake in point of view; the reader shares particular characters' perspectives as the story unfolds to accentuate how history is arbitrated through a network of viewpoints, and the characters whose angles of vision are pointedly excluded stand as markers of what is lost in the larger historical narrative. Furthermore, there are still many historical atrocities levelled against large groups of people that are *also* disavowed. The next two chapters will be concerned with the ethical positioning employed in two different graphic narratives that deal with atrocities in the history of the United States. In these cases, structural racism and violence is made more legible to assumed white audiences through the manipulation of point of view and through character identification, and a call is made for a reintegration of individual experience into the larger narrative arc of history. However, the authors employ different means to arrive at related messages about knowledge and history. In the next chapter, my exploration of *Scalped* will highlight a single flashpoint in American Indian history used to interrogate individual and cultural memory.

CHAPTER 3

"WE'RE STILL HERE"

Authenticity and Memory in *Scalped*

I felt so conflicted about having fled the rez as a kid that I created a
whole literary career that left me there.

—Sherman Alexie

We have lived upon this land from days beyond history's records, far
past any living memory, deep into the time of legend. The story of my
people and the story of this place are one single story. We are always
joined together.

—Taos Pueblo Man (qtd. in Sharon O'Brien's *American Indian Tribal
Governments*)

THE REPRESENTATION of American Indians ranges from the image of the
savage promulgated by Westerns; the firm, strong jaw or cartoonishly smil-
ing mascot; to the primitive with "special knowledge" of the natural world.
These images still have a powerful hold on popular conceptualizations of
Native identity and can be seen in a range of media, including comics. As
Marc Singer notes, because "Comics rely upon visually codified representations in which characters are continually reduced to their appearance [. . .]
The potential for superficiality and stereotyping is dangerously high" (107).
This danger, however, is balanced with the exceptional potential for comics
to disrupt stereotypes and pat narratives about race, a potential increasingly bearing fruit in newer titles. Through the careful manipulation of the
reader's relationship with characters and the text, graphic narrative authors
can make highly complicated arguments about race that undercut stereotypes and reintegrate forgotten histories of marginalized racial groups.

As a visual medium, comics directly express the "visibility" of race
and all the complications thereof, including stereotypical representations,

awareness of appearance, and questions about identity and categorization. They also make arguments about the way in which we read race and how we are taught to read—and to perform—particular identity formations. Furthermore, "authors may expose, either overtly or through tacit implication, certain recognized or even unconscious prejudices held by them and/ or their readers" (8), argues Derek Parker Royal, wherein there is acknowledgement of the work occurring in a network of difficult conversations about race in which most readers hold unconscious biases.[1] Readers may not always be aware of their implicit attitudes or associations, but the structure of graphic narratives, particularly their employment of imaginative closure and iconicity, can make powerful statements about race. In the case of iconicity, graphic narratives may employ and alter stereotypical representations in order to expose latent expectations about racial performance, while imaginative closure may prompt readers to expose assumptions they make about racial identity performance.

The evolution of the graphic narrative has been heavily inflected by race from the beginning. As a form frequently employed by Jewish authors to, on one hand, describe Jewish experience (as with Will Eisner's *A Contract with God*) or to produce a hero that could defend the defenseless in the age of fascist anti-Semitism (as with Jerry Siegel and Joe Shuster's Superman), graphic narratives are rooted in questions of racial identity, marginalization, stereotypes, and social justice. However, graphic narratives have also frequently been the sites of egregious promulgation of damaging stereotypes, as with *Tintin in the Congo*. Responding to such depictions, in *Black Skin, White Masks*, Frantz Fanon asserts that "all those comic books serve actually as a release for collective aggression. The magazines are put together by white men for little white men" (146). Fanon's argument is concerned with adventure comics, a mode that expressed the classical depiction of the "civilized" versus the "savage" and generally figured "the Savage [as] always symbolized by Negroes or Indians; since there is always identification with the victor, the little Negro, quite as easily as the little white boy, becomes an explorer" (146). But in the case of the former, Fanon argues, the act of identification "subjectively adopts a white man's attitude" (147), which splits the consciousness against itself.[2]

---

1. A useful illustration of this can be found at Project Implicit, an ongoing Harvard research project that administers Implicit Association Tests on topics like race and gender.

2. It is worth noting that there are similarities between Fanon's argument about race and Mulvey's argument about gender referenced in the previous chapter.

The ambivalent relationship between graphic narratives and racial representation has continued into the present, and while comics still often employ stereotypical representations or racist attitudes, there are many more comics that engage in nuanced ways with the concept of race. Questions about "authentic" performance of a racial identity, the experiences faced by those of a particular phenotype, the heritage of a group, methods of negotiating a place in the larger social structure, and, of course, disremembered histories are all subjects of meditation in recent comics. In historio-metagraphic treatments, the reintegration of marginalized voices and historical events serves to comment on how the form was responsible in part for erasing the humanity and subjectivity of characters of color and to amend that issue. In recent decades, fictional comics have frequently included recognizable historical facts and representations of the lives of racial minorities as an ethical project in that they explicitly engage with subjectivity in relation to historical events. While the objective pose is frequently seen as a positive trait in historical (and scientific) accounts, historio-metagraphics instead highlight the ethical dimension of writing and consuming narratives of marginalization. Fanon's initial remarks about subjectivity and race are crucial to this discussion because they provide the background whereby historical narrative's already-existing subjective approach is highlighted. For example, Ankersmit notes that "obvious histories of tragedies such as the Holocaust would fail to meet even the most elementary standards of taste and appropriateness if they were to observe a complete moral neutrality regarding the unspeakable atrocities that were committed against the Jews" (93). By rejecting the pose of "moral neutrality," a complex set of ethical questions arise in relation to the representation of historical outrages suffered by American Indians.

These outrages are purposely forgotten in American culture because memorializing the atrocities in the past would also call attention to their continued effects on the present, which I will explore in more detail below. You will note that above, the reference Ankersmit uses to critique moral neutrality in historical writing is the Holocaust, recognized nearly universally as one of the greatest tragedies of modernity. However, the fervor with which Americans in particular memorialize the Holocaust is not matched by a similar interest in atrocities closer to home. Rather than museums or holidays, Native history has largely been erased, and this erasure takes place in part by the cultural choice to remember the Holocaust at the expense of other upheavals in which the nation was stained with the same evil because in the Holocaust we were among the "good guys." Rothberg argues that a "screen memory stands in or substitutes for a more disturbing or painful memory that it displaces from consciousness [. . .] The mechanism of screen memory thus illustrates concretely how a kind of forgetting accompanies acts of remembrance, but this kind of forgetting is subject to recall" (13). Recently, historio-metagraphics have been highlighting how the screen memory of the Holocaust obscures the historical marginalization of American Indians and problematizes that forgetting, including Jason Aaron and R. M. Guera's *Scalped.*

Before delving into *Scalped,* providing some historical background is essential for understanding Aaron and Guera's project in this series. Most of what is provided here is referenced, although not directly explained in its pages. *Scalped* began its run in 2007, intervening at a particularly low point in discussions of American Indian life and identity. After 2002, the Leonard Peltier case faded somewhat from the liberal cultural consciousness, as Paul DeMain, a well-known journalist, withdrew his support from the decades-long campaign supporting Peltier's release from prison. In 1975, two FBI agents on the Pine Ridge Reservation in South Dakota were shot and killed. The ensuing investigation located several members of the American Indian Movement (AIM), a radical organization that had previously occupied Wounded Knee in 1973. The members of AIM used such actions to draw attention to the plight of those on these reservations, where conditions have been consistently poor since the reservations' inception. For example, Joseph Stromberg notes that the Pine Ridge Reservation is home to the lowest life expectancy in the Western Hemisphere aside from Haiti (4). Stromberg notes that a study by Fenelon found that "federal policy shifted from indirect colonialism to termination from the 1940s through 1960s. At best, termination was an attempt to assimilate Natives into the American mainstream. At worst, it was an attempt to erase the existence of tribes and reservations as sovereign political units in order to void treaty obligations" (17). This was the background of the era of AIM in the 1970s, during which "tribal politics for the Oglala Sioux Tribe [were] embroiled in a controversial struggle between traditional and progressive ideologies, catalyzed by the arrival of the AIM. In part based on the Black Panthers, AIM's philosophy was one of uncompromising sovereignty, pan-tribal alliance, and traditionalism" (23). The legal maneuverings surrounding Indian rights and citizenship were problematic because of this tension between poles seeking to eliminate or assimilate.

In *Our America,* Walter Benn Michaels argues that "if the purpose of the Johnson Act was officially to exclude groups of people from citizenship, the purpose of the Indian Citizenship Act was just the opposite. Throughout the nineteenth and early twentieth centuries, Indians had been anomalies with respect to American citizenship" (30). Legal redefinitions of citizenship served to further complicate a relationship with a historical past that was increasingly unrecoverable. Interestingly, these two acts "participated in a recasting of American citizenship, changing it from a status that could be achieved through one's own actions (immigrating, becoming 'civilized,' getting 'naturalized') to a status that could better be understood as inherited" (32). The constructed nature of "citizenship" was obscured further by legal action, while the constructed and performative natures of other components of identity became vital to promoting American Indian identity as something separate and unique.

In addition to acts and mandates that attempted to restructure American Indian identity, Stromberg notes that blood quantum requirements have played a major role in the historical formulation of the identity of Lakota and that mixed-bloods dominated the politics of the tribe until the introduction of AIM, a group that was supported by full-blood traditionalists. The chairman of the tribal council at the time, Dick Wilson, was a mixed-blood assimilationist whose policies, including inviting federal agents to quell unrest, led to AIM's occupation of Wounded Knee, an act that contributed to an atmosphere of panic that later resulted in the deaths of the two FBI agents Peltier was convicted of killing. This chaotic mix of historical influences can be seen in Aaron and Guera's *Scalped,* which calls into question how "the intertexts of history and fiction take on parallel (though not equal) status in the parodic reworking of the textual past of both the 'world' and literature" ("Historiographic Metafiction" 4). Given many of the persistent questions surrounding land, blood quantum, and the history of violence, poverty, and violations of sovereignty, factors that have all contributed to the formulation of the Oglala Sioux identity, *Scalped* "offers a sense of the presence of the past, but this is a past that can only be known from its texts, its traces—be they literary or historical" (4). Far from being a stable set of characteristics, history and identity are under constant contestation because of the precarious placement of the people in history and the precarious claim the people have on the land. Because identity is contested on the basis of blood, historical commitment to "the cause," and experience within the social context of the Pine Ridge Reservation, claims to "authentic" identity inevitably fall short.

The notions of special knowledge, historical ties to identity, and the policing of the boundaries of identity all come together in *Scalped.* This comics series deals with the lives of the inhabitants of the Prairie Rose Reservation of the Oglala Sioux, a fictionalized representation of the Pine Ridge Reservation in South Dakota where the shoot-out in 1975 left two

FBI agents dead. Peltier was incarcerated for the crime, although doubts
about his guilt persist to this day. The series follows Dashiell Bad Horse,
who returns as an FBI informant to the reservation on which he grew up.
He shields his status by working for Red Crow, the shady leader of the
tribe who was involved in the fictionalized version of the Pine Ridge Shoot-
out when he was a young man. The characters who were involved in this
shoot-out are important to explore in terms of historiographic metafiction
and the construction of identity because they typify an array of possible
reactions to history within their attempts to perform "authentic" American
Indianness. The primary group involved with the murder of the FBI agents
in *Scalped* are Lincoln Red Crow, the current leader of the Oglala Sioux,
who is opening a casino at the beginning of the series; Catcher, a former
Rhodes scholar who has, over the years, transformed from a radical intellectual into a seminomadic alcoholic; Gina Bad Horse, Dashiell's mother,
who has remained committed to political action on behalf of American
Indian rights; and Lawrence Belcourt,[3] who was imprisoned for the murder even though he did not commit it. While these characters are not the
primary subject of the series, their actions at Pine Ridge and their historical
commitment to American Indian activism create the backdrop for the major
story line and demonstrate that history constitutes a disruptive force in the
formulation of identity.

Scalped follows a much larger constellation of characters as they negotiate life on the Prairie Rose Reservation. Agent Nitz is an FBI agent intent on
convicting Red Crow for Nitz's suspicions about the latter's involvement in
the shoot-out in 1975, and he is particularly invested in this case because
the victims were two of his friends. He alludes frequently to the fact that he
helped incarcerate Belcourt, who he knew to be innocent. Granny Poor Bear
is an elder and has refused to move into town, preferring more traditional
modes of life, but is nonetheless subject to the privations and dramas of
the reservation. Dino Poor Bear, a teenager with dreams of a better life off
the reservation, is slowly sucked further into drug trafficking. Shunka, Red
Crow's assistant, is a burly, closeted homosexual whose jealousy grows
over the favoritism Red Crow shows for Dash. A blowhard white sheriff
one town over from the reservation slowly begins to realize that his lies
about his glory days have stood between himself and his potential. Red
Crow's daughter, Carol, who uses drugs and sex to cope with the loss of
her pregnancy years before, a pregnancy that ended because her child's

---

3. In addition to standing in for Leonard Peltier, Belcourt's name also recalls
Clyde and Vernon Bellecourt, who were Ojibwe activists and AIM leaders who were
at the Wounded Knee incident. Clyde served as a liaison between activists and police,
while Vernon attempted to raise awareness and funds to assist the protestors.

father stole money from her own father, who sent thugs after them as they tried to flee. While I will be bracketing the bulk of these characters except for when they play into the plot thread under examination, the sheer number and competing concerns attests to the complexity of the series.

Each character in *Scalped* has a fraught connection to the past, and memory and the present are frequently depicted as conjoined, even overlapping. Memories bleed into current circumstances, erupt into the consciousness, distract the characters at critical moments. Furthermore, memories frequently change attribution midway through their narrative; while the reader is offered one character's point of view at the outset, this sometimes changes either nearly imperceptibly or shockingly abruptly, confusing the normal pathways for identification and empathetic engagement and insisting that memory has its own force and weight aside from those who carry it.

Pine Ridge was the site of some of the most famous conflicts between whites and American Indians in history, including the Wounded Knee massacre in 1890, in which at least 150 and possibly as many as 300 Lakota were killed by the U.S. Cavalry. The cavalry had come to the camp to disarm the men, and accounts vary on what precipitated the massacre, but it is clear that U.S. soldiers pursued men, women, and children as they fled in order to kill them. As discussed above, nearly a century later, Pine Ridge became a hotbed of American Indian Movement activism in the 1960s and '70s, and in 1975, two FBI agents were shot and killed there. The resulting Leonard Peltier case came to stand in for the more generalized mistreatment of American Indians and raised significant awareness of the traumatic elements of reservation life, including an unemployment rate of 33 percent on the Pine Ridge Reservation, while 24.5 percent of residents exist below the federal poverty line and have shorter life expectancies.[4] While those in the general population of the United States are vaguely aware of the difficulty of reservation life, the statistics reflect conditions more well suited to those collected in a developing country. These statistics illustrate that reservations have become not a place where American Indians can preserve their cultural heritage but instead are subject to grinding poverty and humiliating conditions most recently made public by photographer Aaron Huey's photo essay, published in *National Geographic* and publicized in *Slate.com*. The photographs alternate between capturing the preparations for ceremonies and illustrating the living conditions of reservation residents, including photographs of overcrowded houses and alcoholics passed out beside

---

4. All statistics drawn from the U.S. Commission on Civil Rights report in July 2003 entitled "A Quiet Crisis: Federal Funding and Unmet Needs in Indian Country."

dilapidated trailers. In the introduction to her article on Pine Ridge accompanying Huey's photographs, Alexandra Fuller remarks that

> almost every historical atrocity has a geographically symbolic core, a place whose name conjures up the trauma of a whole people: Auschwitz, Robben Island, Nanjing. For the Oglala Lakota of the Pine Ridge Indian Reservation that place is a site near Wounded Knee Creek, 16 miles northeast of the town of Pine Ridge. From a distance the hill is unremarkable, another picturesque tree-spotted mound in the creased prairie. But here at the mass grave of all those who were killed on a winter morning more than a century ago, it's easy to believe that certain energies—acts of tremendous violence and of transcendent love—hang in the air forever and possess a forever half-life. (1)

Fuller emphasizes the centrality of place in the history of American Indian experience and seeks to connect space to specific historical contexts that have created resonances moving across time. Responses to the rigors of reservation life often focus on high rates of alcoholism, racist characterizations of the populations as "lazy," and insistence that American Indians adapt to the changing nature of the economy and the country at large, at the expense of preserving their culture. These responses conveniently sidestep the history of atrocities against American Indians, taking comfort in the pernicious specter of forced assimilation, itself a significant part of this history. Like *Scalped,* Huey's photography seeks to expose a range of experiences central to American life that are largely papered over with childhood plays about giving and friendship during Thanksgiving—and utterly ignored for the rest of the year.

As discussed above, the image of American Indians has been subject to a range of anxieties in the larger cultural consciousness in the United States. From children playing "cowboys and Indians" to spaghetti Westerns elaborating a mythos of an untamed frontier to the "friendly natives" of the Thanksgiving myth to the attribution of "special knowledge" of the land, American Indians have been viewed as wily aggressors and patient stewards of the earth. They are, however, rarely seen within the context of present-day reservations, and aside from authors like Louise Erdrich, M. Scott Momaday, and Sherman Alexie, their stories are not widely read by the general public. Reservations are a semiforgotten space in American life, a space that *Scalped* seeks to reintegrate as central to the American consciousness of what the nation *is*.

Scalped uses Wounded Knee, the Peltier case, and other confrontations between whites and American Indians as historical intertexts by which present-day life on reservations can be exposed and questioned. The story is set in the present day and follows characters who were either directly involved in the fictionalized shooting or were connected with characters who were. As a reminder, the characters present at the shooting were Lincoln Red Crow, who is now the Chief of the tribe and has recently opened a casino on the reservation; Catcher, who was a Rhodes scholar and intellectual but has become a drunk vagrant; Lawrence Belcourt, who was a young activist at the time of the shooting and has since spent his life in prison (the fictional version of Peltier); and Gina Bad Horse, who was dating Lincoln Red Crow at the time and now is widely known in the present at as staunch traditionalist, opposed to the casino Red Crow has opened. Each of the introductory scenes use one panel that depicts a stereotyped representation alongside a panel that depicts the character as round.

Aaron and Guera use both textual and imagistic historical artifacts as inspiration for this tale of contemporary reservation life, in order to explore how historical trauma results in intergenerational cycles of poverty and violence. Over the course of the series, the writer and the artist manipulate point of view in individual comic panels in order to transfer readers' allegiances and, more importantly, in this process cause the reader to acknowledge her own distance from these events. However, Aaron and Guera simultaneously open up pathways for identification, including the use of character point of view, as a method of relocating the events of the story as a historical *present*, illustrating how the tragic and violent past is intimately connected to the marginalization and deprivation in the present. Furthermore, they attempt to show how the locations of massacres and shoot-outs resulted not only in a forgotten history but forgotten *locations*. The setting and the relationship between the reader's viewpoint and that of the character work together to craft a sense of places that signify an eruption of the historical past into the lived present.

Scalped is preoccupied with what it means to perform an "authentic" Native American identity, and through this preoccupation, Aaron and Guera seek to explore how a legacy of violence and marginalization has explicit effects on both memory and the transmission of trauma from generation to generation. Using Wounded Knee as a point of departure, they explore how Native Americans were progressively more marginalized during the early stages of the twentieth century, until this was brought to a head during the "incident at Pine Ridge" and what follows in the late twentieth and early twenty-first centuries.

NATIVE INTELLECT

Early in the series, the reader is frequently positioned as an outsider looking in on the characters. For example, at the end of a chapter introducing
Dash as coerced into becoming an FBI informant by Agent Nitz, a racist
agent bent on destroying tribal leader Lincoln Red Crow, a panel depicts
Dash eating at a local restaurant. We are observing him from across the
room. Our distance from his internal life—his thoughts and emotions—is
heightened by the realistic rendering of the surroundings. Guera is careful
to offer a convincing, almost photographic rendering of Dash's face and
the corner of the restaurant, including details like the grain of the wooden
floor, the screen on the window, and the specials board. The specials board
itself heightens the distance between the reader and the character, as it
refers to food relatively uncommon among the assumed readership—hard-
tack and prairie oysters are likely unfamiliar terms. Several photographs
are tacked to the wall, depicting familiar scenes of teepees and tribe members posing for the camera, looking out into the squalor of the restaurant.
Aside from the specials board, the only text is drawn from a previous panel
depicting Agent Nitz remarking that he doesn't care whether or not Dash
is hurt in the process of trying to gain evidence against Red Crow. His final
remark is that "it would suit my fuckin' needs nonetheless" (2.1.29). His
remarks stand in for a broader consensus on conditions on reservations.

While Nitz harbors more vitriol toward American Indians than most,
the "accidental" conditions of deprivation derive from a history of systematic impoverishment through the Dawes Act, which served to allot reservation lands to individuals rather than tribes in order to promote agriculture
but in fact frequently burdened families with isolation on land ill-suited
for farming. While the results of the Dawes Act were catastrophic for reservations and individual American Indian families, even today the governmental website devoted to documenting the historical contexts for acts
explains that

> very sincere individuals reasoned that if a person adopted white clothing
> and ways, and was responsible for his own farm, he would gradually drop
> his Indian-ness and be assimilated into the population. It would then no
> longer be necessary for the government to oversee Indian welfare in the
> paternalistic way it had been obligated to do, or provide meager annuities
> that seemed to keep the Indian in a subservient and poverty-stricken posi-
> tion. ("Dawes Act" 1)

Instead of identifying the problematic presumption that white behavior was preferable to "Indian-ness," critiquing the "necessity" of governmental paternalism, or noting how the current position was a result of previous governmental policies, the authors of this act are instead described as "very sincere," and this is a current account. While Nitz is clearly positioned as a villain, even present-day remarks about historical contexts suggest an assumption of the superiority of dominant white culture as well as a convenient historical amnesia as to what brought about such conditions. Nitz as a character reintegrates the vicious stereotypes at the core of such explanations.

The following chapter opens with an explicitly historical scene recounting the experience of Lincoln Red Crow as a child on one of the boarding schools designed for American Indian children in order to promote assimilation and minimize contact with their heritage. In his "Taking the Indian Out of the Indian," Donald A. Grinde Jr. notes that the racism at the core of the boarding schools was not about racial inferiority but rather *cultural* inferiority.[5] Grinde goes on to explain how the schools did not seek to create a nexus of two types of knowledge—one Native and one white—but instead insisted that white knowledge *replace* traditional forms of knowledge and religious practice. Students were banned from speaking their tribal languages, wearing traditional clothing, and participating in ceremonial practices. Red Crow's experience replicates these experiences, the first panel depicting a bleak house on a rain-swept hill, a location visually steeped in sorrow. Tagged as "Our Lady of Mercy Indian Residential School," an overlain text box asks, "Are you ready to pray now, number six?" (2.2.1). A panel inset shows the scene from approximately the position of the priest, his hand holding a ruler as a boy cowers on the floor. The reader shares nearly the point of view of the priest, the aerial of the boy enhancing his degradation even as he responds to "Or shall we continue?" with "Ohnzeh. Kangi luta emaciyapi." They leave this untranslated, underscoring the assumed white reader's connection with the priest, who responds with "Stop that infernal gibberish!" It is not, of course, gibberish,

---

5. "In analyzing the theory behind boarding schools for American Indians, it is important to note that Colonel Richard Henry Pratt's form of racism was cultural rather than racial. To Pratt and his followers, American Indians were human beings like everyone else. Uniformly, Pratt rejected any notions of inborn racial inferiority. Hence, Pratt's policies were to strip the American Indian of his Indianness and replace the traditional Native culture with a new set of religious and social attitudes and skills in concert with the values of the dominant white society" (Grinde 28–29).

instead roughly translating as "my name is Red Crow," reasserting both
the Lakota language and the tribal name, thus his connection to his heritage. The priest argues, "This is for your own good, number six! We must
kill the Indian inside you in order to save the man! When are you going
to learn that?" In this statement, the dehumanization of being stripped
of one's culture is emphasized through the replacement of a name with a
number and, furthermore, the idea that one segment of one's being—ethnic
identity—must be annihilated in order to salvage one's personhood. The
assumption here rests on non-normative culture as poisonous to humanity, an assumption embodied by the boarding schools of this period. While
the reader is undoubtedly encouraged to feel sympathy for and admiration
of Red Crow's strength as a child, the tension of the untranslated words
underscores readerly complicity in the scene, partly through the policing of
English as a necessity of American life.

However, this scene immediately transitions on the following page
to a scene of an adult Red Crow in his casino, smiling for cameras and
surrounded by dancers attired in parodies of more traditional garb. The
text boxes relate that "The meek shall inherit sweet fuck-all. That's what
I learned from them sadistic little shits, the Jesuits." He refused to be
stripped of his identity as a Lakota, but in spite of that, he is capitalizing
on racial caricature within a building that is a monument to greed and gull-
ibility. His insistence on maintaining his identity even at the expense of
repeated beatings has led him to a different type of trap. In addition, when
the reader is given closer proximity to the characters early in the series, it
is frequently used in relation to characters that are to some extent *unsympathetic*. In this panel, the reader's viewpoint is *within* Red Crow's posse as
they descend into the casino. The arrangement of individuals around and
in front of the viewpoint gives the illusion of proximity in the over-the-
shoulder point of view, but the previous installments have already primed
the reader to resist identifying with Red Crow because he runs the reservation more like a mob neighborhood, lacking the expected wisdom and clarity of a tribal elder.

Catcher, mentioned above as another one of the young American Indian
activists involved in the FBI shoot-out, has aged poorly and is depicted as
a thin, grizzled old man riding his gaunt hose around the reservation. On
the first page of the fourth chapter, he recounts various indigenous creation
myths, apparently thinking to himself, but his only verbalized commentary is a quotation of the opening lines of Samuel Taylor Coleridge's "Kubla
Khan": "In Xanadu did Kubla Khan a stately pleasure dome decree." As
he gazes at the searchlights marking the location of the new casino, Catch-

er's literary reference seems out of place with the creation stories he was contemplating. However, "Kubla Khan" is preoccupied with the fall from an original state of grace and oneness with nature, also meditating on the potentially productive tension between nature and art. Beyond Catcher's use of the poem as a commentary on the casino, his casual knowledge of it suggests a background with a classical education distinctly at odds with the traditional stories he tells himself and at odds as well with his appearance.

After a tense visit to Red Crow and a remark to Dash that indicates he knows Dash is working with the FBI, Catcher goes to phone Gina, thinking to himself that "Only by returning to those old ways can we ever again be at peace with Mother Earth. And at peace with ourselves." This traditionalist understanding of the salvation of his people is followed by an account of Wakinyan, a thunder deity and provider of visions. The vision Catcher experiences is not pleasant; unlike the "vision quest" usually imagined by those who romanticize indigenous peoples' connection to the earth, this vision is violent, bloody, and filled with jagged edges.

The reader is positioned to see through Catcher's eyes as the vision shows the dead FBI agents, a fight, Gina kissing Red Crow as young lovers, Gina's head smashed open on a rock, crows picking at the corpse of his horse, and, finally, the casino engulfed in a blaze (see fig. 3.1). This vision is multidirectional, imbricating the past and future with no textual cues as to which temporal category each image belongs or how the visions in either the future or the past have come to be. The vision to a certain extent mimics the way conditions on reservations have historically been treated, as if they did not exist within a network of historical circumstances that wove together to create the tapestry of despair. The pages leading up to and following the vision are also temporally unstable—he is at the casino talking with Red Crow and Dash, he is on the phone, he is having his vision, he is far outside of town talking with Granny Poor Bear, he is remembering Gina—and one can determine the actual order in which events unfold only in retrospect, after he leaves Granny Poor Bear and stands before a broken mirror in a trash heap. Walking toward the mirror, he continues the poem, text boxes relating his many accomplishments, including Oxford graduate, Rhodes scholar, and acquitted murderer. As he gazes in the mirror at himself and his spirit guide, an owl, the reader occupies his perspective, but the mirror is cracked and he is dejected, having been unable to accomplish the goals set out for him, recounting that "This is the story of a mighty vision given to a man too weak to use it" (2.4.97). It was not the man but the vision that had power, he tells himself, and his only defense against his own thoughts is violence. He shoots the mirror, destroying his own image.

FIGURE 3.1. Catcher's vision. Aaron, Jason, and R. M. Guera. *Scalped—Casino Boogie*. Vol. 2. New York: DC Vertigo, 2008.

PINE RIDGE SHOOT-OUT

The Pine Ridge Shoot-out has loomed larger in the American cultural memory than most events involving American Indians. Only two years after the Wounded Knee Incident, when AIM activists took over the town for two months demanding better treatment by the federal government and that their own chief step down because of extensive corruption in the administration, two FBI agents were killed nearby. In 1975, *Time* reported:

> The victims were two FBI agents, slaughtered by a band of Indian militants, and one of their attackers. The trouble began when four Indians kidnapped two young whites, releasing them a few hours later. [. . .] Indians apparently opened fire on the [agents'] car from both sides. Coler and Williams radioed a desperate Mayday call and succeeded in turning the car around, but could not get away. Their assailants apparently dragged both men—by then presumably dead—from the car, stripped them of their belongings and shot them in the back of the head.

The circumstances surrounding the deaths were complicated, and who was actually responsible for the murders was questionable. In a trial riddled with problems and inconsistencies, Leonard Peltier was eventually convicted of the murders in 1977, partly resting on evidence extracted from Myrtle Poor Bear under apparent threat by the FBI.[6] Mark Meister and Ann Burnett argue in "Rhetorical Exclusion in the Trial of Leonard Peltier," that "the power exhibited by the federal legal system during Peltier's trial limited the cultural legitimacy of Indian cultures and traditions. Moreover, the federal government's case against Peltier attacked the Indian cultural conceptions of power not only for the purposes of conviction but also to de-legitimize Indian lifestyles" (720). *Scalped* takes up this case in order to illustrate the problems with memory and perception tied to witnessing events as well as the way in which narrative reframes memory.

The way in which the scene of the shooting is depicted varies according to the character who is doing the remembering at the moment. When Gina is dreaming of the scene, the main panel shows the two FBI agents' abject fear, and the viewpoint is gazing slightly upward, placing the reader in nearly the same position as them. Being set slightly below characters who are fearful tends to evoke compassion for the characters in the reader, as the vantage point from below tends to suggest that same groveling posi-

---

6. See page 731 of Meister and Burnett.

tion. In the third panel on this page, the point of view abruptly shifts to that of Gina, who is apparently remembering her own role in the shooting (see fig. 3.2).

The reader sees through her eyes as she holds a gun to the terrified man's head, as he pleads with her for his life. In this superior vantage point, however, the reader is not necessarily primed to identify with Gina because he has already felt sympathy for the men she is holding at gunpoint. In spite of having significantly more of Gina's story to draw from, this panel arrangement suggests that the reader reject a sympathetic engagement with her character. This is underscored in the final panel on the page, when her face is realistically rendered, and she threatens the men's lives.

However, after an interlude in which Gina has an exchange with the incarcerated Lawrence Belcourt, this page is followed by a completely different way of remembering the situation, once again from Gina's vantage point. Gina is asleep in the present day, dreaming of that night. She threatens the agents, but Lawrence whispers to her "are you *crazy?* These guys are the FBI" (2.138), a warning Gina shrugs off. She tells him, "I know what I'm doing," but one of the agents interrupts: "You don't know *shit*, you stupid bitch . . ." (2.138). The reader is compelled to withdraw sympathy from the FBI agents, as their faces change from terrified to explicitly menacing. One mocks, "pull the trigger, sweetheart—and help us put an end to *you* motherfuckers once and for all" (2.138). This suggestion a lingering threat—that killing them will only serve their purpose—indicates that the goal is to wipe out Natives who seek to conserve their culture. While both the young Red Crow and the young Catcher attempt to talk her down, the final panel on the page is vital in terms of context. While these scenes take place in Gina's dream, she herself is depicted from outside of herself in her own memory, and in this final panel, she realizes that "No, this ain't right. This *ain't* how it happened" (2.138), suggesting that, while she was present, she has already misremembered a history that only the people present can in fact know.

At this point of understanding how her memory is reconstructing the narrative, a succession of characters who were not there at the shoot-out appear, each criticizing her for both action and inaction. Crying, she raises the gun, asserting, "I'm not running away anymore" (2.139), but rather than showing the murder, it shows her finger on the trigger, a murder of crows poised on a branch, the sound of the shots, the bodies, and, finally, Gina stumbling into the woods and retching. The scene strongly directs the reader toward the conclusion that Gina in fact is responsible for the murders that sent Belcourt to prison, but much like the trial itself, the reader

FIGURE 3.2. Gina's changing memories. Aaron, Jason, and R. M. Guera. *Scalped—Casino Boogie*. Vol. 2. New York: DC Vertigo, 2008.

lacks reliable eyewitness proof. These tensions between different series of images prompt the reader to question which memory is a depiction of the "real" story or if either memory represents the historical reality. However, neither series offers proof, and moreover, the panels depicting the moments in each series themselves, partly through point of view, partly through the gutters between them, and partly through the conflicting accounts in the content, highlight the extent to which the "real" story is mediated through conflicting narratives and demands. Gina's dream prompts her to make a decision—to reveal who the actual murderer was—in order to both alleviate Belcourt's suffering in prison and to expose the justice system for its fraud in convicting an innocent man, but she never makes it. The following morning, her body is found out along the highway by a group of teenagers, killed in a manner eerily similar to that of the murdered Anna Mae Aquash, an AIM member whose murder was never solved.

Red Crow sits out near Gina's corpse holding vigil, and as he remembers her, he glances at each part of her body contained in the memory. The soft charm of her tucking hair behind her ears is replaced by the bruised wrist, kissing Red Crow himself is replaced by the blood splatter framing her slack lips, and her hunched-shouldered sadness and frustration is replaced by the blank stare of her lifeless eyes. The reader shares not only Red Crow's point of view but also his memory in this moment, experiencing how her physical body connects to the circumstances that brought her to this place. As a stand-in for the national body of the Oglala Sioux, Gina's death represents the death of potential, mourned not only by a man who sold off much of that potential but also existing now only as a reconstructed memory.

In a similar scene of memory later in the series, Aaron and Guera employ the same transitional method and color scheme to create a visual as well as textual conflation of the different points of view represented in the memory of the shoot-out. In a transitional page, an independent "good cop" character, Officer Falls Down, peruses the files on the FBI murder representing the basic, indisputable facts of the case. The scene begins from within Falls Down's point of view as he pulls a crime scene photograph of one of the murdered FBI agents from a folder, replicated two panels later in the transcript of the evidence. In text boxes, the known times and circumstances are recounted from the position of the investigators, and the scene transitions from Falls Down sipping coffee at his desk as he wades through files to Belcourt, viewed from above, trying to sleep on his prison cot. The reader is offered three distinct points of view in this passage, all from various positions inside the justice system. In one case, we have the perspective of an officer combing for clues and at the other pole is the view inside of the carceral cell, but the third is the pure documentation. As Belcourt turns over, the remarks in the file hang above his head: "To this day, debate continues as to who actually fired the fatal shots. No one present at the shooting has ever spoken publicly about the events of that day, and presumably never will" (5.4.11). The bureaucratic reportage on the incident is utterly divorced from the circumstances of reading it, as well as the outcome of the investigation, cueing the reader to the way in which the narratives of the night of the shooting are separated not only by their content but also by their form. Meister and Burnett note, however, that we personify institutions, arguing that "the law is more than simply a set of statutes; the embodiment of the law is manifested by those who enforce it, interpret it, and change it" (722). They link this idea of the personified law with the multivalent operations of power, in which individuals can be excluded from producing certain types of discourse, legitimizing one method of telling a story while silencing voices which may contradict that story. When the voice of the legal document overlays Belcourt, silently worrying himself to sleep in prison, it is a visual demonstration of how certain narratives are privileged at the expense of others and also an indication of who in fact has the right to speak as to a subject. While the document opines that none involved have come forward to tell their stories, in fact, the actual complaint is that none have told their stories in a way that is satisfactory to the parameters required by the court. Belcourt is innocent and has said as much, and although he is the only one of the four involved who can certainly be exonerated, he remains the only one penalized for the crime.

Transitioning into memory, the reader is suddenly confronted with a page of violence in which she occupies a first-person point of view. While the scene is framed by Belcourt, suggesting that we are viewing his memory or dream, the point of view rapidly shifts between characters, destabilizing the reader's perception of the scene and, for all that, perhaps more accurately rendering an actual scene of violence. Gina's memory, explored above, was comparatively stable in spite of the eruptions of other characters and narrative threads nagging at her conscience. In this scene, a flurry of gunfire and running tells a different story than the one recounted in the legal documents on the previous page. The documentation indicates that "June 26, 1975, 6:15pm—Agents Bayer and Berntson come under heavy fire after driving onto land occupied by Native American radicals, the Dog Soldiers Society" (5.4.11), while the following page begins with nearly the same time and date stamp, "June 26, 1975, 6:19pm" (5.4.12), a full four minutes after that enshrined within the investigative report. Instead of depicting the FBI agents coming under "heavy fire," as is codified, we see a young Lawrence Belcourt in obvious fear, screaming, "Jesus Christ, they're gonna kill us all!"

Unlike the report, the opening panels suggest not that the activists began the shoot-out but rather the agents, although we don't see the opening shots fired. The tension between the verbal—the report—and the visual, this rendering, once again subverts truth claims. The panels rapidly cycle between the Dog Soldiers and the agents firing at one another. After the opening salvo, a scene from within the activist encampment illustrates them returning fire and finding cover, overlain with a text box relating the "Native radicals known to have been present that day" (5.4.13). Each name overlays a panel depicting the individual's role in the fight. Lawrence is terrified, saying, "They just came outta nowhere and started shooting," while Gina demands that Red Crow stop returning fire. Notably, Red Crow is identified as "John R. Bustill, A. K. A. Lincoln Red Crow," and Catcher is identified as "Arthur J. Pendergrass, A. K. A. Catcher," while neither Belcourt nor Gina are identified in terms of both name and alias. Their names stand alone as their identity markers, while Red Crow and Catcher both have white names that are listed as primary, their Native names as aliases. The power to name has always signaled a measure of control over an individual, and in this moment, as the report re-erupts into the scene, two of the participants are not allowed the names they prefer but are rather soldered to names that efface their identities.

Even at the time—or in the space of the memory of the incident—it's unclear who fired the first shot. After the agents throw down their guns, Gina shouts at them, asking "why the hell they just tried to kill us!" (5.4.15), one of the agents immediately responds: "Fuck you! Your people shot first!" (5.4.15). Gina claims, "You people came in guns blazing! You coulda killed somebody!" (5.4.15), while at the same time holding her revolver to the temple of one of the agents. In both speech and visual layout, it is unclear who is responsible for the first shot that sparked the firefight, and both are equally plausible. In the real world, FBI agents had already been documented harassing local groups like AIM, and AIM had already used violent tactics in response. Aaron and Guera preserve the true ambivalence in the historical record, rather than propagating the story that was largely told by the media—radical activists killed the agents in cold blood—or the counterstory that had the activists as victims only defending themselves. The reality was likely much more complicated than either neat tale of heroism, although the more complicated version of the story is seldom acknowledged.

The following page depicts the murders of the FBI agents (see fig. 3.3).

In three of the five panels on the page, the reader is set in the uncomfortable position of being the inflictor of violence. Gina's gun is foregrounded against one of the agents as a shot spikes through his head coming from a different location, and the other begs before a panel depicts a bullet fired through his pleading hand directly through his eye. The only panel that doesn't depict their deaths shows Red Crow, Gina, and Belcourt, clearly set at a remove from the violence, Gina asking in confusion, "What just . . . what just happened . . ." (5.14.16). Red Crow is in closest proximity to the viewer, suggesting some complicity in the murders, while Gina is a bit further away, expressing confusion. Belcourt, the man convicted for the crime, is all the way at the back, the smallest part of the scene. On the following page, Catcher is depicted with the gun, remarking only "hecheto aloe," which means "it is finished." As he walks away from the group, it becomes clear that all five of the panels on the previous page depicted approximations of his point of view. What does this mean for the reader? While the reader shares his position, they have been primed over the last few pages for a certain amount of ambivalence in relating this tale. In addition, they have already seen versions of this scene play out, none satisfactory, and none that claim to be the "truth." The coloring is similar to that in Gina's dream, and this visual similarity suggests that, once again, this depiction of the crime is less about the historical fact of what happened than about the emotional truth that those involved carry with them.

However, that the reader is completely immersed in Catcher's point of view leaves a nagging uncertainty about the relative truth-value of the memory/dream. While we were primed to view these events from the perspective of Lawrence Belcourt, we instead have a contest between the bureaucratic version and what slowly becomes clear is the *real* story. The uncertainty about who began shooting, the ambivalence about fault, these suggest a verisimilitude not available in Gina's dream. Furthermore, there is no questioning of the events from any of the characters' perspectives, no cautionary questions of the memory or assertions that "this ain't how it happened." In the final panel on the page, Catcher stares blankly out, the object of his gaze not the corpses or his friends but instead the reader. This panel is a moment in which the reader is directly addressed—a rarity in historio-metagraphics—and the form of that address is midway between a plea and an indictment. Most comics readers (and creators) are white,[7] and while this panel coupled with those from Catcher's point of view invite—

---

7. An estimated 79 percent of comics creators are white (Hanley 1).

FIGURE 3.3. First (or second?) person shooter. Aaron, Jason, and R. M. Guera. *Scalped—Casino Boogie*. Vol. 2. New York: DC Vertigo, 2008.

even insist on—identification with his position, what does that identification mean? On one hand, it seems to be a plea for some measure of understanding, telling the reader that "now that you have seen how complicated and confusing it all was, perhaps you can see how this happened." On the other hand, it also registers as an indictment of the audience as well.

The integration of legalese in the documentation of the crime—revealed in the scene to be erroneous at best—alongside the reader's vicarious participation in the crime, coupled with the tacit acknowledgment that because of this framework certain people (specifically, the Dog Soldiers) are denied even the right of self-identification, much more so credibility in U.S. courts of law, the reader exists as a *beneficiary* of incursions on Native identity. Charles Mills's elaboration of *The Racial Contract* notes that "*all whites* are beneficiaries of the *Contract,* though some are *not signatories* to it" (11, emphasis in original), meaning that willing and open collaboration with the structures of power that marginalize American Indian voices is not necessary to be implicitly responsible for the conditions wrought by racism and paternalism. Indeed, this direct gaze designates the reader as a witness and a collaborator, not in Catcher's crime but rather in the crimes that produced the conditions against which they are protesting. Given the age demographics of the readership, most of the audience was probably not yet of age when the real-life intertext of the shoot-out at Pine Ridge occurred, but the bulk of the series is informed by and embedded in this history but is not only about the shoot-out. Instead, *Scalped* exposes contemporary life on the reservation, showing the reader that it is not enough to say "not me."

The uselessness of the denial of responsibility is underscored by Lawrence Belcourt's own remarks to Gina before her death. Near the end of the second volume, when visiting him in prison, Gina expresses remorse that she didn't tell the whole story, but Belcourt insists, "Stop it. Just stop it right there. I knew the risks going in [. . .] Yeah, I was a kid back then. But look at me now. . . . I've done more for the movement locked up in here than I ever could've done out there" (2.6.11). While one of the group—Catcher?—is responsible for the murders, the conviction of a clearly innocent man drew more attention to the problems between the U.S. government and American Indians, as well as the conditions of life on reservations, than simple protests. Because Belcourt's case stands as an emblem of the misuse of power by the justice system, exposing all of the methods by which American Indian voices are silenced, Belcourt's own seeming silencing stands instead as a gaping hole at the center of the rhetorical construction of "justice" within government-indigenous relations.

BE(COME)ING "INDIAN"

In terms of identity, among those who were present at the shooting, Gina Bad Horse and Lawrence Belcourt have the least to question in terms of their own authenticity. While both Red Crow and Catcher have their white names serving as privileged identifiers in spite of their own stylings, Gina and Belcourt are only identifiable through names that remain stable in whatever social context they find themselves. Their political commitments have been consonant with their self-perception, and while Gina has certain regrets, Lawrence is reconciled with his lot. Lawrence, rather than understanding his identity in terms of those things he has been denied from experiencing that constitute much of Red Crow's identity, instead considers his incarceration, false in its premise, as the most authentic component. Their involvement with the American Indian Movement and the murder of two FBI officers interpellates historical realities into a series that interrogates all claims to authenticity.

Authenticity is an unstable concept partly because of the historical realities of blood quantum laws, which delineate identity based on percentage of American Indian heritage. For example, the most restrictive tribes require members to have half-degree blood quantum, while the least restrictive tribes require members to be descendants of enrolled members.[8] In addition, alienation from the land has remained a historical problem, given early U.S. government policies of extermination and later efforts to consolidate American Indians on reservations that generally include only a small portion of previous territories.

Gina is even more problematic in these terms than Lawrence, partly because Gina is our first window into the scene that disrupted the lives of the group. In the dream about the night the agents were murdered that is explored above, she is holding the gun and is acting out a role of leadership within the group. In the sequence she is the instigator, but her claim that "this ain't how it happened" illustrates how memory can valorize and victimize (2.6.16), even when it purports to archive the "truth." While Gina's history is shaped by this single night, it remains inaccessible in its entirety in her memory, primarily because it forced a choice between her self-perception and her social identity. In her dream, Gina is operating both as the

---

8. Jack Forbes makes a cogent argument in "Blood Quantum: A Relic of Racism and Termination," while Paul Spruhan reports on legal maneuvers in Navajo membership debates in "The Origins, Current Status, and Future Prospects of Blood Quantum as the Definition of Membership in the Navajo Nation."

rejected but necessary thing and as the repressed memory within a larger history of the people.

This larger history, however, is subsumed by an outsider culture—the white culture that requires sacrifice based on the deaths of its agents of intrusion. This sacrifice is not limited to Lawrence Belcourt, however; instead, the sacrifice also takes the form of corruption of the idea of a Sioux identity, particularly the part of that identity that is radicalized. This is typified in the ways in which Red Crow, a former revolutionary who worked alongside Gina, navigates his own increasingly problematic identity in the face of his own history and that of his people. Red Crow has invested an enormous amount of money in a casino, which is being protested by many locals as an unnecessary and insulting expenditure. Red Crow is an interesting figure for the way in which he operates in terms of identity, laying claim simultaneously to an "authentic" Indian identity while still operating through a white business model. This is clearly articulated while he is reprimanding Dashiell for beating up his lackeys, saying that they are

> looking at the president of the Oglala Tribal Council. As well as Sheriff of the Tribal Police Force, chairman of the Prairie Rose Planning Committee, treasurer of the highway safety program and Managing Director of this here brand spankin' new casino. But I can see that don't mean sweet fuck-all to a bona fide shitkicker like yourself, right? [. . .] You see this knife? [. . .] This knife is 200 years old. It's claimed more men's lives than typhoid. (18)

Red Crow occupies a place between identities, laying claim to both. This contradiction can be seen in his assertion: "'Most important, I still know how to take a big knife, make an incision from the forehead to the back of the neck . . . and tear someone's fucking scalp off" (16). His ambivalent vacillation between the relative importance of the knowledge of two identity formations is interesting in regard to the way in which we read identity in a comic that is primarily focused on one marginalized subject position. Here, Red Crow is arguing that he did not, as Žižek argues, give over his desire to become a member of society but rather that he has re-created and shaped the social fabric to be consonant with his desires.

The Prairie Rose in *Scalped* is inscribed as embedded within and subject to the white world and white power. Red Crow's claims to authenticity are significant in respect to this scenario, for he uses "traditional" Native American rituals in the context of his work within the white bureaucracy while nevertheless arguing that the authenticity of the acts that define

"Native American identity" are more significant to reading his body than those that define him as a puppet of whites. He locates himself at the heart of a political movement that actively and violently resisted white incursion onto the land is an attempt to articulate a stable subject position in the present, as he is trying to create a narrative of continuity between his younger self as a political reactionary and his older self as a businessman.

However, this continuity is repeatedly disrupted by flashbacks to and conversations about the day on which the federal agents were killed, as that is the point at which he betrays one of his own to save himself. Gina Bad Horse also disrupts Red Crow's narrative by reminding him of this past, particularly when she shouts at him to remember it: "You remember Lawrence Belcourt? Poor kid, rotting away in Leavenworth for two murders he didn't even commit? I suppose not. I suppose a big shot like you doesn't bother to remember a little thing like Lawrence, or that day in 1975 when we—" (1.84). She is contesting his right to locate his identity, particularly given his actions, actions that she deems sufficient to destroy any claim to authenticity. This contestation coincides with Red Crow's own ambivalence about his identity, an ambivalence heightened partly because it reifies the gulf between the two identity formations he claims to occupy, traditionalist and progressive. Bhabha articulates this as being located partly in the gaze, in the need "to fix cultural difference in a containable, *visible* object. The desire for the Other is doubled by the desire in language, which *splits the difference* between Self and Other so that both positions are partial" (72, emphasis in original). This split in identity can be seen in the contradictions of Red Crow's character, for he is a character who must be simultaneously read through two cultural lenses. Bhabha further argues that

> cultures come to be represented by virtue of the processes of iteration and translation through which their meanings are very vicariously addressed to—*through*—an Other. This erases any essentialist claims for the inherent authenticity or purity of cultures which, when inscribed in the naturalistic sign of symbolic consciousness frequently become political arguments for the hierarchy and ascendancy of powerful cultures. (83–84, emphasis in original)

In keeping with this, Red Crow argues that he is powerful because he has acquired the symbols of power in both white and Sioux cultures, but Gina disrupts this fantasy of dual and coequal subjectivity by articulating the past, a moment of resistance to white incursion on the land, as Red Crow's failure, a failure that sacrificed another in place of the self for his continued freedom.

While Catcher was involved in the activist group and was present on the night the FBI agents were killed, even taking a bullet in the process, he has since largely abandoned his ties to other members of the tribe and primarily roams around on his old horse. However, since the beginning of the series he has experienced a series of disruptive flashbacks to the night on which the FBI agents were killed, visions that are also coupled by his seeing other's animal totems. On his way to confront Red Crow on the opening night of the casino, Catcher stops to talk with Granny Poor Bear. In their exchange, during which he asserts that he is having visions sent by the Thunder Beings, Granny Poor Bear mocks his pretensions to authenticity: "I told ya before, Catcher, just 'cause you got drunk and started seein' things, that don't mean you had no vision" (2.4.8). Her mocking of his claim to authenticity is important in respect to its anachronism—Granny Poor Bear, in spite of being an elder, recognizes the problems with the incorporation of long-held beliefs into the contemporary social fabric. Not only is she pointing out Catcher's faults as a character, but she is also pointing out that he is a parody of these beliefs. In spite of this, Granny Poor Bear contrasts Catcher with Red Crow and Gina, both of whom she finds lacking in character, while Catcher could have been their leader: "but you . . . You coulda been the leader we all needed" (2.4.18). In spite of her anger at and mockery of him, on the following page, the reader briefly occupies his perspective, and through his eyes, we see her totem behind her. More importantly, his vision after meeting with Granny Poor Bear is framed by a narration of the role of the Heyoka, described as "the sacred clown or thunder dreamer," chosen by Wakinyan, who sends the Heyoka visions. This dual role, as someone who imparts the knowledge of deities as well as the one who is a fool for them, is a significant example of the simultaneously parodic and sacred—the truth, in the Heyoka, can only be inscribed as it is being undermined.

Catcher is, in some senses, similar to Red Crow in his work to negotiate his identity after the murder of the FBI agents. However, rather than attempting to gain power in both cultures, he largely renounces both. He rejects his incorporation into any social fabric, but like Red Crow's embrace of both worlds, Catcher's rejection ultimately fails. As Catcher attempts to call Gina, the vision explored above that shows both past and future instances of violence comes, half disruptive PTSD flashback and half harbinger of things to come. His vision incorporates the past and the future, the panels revealing the way in which they are not only placed alongside one another but are woven together by the gaze. The murder of the agents constitutes a debt to history—a debt in keeping with Žižek's argument that "The unpaid symbolic debt is therefore in a way constitutive of our existence: our very symbolic existence is a 'compromise formation,' the delaying of an encounter" (26). This relates in a sense to the reader's confrontation with the tensions on the comics page as well as a commentary on the way the characters negotiate identity within the pages. In this context, the vision is a forced encounter with the past that reinscribes the limits on identity. Catcher's hallucination is, in itself, the disintegration of the concept of authenticity in that "madness designates the collapse of the distance between the symbolic and the real, an immediate identification with the symbolic mandate" (251). Rather than only an eruption of the past into the field of vision of the present, the hallucination is also the recognition of the ways in which memory normally screens the reality of the past and, therefore, also the reality of the identity.

LIVING HISTORY

Hutcheon remarks that "we can only 'know' (as opposed to 'experience') the world through our narratives (past and present) of it, or so postmodernism argues" (*A Poetics of Postmodernism* 9). In *Scalped* the narrative of the shooting, which is the historical moment that, to a great extent, has defined the lives of this constellation of characters, is an unstable memory. Each character references the shooting in different contexts: Belcourt by living its consequences and finding solace in his visibility, Gina by reliving the scene, Red Crow by reformulating his strategy to better suit what he perceives to be the conditions of the world, and Catcher by attempting to or being forced to recuperate and reconstitute the past. That "the past really did exist, but we can only 'know' that past today through its texts" (10), connects not only to the literariness of history and to interrogations of the legitimacy of texts, but also to memory and to the ways in which we articulate the body based on the social context provided by a reading of history.

After Gina is killed, but before Dash knows of her death, he has another installment of a regular anxiety dream in which he is about to be exposed as an FBI informant and killed by Red Crow. However, as Red Crow's henchmen approach from behind, they are shot by Dash's mother. Gina tells him that

> when Crazy Horse was a young man, he realized that the world we see
> around us with our waking eyes is only a pale shadow of the real world,
> and the only way to pierce the veil is through dreams. So Crazy Horse
> began dreaming himself into the real world before going out into battle,

and that made him unbeatable. Do you understand what I'm trying to tell you? (3.1.11)

Gina is attempting to warn him about the future, of course, but she is also recalling the past and trying to impart some memory of their heritage. The warning is not only about the risks he is running working for Red Crow and as an FBI informant, however; it is also a warning about placing too much trust in the senses, in the perception of the world surrounding him without paying adequate attention to the invisible contexts that *created* the present. On the following page, they stand in the midst of the bodies of those massacred by the U.S. Cavalry at Wounded Knee. Those in the foreground are dead, although the cavalry men in the background mill about the battlefield collecting the corpses. The perpetrators are merely a backdrop to the fact of so many deaths. It is not a visual exoneration but rather a reframing of the scene that privileges the vantage point of the victims at the expense of the powerful. Gina tells him, "If you're gonna live through what's coming for you, Dash, then you're gonna have to open your eyes and accept who you are" (3.1.12). Both are shot, and as they lay on the ground, Gina tells him, "*This* is who you are" (3.1.12). She is not attempting to tell him that he is a "dead man" or anything so prosaic. Instead, she is reminding him that he must carry his heritage with him, recognize it and use it, in order to survive, not because it is something that should be done to honor his ancestors, but instead, the history will tell him about his place in the present. The "world we see around us with our waking eyes is only a pale shadow" because it shows only the fact of what is there, rather than illuminating how the conditions came to be. Recognizing how things came to be is more important in the resolution of problems than simply identifying what appears before us.

Identity here is neither strictly relegated to the categories of "ownership" or "performance," but is rather an approach that involves recollection and the mobilization of memory in order to make the present legible. On the following page, she identifies his heritage as the nooses that are knotted around their necks, the hanging, the violence of legitimized power exerted on the bodies of those without voice. On the third page of the dream journey, they are both suffering from smallpox, and when he asserts that he wants to wake from this dream, Gina tells him, "There's no waking up son, not from this. Just look around . . . this is no dream. This is what the white man thinks of you" (3.1.14). In this moment, we view piles of dead corpses over Gina and Dash's shoulder as a man carrying a U.S. flag rides among the bodies. Gina's remark is meant to indicate not only stereotypes about

American Indians but also the ways in which the material conditions of their genocide, as well as their continued historical oppression, have been legitimized through various branches of power and through popular discourse: a history of victim blaming, in which the indigenous people are at fault for every tragedy, whether purposeful or accidental. She tells him that what he is fighting for isn't worth it. "The ground you're standing on. The people who live on it . . . Your people. Your heritage. Those are the only things in life worth dying for" (3.1.15–6). From her and Dash's perspective, the reader is presented with hundreds of American Indians both past and present, standing beneath Mt. Rushmore, which bears the graffiti "You are on Indian land," a textual reintegration of ownership of the land laid over one of America's most treasured national symbols. This assertion of rights to the land is painted over the face of George Washington, as a reminder that the nation's "founding" was at the expense of those already here, a reclamation of American Indians' place in history, which is too often rhetorically sidelined even in terms like "founding." It is a reminder that the story of the "founding" is told at the expense of other stories and in fact erases other stories so that its own narrative may exist.

Against the backdrop of these characters' negotiations between identity, history, and their own senses of power and control is the reservation itself. In the interest of space, I have bracketed the vast majority of narrative threads in *Scalped*, but at the close, it is worth remarking on the extent to which place plays a significant role in this work. Panels illustrating the ravages of alcoholism and the drug trade, scenes showing families with unsure futures, characters that I did not have room to mention living and dying in squalor and frustration, all of these elements play a role that is foregrounded against the grand historical narrative that I traced above. *Scalped* is not only about its primary protagonists and antagonists, and those terms fail to capture the complex histories and motivations of the characters in question anyway. It instead seeks to highlight how the history has material consequences for those existing within the narrative arc.

Scalped focuses on the question of identity as it is read as a historical construct and explores the importance of the performance of identity, indicating that the biological construct of race is insufficient to denote an authentic subject position, and because of this, identity only exists in its repeated performance. This anxious repetition is complicated by legal and cultural histories, which compromised self-reflexive assessments of authentic identity performance by shaping a symbolic heritage around the real — in this case, the disruptive moment of violence that reshaped the identities of the characters around an act of failed resistance to white intrusion. In keeping with this, Bhabha asserts that "It is from this *instability* of cultural signification that the national culture comes to be articulated as a dialectic of various temporalities—modern, colonial, postcolonial, 'native'—that cannot be a knowledge that is stabilized in its enunciation" (218–19). The destabilization of the narrative framework through the temporal dimension of the experiences of multiple identities disrupts concepts of historical and cultural truth. *Scalped* uses this disruption to question the way we read in terms of race and in terms of historical realities by creating a world in which Fanon's critique of the adventurer mode of comics is subsumed in a larger narrative of identities discordant with history.

Graphic narratives as a genre are ideal for questions of race, as the visual element underscores the concept of the visibility of race while simultaneously interrogating the ways in which race, ethnicity, and identity in general are socially elaborated and policed. The "collective aggression" that Fanon identified is therefore not necessarily located only in the white consciousness but instead is rather a form of address native to comics because of the way in which the genre simultaneously deploys race and subverts the expectations raised by visual mediums. Bhabha notes that "this image of human identity and, indeed, human identity as *image*—both familiar frames or mirrors of selfhood that speak from deep within Western culture—are inscribed in the sign of resemblance" (70, emphasis in original), going on to argue that there is a problem with the primacy of the image of the self because it entails, in terms of the Lacanian mirror stage, a fundamental misrecognition. And this misrecognition, in all of its ambivalence, is where comics are most useful in terms of articulating the instability of the subject.

Ultimately, the choice faced by the characters in *Scalped* hinges on the same question posed to both the problem of identity and the problem of memory: "assimilate or resist?" In terms of memory, the only way in which a traumatic memory can be conquered is to assimilate it into everyday functioning—to bring it out of the shadows and into the light of day so that it holds less power over the psyche. In terms of American Indian identity, the question of how to preserve traditional culture is becoming increasingly fraught in the present day, as life on the reservation is plagued with the problems associated with assimilation—without traditional modes of living, things like alcoholism and unemployment are major problems. Furthermore, the question of assimilation or resistance is also important in regard to the way in which American Indian cultures are dealt with in larger society. While Natives' reactions to their images being used as mascots and costumes are criticized for being "too sensitive," questions about popular cultural representations conveniently sidestep actual conditions on reservations as well as relegating to history the real abuses faced by tribes from the colonization of America to the present day.

It should be noted, however, that there is one further layer to this critique. Over the course of this chapter, I have looked closely at a very limited segment of the plot. The main thrust of the plot is a battle for power between a semirogue FBI agent and Red Crow, between Dash and Red Crow's right-hand man, Shunka, and between several other characters with competing interests. It is an action-oriented series, full of intrigue, gunfights, hand-to-hand combat, gore, sex, suspense, and pain. It has recognizable elements: white lawmen against "savage Indians," special knowledge of indigenous elders, and other stereotypical plot points, although each one has been twisted. The white lawmen are clearly positioned as enemies, the elders are less patient and wise than they are irritated. The gunfights are so frequent and relentless as to be almost comical. Between lurid close-ups of wounds and fight scenes that extend for sometimes as much as ten pages, the careful attention paid to character development and historical accuracy may seem—at its surface—somewhat beside the point. *Scalped* manages, in spite of being action packed, to offer a tight historical ledger of the experiences of those on the Pine Ridge reservation from Wounded Knee to the present, tucked in between a series that is more clearly classified as resting between an action comic and a detective caper. The series as a whole manages to educate its audience in spite of themselves, while tacitly acknowledging that the only way most people will become aware of this history is if it's wrapped inside something suspenseful and exciting.

Scalped insists that this history *matters* and that in fact the history is not in the past but is rather a traumatic memory that erupts into the present at every turn. The "screen memory," *Scalped* argues, is not worth the work it takes to maintain the illusory at the expanse of the real, and moreover, reality is not a strictly objective accounting of "winners" and "losers" but rather a subjective assessment of what truly matters and why. As an artifact of popular culture, it intervenes in the debate about American Indian heritage at an awkward point. By virtue of its form, it is part of the very legacy of stereotypes and marginalization that threaten actual American Indians' lives today. By using this particular *form*, Aaron and Guera are promoting a representation of American Indians that recalls their history of oppression and explicitly connects it to present-day circumstances on the reservation. Moreover, they use stereotypes and questions about identity in order to underscore the complicity of popular culture in circulating negative images, while simultaneously drawing the reader into conversation with the complex frustrations of very real human lives. I take up similar questions in the next chapter, in an exploration of African American identity, in order to illustrate an alternate method of dealing with the tensions in memory and experience in the graphic narrative form. While *Scalped* utilizes memories that question one another, the next chapter addresses *Bayou*, which develops a concept of cultural memory and trauma that reintegrates unspoken histories into the visual field.

CHAPTER 4

MY CHILDREN WILL REMEMBER ALL OF THE THINGS I TRIED TO FORGET

Bayou and Intergenerational Trauma

Is it possible for white America to really understand blacks' distrust of
the legal system, their fears of racial profiling and the police, without
understanding how cheap a black life was for so long a time in our
nation's history?

—Philip Dray

PRACTICES OF memorialization sanction what is remembered and how
it is remembered, while our conceptualization of memory also has repercussions for the enshrining of historical "truth." Ethical questions follow
from these parameters, particularly, as I mentioned early in the previous
chapter, that the Holocaust has in some ways served as a screen memory
for more geographically pertinent historical traumas in the United States.
Gilda Graff begins her essay "The Intergenerational Trauma of Slavery and
its Aftermath" by recounting Jane Lazare's "mus[ing] that there is no per-
manent slavery museum in the United States, though there is a Holocaust
Museum" (181). Museums are structured as models for remembrance, and
the disavowed history of structural racism in the United States is emblematized in this lack of a museum. As discussed in the previous chapter, certain
cultural tropes sanction certain types of memory, but memory functions not
as a stable set of artifacts but rather a set of negotiations. The museum as a
metaphor for memory is profoundly deficient for understanding how memory works, but graphic narratives like Jeremy's Love's *Bayou*, a two-volume
comic that follows a young African American girl as she negotiates life in
1930s Mississippi, provide an alternative metaphoric model for memory

that more accurately reflects the play between past, present, and future that is core to the practice.

We traditionally envision memory as an archive, a metaphor that firmly links memory with the structure of the museum in which artifacts from the past are stored and may be accessed at our leisure. In this model, the past is conceived as static and composed of a series of specific "pictures" that are the discrete units of memory that—when taken together—compose the identity of an individual. The last decade of research demonstrates that memory is less an archive of videos than a narrative.[1] Charles Fernyhough contends that "a memory is more like a *habit*, a process of constructing something from its parts, in similar but subtly changing ways each time, whenever the occasion arises" (6). Recent cognitive research has shown that memory is rooted in narrative, and the relative "truth" of a memory is mediated by present demands. Daniel Schacter, professor of psychology at Harvard, has highlighted these alterations as a method of preparing for the future. He remarks that these modifications do not represent a "fabrication" of the past; instead, they are the result of changing demands placed on past experiences in the present. Similarly, Wolfgang Müller-Funk asserts that "The point is not that there is no 'reality'—pain, death, war, hunger, exploitation—but that this reality can only be understood through the specific narratives" (209). Memory serves the extant rather than the bygone.

The hold of the present over the past also suggests that the screen memory is not merely that which is put in place between the individual and a past too traumatic to immediately integrate but also that the screen memory is an attempt to overhaul the past, to retell it so that the trauma will have never existed. It's a neat trick. Martin Conway succinctly encapsulates this in the assertion that "memory is motivated" (594), meaning that memory functions to prepare the individual for changing demands and to organize a coherent sense of self by "making memory consistent with an individual's current goals, self-images, and self-beliefs" (595). It is not that memory is "purely" a story; what happened in the past shapes our present reality. However, there is a more complex back-and-forth. Memory is a process of narration *rather* than the raw materials by which we construct a narrative. The raw materials are indeed stored in some fashion, but how we fit them together depends on the situation in which we're telling the story. As with the previous chapter, in which the characters sought to use scripts to perform "authentic" identities while simultaneously grappling with provi-

---

1. Literary criticism includes James Olney's landmark *Memory and Narrative* and Andreas Huyssen's *Twilight Memory*.

sional memories of the past, memory is mediated by the person's relationship with himself, with others, and with history.

The centrality of narrative to memory is acknowledged by psychologists partly in the treatment of PTSD, while PTSD itself is a memory that cannot be controlled. Cathy Caruth claims in her introduction to *Trauma: Explorations in Memory* that the "simple definition [of PTSD] belies a very peculiar fact: the pathology cannot be defined either by the event itself—which may or may not be catastrophic, and may or may not traumatize everyone equally—nor can it be defined in terms of a *distortion* of the event [. . .] The pathology consists, rather, solely in the *structure of its experience* or reception: the event is not assimilated or experienced fully at the time, but only belatedly, in its repeated *possession* of the one who experiences it" (4). It is not the event itself but the remembering of it that is the locus of traumatic experience. Cathy Caruth, Bessel van der Kolk, and other trauma theorists frequently note that the traumatic memory only loses its power to disrupt an individual's life when it has been adequately narrated into the larger life story. How, then, does this work at a cultural level? As briefly discussed in the introduction, Holocaust scholarship has long discussed the transmission of trauma across generations—through the terms "intergenerational trauma" or "transgenerational trauma"—and has attempted to decipher how a group or a culture can transmit feelings of helplessness or loss across time.[2] A similar concept is "cultural trauma," which "refers to a dramatic loss of identity and meaning, a tear in the social fabric, affecting a group of people who have achieved some degree of cohesion" (Eyerman 160). Eyerman goes on to explain that a cultural trauma can be as central to the identity of a group as a sense of success, the latter being a more common way of defining the group's source of unity. While the Holocaust has long been a primary focal point for trauma theorists, slavery and its aftermath is increasingly becoming an object of concern in discussions about intergenerational or cultural trauma.

---

2. Transgenerational trauma was first identified in the children of Holocaust survivors, many of whom increasingly sought therapy in the late 1960s and 1970s. Selma Fraiberg's foundational concept of "ghosts in the nursery" highlighted how parents can unconsciously reenact their own moments of fear and transmit them to their children. The transmission pathway was initially conceived of as between mother and child, although later works, including those of Paul Barrows, broadened this concept to include the father-child relationship and the relationship between the parents. Fraiberg's work spawned a generation of discussions about the ways in which parents could "infect" their children with their own traumatic experiences. It should be noted that Alicia Lieberman's concept of "angels in the nursery" acts as a counterpoint, establishing positive caregivers as bastions against trauma.

Unlike the Holocaust, which is clearly memorialized by the German people, the United States has never adequately dealt with its heritage of slavery. The two pathways of remembrance outlined above can come into conflict when one group is responsible for the suffering of another group, particularly when the group who perpetrated violence or loss chooses to dis-remember that aspect of their history. For most people, the stories that they choose to comprise the self are tied to an image of themselves as a "good" person. Bracketing stories in which that "goodness" is compromised is normal for both individuals and nations because the demands of the present often insist on moral rectitude in the past. However, this retelling of history can inhibit adequate understanding of the suffering of others, circumventing the possibility for empathy and/or atonement because of a refusal to acknowledge the damage of the past. Purposeful forgetting has consequences for those who were victims in the past not only because their heritage is minimized or denied but because their history also affects the present in both material and affective ways.

At the affective level, trauma does not go away if one simply ignores it, whether one is suffering from a traumatic memory or someone perpetrated a trauma on another. In fact, recent cognitive studies have demonstrated the resiliency of aversion across generations.[3] In a study published recently in *Nature Neuroscience*,[4] researchers found that mice may indeed transmit aversion between generations by nonsocial means.[5] Somehow, this fear is genetically encoded, etched into the make-up of these animals. Brian G. Dias and Kerry J. Ressler studied "how environmental information may be inherited transgenerationally" (89). The possibility that there is a noncultural transfer of memory sanctions many of the theoretical explorations of intergenerational trauma in the humanities, which, while not scientific, cer-

---

3. "Aversion" is often a component of but is not equivalent to trauma. The symptom profile of PTSD in the DSM-V includes "intrusive thoughts or memories," "avoiding thoughts or feelings connected with the [traumatizing] event," "avoiding people or situations connected with that event," and others, including most significantly for this chapter, "Memory problems that are exclusive to the event."

4. Briefly, the study exposed mice to the scent of cherry blossoms along with electric shocks. The gametes of the mice were harvested and mice who had not received the fear conditioning were inseminated, so that no cultural contamination would occur. The next generation showed aversion to the scent.

5. It is important to note that this study has been criticized, most notably by Gregory Francis, who argues in "Too Much Success for Recent Groundbreaking Epigenetic Experiments" that Dias and Ressler's account "likely overestimate[s] the effect magnitudes because unreported unsuccessful outcomes usually indicate a smaller effect than reported outcomes" (450). Dias and Ressler dispute this. Francis does not dispute that there *may* be a nonsocial transfer of environmental information, however.

tainly examine a phenomenon that may have more dimensions in terms of cultural relationships and ethics than previously suspected. However, there are some issues with overapplying this lens.

Trauma is not simply an unruly memory, but rather, it is *already* a narrative but one that disrupts present demands rather than preparing the sufferer for the future. The "possession" metaphor employed by Caruth and others ultimately evacuates agency from the victim and, furthermore, "transform[s] the experience of trauma into a basic anthropological condition" (Kansteiner 204). Trauma is not, however, a general experience, and it is not equal to difficulty in representation. In fact, even in the case of traumatic memories, the individual frequently *remembers* and can narrate the event as well as any of us do but has failed to contextualize it in a way that allows them to live normally—it is less a problem of the narrative itself than the lens through which they tell it.[6] We are often inclined to think of "normal" memories and traumatic memories as two distinct *types* of memory—categorically dissimilar. Normal memory can be filed away, as in the museum model, while traumatic memory is disruptive.[7] While traumatic memory is different, we are inclined in literary studies to overstate this case rather than understate it.[8] While an individual experiencing PTSD is most certainly overwhelmed by memories, research has repeatedly demonstrated that traumatic flashbacks and memories consist not only of the event but also of "what we feared *might* have happened" (Fernyhough 185).[9] Trauma is *not* a haunting or a possession. It is a narrative that is debilitating in the present. Approaches to therapy always focus on being able to narrate an experience in a more productive way. This metaphoric linking with the supernatural—while illustrative of some of trauma's more pyrotechnic effects—simultaneously obscures its roots in very real, very lived experiences of individuals in the material world. Furthermore, memory in this sense is an *owner* of the subject, rather than a product of

---

6. See Ruth Leys's *Trauma: A Genealogy.*

7. Strictly speaking, traumatic memory differs in some ways, primarily in the "'overconsolidation' of the memory of trauma" (Debiec and LeDoux 521). This "overconsolidation" is less a difference in *kind* than in amplitude, however.

8. Karim Nader has presented these findings in various formats, including on the RadioLab podcast, episode "Memory and Forgetting." Brunet, Alain, et al. "Effect of Post-retrieval Propranolol on Psychophysiologic Responding During Subsequent Script-driven Traumatic Imagery in Post-traumatic Stress Disorder." *Journal of Psychiatric Research* 42.6 (2008): 503–6.

9. Dorthe Berntsen and David C. Rubin, *Understanding Autobiographical Memory*; Richard J. McNally, *Remembering Trauma*; and M. I. Good, "The Reconstruction of Early Childhood Trauma."

a subjectivity. It has important repercussions for how fear and danger are assessed. Goldie notes that "the class of dangerous things has no unifying feature or features that can be captured in the language of the sciences [and that the dangerous] is an evaluative property" (*The Emotions* 30). That which is deemed dangerous is based on cultural position or point of view, and the recognition of a danger inspires not only aversion but also fear. This has significant repercussions for memory and conflict between groups.

Love's *Bayou* explores in part how the effects of slavery and racism in the United States are the shared history of all citizens of the nation, though the way in which that history is framed differs by race. African Americans share a cultural memory of a time when their families could be broken up by a whim, when their labor and children were stolen, when their women were subject to rape with impunity, and their men could be killed for mild transgressions. This shared history formed a collective identity based in part on a narrative of resilience, but it is also based on a shared cultural trauma, which Eyerman explains is renegotiated through narrative in successive generations, wherein grappling with their shared sense of history creates (or makes accessible) different stories at different cultural moments. As I will explore in more detail below, Love explores this renegotiation of trauma in 1930s Mississippi, at the height of the lynching era.

White Americans, by contrast, do not necessarily share a cultural memory of slavery, and they negotiate the historical realities of slavery in a wide variety of ways. However, many white Americans find the discussion of race and the history of slavery uncomfortable and compartmentalize their ancestors' actions as something that occurred in the past so as to ease a collective sense of guilt. This denial of the persistence of the effects of slavery, a kind of cultural amnesia, divides whites' perceptions and narratives of the past from those of African Americans. Furthermore, the refusal to acknowledge the historical realities of slavery is to cancel memories that cannot be erased. Acknowledging guilt or complicity or, at minimum, that the narrative of slavery and black history could be positive at the cultural level and at the psychological level, in which narratives of atrocities committed against Africans and African Americans by whites are reincorporated, could serve as a point of healing.

As we consider the ways in which memory functions both biologically and culturally across generations, the narrative core of memory processes is crucial to any radical healing of historical wounds.[10] One possible model

---

10. Wolfgang Müller-Funk's article "On a Narratology of Cultural and Collective Memory" discusses many of the foundational issues with memory studies in which he posits a narratological approach as a reconciliation strategy.

of this can be found in Jeremy Love's graphic narrative *Bayou,* an account of how disruptive intergenerational memory can function as both a reminder of past atrocities and as a cue to readers into their continued *presence.*

MEMORY AS CURATION

Love's *Bayou* is an excellent example of how the traumatic memories of ancestors can be renarrated to effect positive change in the present. Rather than figuring intergenerational memory and trauma as debilitating, Love crafts a world in which the trauma of slavery is integrated into the present by retelling the story in a way that responds to current demands. *Bayou* is a two-volume graphic narrative series that follows Lee Wagstaff, a young African American girl in Mississippi in 1933. *Bayou* uses the material conditions of racism in the South to comment on the persistence of racism in the present day, integrating the familiar story of an innocent black man charged with a crime who is on the verge of being lynched. In a bid to save him, his daughter attempts to find the white friend he is accused of murdering, entering an alternate reality through the bayou that at first glance appears to be a sort of afterlife in which the power structures in the "real" world are replicated; but rather than people, the landscape is populated with monsters and anthropomorphized animals from African American fables.

The borders between the real world and the world through the bayou are permeable and complex. Lee is able to periodically see beyond the real world in moments of terror and is able to go through the bayou to enter this alternate world of her own accord. This porousness of the boundaries between the normal world with its recognizable history and the alternate world that is half afterlife and half fever dream of the era of Jim Crow signifies something beyond a simple mirroring. The alternate world is not only a fun house mirror reflection of the real world but is also a repository for the narratives and anxieties of African Americans in the South during the early twentieth century.

An idyllic cotton field with a shack shadowed against the pale yellow background opens the volume (see fig. 4.1). In the foreground, a fluffy cotton plant delicately frames the vista, and a large tree hangs over the house, the foliage suggesting idle hours enjoying the surroundings. Similarly, the second panel foregrounds a small group of bunnies in a patch of grass, a battered truck trundling down a dusty road. However, rather than a pure Southern idyll as depicted in the cotton panel, this scene also includes a

FIGURE 4.1. Screen memory of the South. Love, Jeremy, and Patrick Morgan. *Bayou.* Vol. 1. New York: DC/Zuda, 2009.

stars-and-bars sign welcoming travelers to Charon, Mississippi. The small inset notes that the year is 1933, and coupled with the rebel flag, the nostalgic effect of the truck and the cute bunnies are counterbalanced by the visual allusion to racism. In the final introductory panels, a crow perches on a "Colored Only" sign, while an inset shows a group of faceless white men looking on at the foregrounded feet of a black man hanging from a tree. The balance illustrated in these three panels gestures toward cultural memory surrounding the South. Often envisioned as a space of tranquility because of images promulgated by slave owners and deeply embedded in cultural memory, the more violent images associated with slavery are nearly completely dissociated with those of the "Southern way of life." The nostalgic depiction of the Southern landscape of the past is always at odds with the atrocities it contained, and the paintings and photographs of landscapes dotted with puffy balls of cotton (as well as the grand depictions of stately plantation houses) coexist—but never overlap with—images of whipped slaves and lynched black men and women strung from trees. These representations exist at odds with one another, each straining for cultural primacy; the idyllic image often becomes a screen memory for the reality of violence inflicted on African Americans. Furthermore, as Hatfield notes, there are "symbols that function non-diegetically—that is, the min-gling of symbols that 'show' and symbols that 'tell'" (40), the former being representational of some reality within the world of the comic and the latter being those that comment upon that world. Throughout *Bayou*, the tension is not only between contested accounts of history but also between those images that represent and those images that comment.

Love replicates this tension in the first and third panel, but he seeks to begin to integrate these conceptualizations of the South in the second, using the symbolic role of the rebel flag as stark contrast to the more sentimental-ized landscapes. Memory, in these panels, is represented as distinct chan-nels, the first of which illustrates a conscious longing for an unstained past, the third of which depicts the marginalized experiences contained within that past that are avoided, and the second of which suggests that within the softened edges of the romantic landscape there is always an ugly truth.

At the beginning of the narrative, Lee dives down into the bayou to retrieve the body of a young African American boy named Billy Glass, who had been lynched for allegedly whistling at a white woman—a clear his-torical allusion to Emmett Till. During these panels, rather than a dialogue bubble, text boxes overlay the scenes that Lee narrates about her experience in the bayou. In the first panel, Lee asserts that "The Bayou is a bad place. Ain't nuthin' good ever happened around there" (1.04), while the second panel merely shows her looking over her shoulder, asking, "Daddy . . . ?" In both of these panels, the reader is positioned at the approximate location of her father and the sheriff. Instead of occupying her point of view, we are given the vantage point of the adults, and while we sympathize with Lee, it is clear that she is narrating this incident from memory, and we are seeing not a reconstruction of her perspective of the scene but that of an outsider. It is revealed after the scene that she is describing this experience to her white friend Lily Westmoreland. This scene of a personal traumatic encounter is filtered through memory, reconstructed for both Lily and for the reader. In fact, although it is Lee narrating the event, we are not wholly submerged into her point of view—instead, we view her mostly from the outside, watching as she swims down into the murky water and seeing her from the perspective of Billy Glass's corpse when she finds him. The only moment at which we are confronted by her point of view is in the dramatic panel at the top right-hand side. When we are embedded in her perspec-tive, it simultaneously draws us emotionally closer to her and, when taken with the other panels, reminds us of our distance from the experience.

As she dives down into the water, we see her from below, and signifi-cantly, her face is erased. Rather than eyes, nose, and a mouth there is a smooth surface without feature. In the following panels, she is depicted in a variety of ways: her eyes are small as she sees Billy Glass's hand protruding from beneath a tree, and they remain small black circles as she looks into a hollow of the tree where his other hand floats in the foreground. The hand mimics the roots in the background, blending into the landscape and suggesting that—given the social climate of the time—the corpse of a lynched black boy at the bottom of a body of water was less remarkable than it was a "feature of the landscape," a peculiar echo of the lynching photography of the period. In lynching photography, the corpse of a black person is usually tied to a tree, a fence, or some other normal feature of the landscape, while a crowd of whites pose for the photograph. Discussed in more detail below, lynching photography served as a public "warning" for blacks, at once propaganda, advertisement, and commemoration. However, the image we see of Billy Glass's corpse is not one carefully posed for effect. We see the corpse through Lee's eyes, momentarily occupying her point of view in a panel that shows his bloated skin and milky eyes, the frayed remains of a rope still knotted around his neck. Lynching photography is repulsive but is also clearly staged for public consumption: the poses, even smiles, the centering of the body in the frame of the shot, the careful lighting. By contrast, Billy Glass's body is hidden at the bottom of a swamp and is seen at this point only by Lee. It is a private vision and a private memory.

Rather than being simply horrific, however, Lee "sees" Billy Glass's spirit, replete with butterfly wings, pausing to watch her retrieve his body. The representation of the girl diving into the bayou is balanced by the symbol that tells: the angelic spirit boy and the corpse are both a part of this discussion. Two of the smaller inset panels switch from Lee's point of view to that of Billy Glass, looking into one another's faces in a moment of closure. However, once Lee emerges from the bayou we see her from a distance, breaking the surface, being helped out of the water and hugged by her father, her face clearly registering shock. Throughout these panels, the overlain text boxes describe her interior experience, and in the last, as she stares out from her father's arms, she struggles to explain that "I was hearing these voices. Sounded like people singing . . ." (1.09). No other sounds are rendered in the panel, though, so the singing clearly exists within Lee's imagination.

On the next page, it becomes clear that the text boxes denoted that Lee was describing this scene to her white friend Lily. When Lee is shown recounting the story to Lily, Lily merely asks what he looked like—what we were viewing on the preceding pages is not what Lily imagined but rather, in this moment, is reframed as what Lee remembered: a reconstruction of herself within the scene rather than the first-person "museum/camera" model of memory. In accessing the memory, Lee reconstructs it in an attempt to adopt a potential point of view for Lily so that she can "see" the scene. In a five-panel spread, Lee remarks that she no longer goes to the bayou because "It's a bad place" (1.10), as she combs her fingers through Lily's hair. Lily asks if "he look[ed] like that Frankenstein picture we saw that one time," attempting to use a shared cultural referent to bring the experience closer to her. Lee says, "He was all pale and puffy and his eyes were bulging out," a description that elicits a shocked exclamation mark above Lily's head. Interestingly, in this panel, Lily's face replicates that of Billy Glass: her face is pale and puffed out, and her eyes are round and wide but have no pupils. The following panel depicts Lily reciting, "My mama said Billy Glass deserved what he got. She said a n***** boy got no business whistling at a white woman," prompting Lee to recoil in surprise, slouching in the following silent panel as Lily blithely whistles.

Lily's whistle, argues Qiana Whitted, is emblematic of the boundaries between freedom and restriction in *Bayou*. Whitted asserts that

> what we hear, then, in Love's visual rendering of Lily's whistle interests me greatly, for those tiny eighth notes generate a tremendous sound. We hear echoes of anti-miscegenation panic, a fear that reverberates unease even as the conversation hastily resumes. We hear the sense of white privilege that attends Lily's ability to whistle freely, carelessly one could argue, in spite of her naïveté as a child repeating her mother's words. But I believe that what Love also wants us to hear in this sequence is the "wolf whistle" of a murdered black child, along with the memory of just how much that sound costs. Perhaps what resonates most deeply in the white girl's whistle are the sounds that Billy (and Emmett) are no longer able to make, were never free to make at all. (1)

Whitted's analysis illustrates the tension in both the sound and the silence in this scene: who is allowed to speak (or whistle), and whose voice is marginalized. Furthermore, it gestures toward whose memories and perspectives matter. While we have just seen Lee's experience recounted for Lily over the course of several pages, Lee's account is annihilated under the weight of Lily's mother's words. Lee is seeking primarily to provide Lily with her perspective, carefully framing the narrative so that Lily can hear the trauma of it. Lily cannot, however, adopt the perspective provided for her and instead parrots her mother's racism then pressures Lee to go down to the bayou.

In his landmark work *On Listening to Holocaust Survivors,* Henry Greenspan argues that there is tension in both the stories that are (or can be) told and how these stories are received. Actual memories do not tend to occur in any recognizable narrative arc—particularly potentially traumatic memories like those associated with genocide—but must be reformulated into a narrative in order to make sense of the experience for the listener. Similarly, while a story may (to the best of the teller's ability) accurately recount these experiences, there are limits to what can be "heard" (i.e., understood) by the audience.[11] While Lee attempts to tell her narrative to Lily, Lily is incapable of hearing the narrative for its heartbeat. This is further underscored as she and Lee walk through a field on their way to the bayou and Lee asks Lily if she can hear singing. Lily remarks, "I don't hear nothin.' You must be losing your head, Lee" (1.13). Lily's inability to hear the singing is not evidence that the singing is not in fact there, as this scene alludes to white people's propensity (both at the time and in the present) to fail to see the evidence of racism even when presented with it. The singing is not simply singing; it is a reminder that black people face experiences of oppression not commonly shared by white people. Lily's response is telling in that she immediately asserts that Lee must be crazy rather than admit that there may be something there that she cannot hear. It should also be noted that, while elsewhere in the comic singing is visually depicted in both musical notes and lyrics, in neither early panel in which Lee purports to hear singing is singing actually visually rendered. This is a tacit nod to the assumed white readers' possible inability to "hear" stories about racism without dismissing them as overdramatic, exaggerated, or misinterpreted, if there is any response at all.

As Lily and Lee walk down to the bayou, Lily asks about Lee's mother, and Lee explains that she died in a juke joint that was swept away in a flash flood in the bayou. Lily wants to swim down in the water to see if the patrons of the juke joint are still beneath the water, and Lee asserts that there "Ain't nuthin' getting me back in that water again" (1.16). In this panel, Lee's face is turned away from the water and her eyes are shut, doubly closing out the bank of the bayou, attempting to avoid even looking at the location of so much trauma. Lily's face is turned away to taunt Lee for her cowardice as a mysterious hand reaches out of the water. Lily asserts, "Ain't nothing in this water, come look for yourself," even as the hand stretches out toward her neck. The tension between the image—which rep-

---

11. For more on this, see Henry Greenspan's *On Listening to Holocaust Survivors,* chapters 1 and 2.

resents a clear danger—and the word—which discounts that danger—also comments on acts of looking, acts of remembering, and acts of narration. Lily is unable to see that there is indeed something in the water because her attention is diverted away from it even as she proclaims to know what is within it, a repetition of the scene above in which she cannot hear the singing. While she has certainly spoken evil by repeating her mother's racist words, she can neither hear nor see it. The traditional aphorism "see no evil, hear no evil, speak no evil" implies a casual linkage in which hearing and seeing define the propensity to speak, but in Lee and Lily's conversation, this is turned on its head. Lily's refusal to hear or see leaves her vulnerable and prompts her to later "speak evil," as will be explored later. While she is busy not hearing the singing, she doesn't see a hand that reaches out of the water and snatches her locket away.

Lee and Lily are depicted in soft focus as Lily worries over what her mother will do when she finds that the locket is missing, the mysterious hand sharply in focus in the foreground. Lee responds to Lily's worries, "Aww, Lily, it ain't that bad, your mama is always buying your stuff," a blithe comment based on Lee's understanding of Lily's circumstances. As the poor daughter of a sharecropper, Lee understands primarily that Lily is well dressed and well fed, but Lily's eruption of "I just can't take another beatin' by mama, I just can't" exposes her own difficult circumstances (1.18). The exposure of her bruise in the right-hand panel draws the eye, as it is on the back of her shoulder, a place normally hidden by clothing, suggesting that Lee didn't know of Lily's mother's abuse. Interestingly, this mirrors to some extent Lily's own dismissal of Lee's experience pulling Billy Glass's body from the bayou. Both girls attempt to use visual aids to help illustrate their stories—Lily her bruise and Lee her description of the corpse—but neither is sufficient to prompt the type of sympathy that either seeks. Both fail to hear the root terror at the heart of each story. When her father calls, Lee runs off even as Lily begs her to go into the bayou to look for the locket. However, the bayou is itself the site of a primal fear for Lee, having destroyed her mother and being the site of her own confrontation with death, so the impasse is at its core an inability to reconcile the weighty symbolism of the bayou on the part of Lee with the utter lack of symbolism for Lily.

This lacuna between two modes of understanding the bayou is meant to replicate the gulf between two understandings of race relations in the United States at the present. On one hand, a white child who legitimately has a family problem—being beaten by her mother—is seeking to minimize her vulnerability. However, her beatings are neither Lee's responsibility nor equivalent to systemic racism. In this text, they are represented as an individual problem. On the other hand, Lee's experience of seeking out Billy's body in the bayou is an individual traumatic experience to be sure, but it is also an emblem of a larger social problem. At a time when "Black Lives Matter" is met with the response "All Lives Matter," one cannot help but connect this tone-deaf response with much of the white community's inability to distinguish between problems that exist for all and problems that are experienced *because* one is a person of color. Lily's experience of abuse has—to be sure—been shared by millions of children of all races, but it has not occurred *because* of her race. This doesn't negate the problem but rather signifies a difference in category.

Compounding this problem, Lily blames the necklace's disappearance on Lee. After working in the field with her father, Lee is cooking supper for the two of them when Mrs. Westmoreland, the sheriff, and Lily arrive. As the adults "negotiate" about Lee working off the value of the locket, Lee is once again turned from the point of action and has shut her eyes. Lily peers at her, stuttering her name, comprehending only that her friend has been hurt in same way that she is and failing to understand that the consequences of her lie have bought her friend a year of labor . . . as a child. At this moment, the reader is positioned at child height but sees the scene from neither of the focalizing characters' perspectives, indicating an affinity but without full closure. The reader is of course sympathetic to Lee, but the ambivalence in this positioning also acknowledges that the assumed reader is in some respects closer to the uncomprehending Lily than the frustrated Lee. Lily's failure of empathy doesn't allow her to predict the consequences of her lie, nor does it allow her to understand the difficulty of these consequences for others. This failure of empathy is emphasized as Lily later follows Lee across a field, saying, "You can't still be sore at me," phrased as much as a command as a question (1.34).

Lily's guilt over lying prompts her to go down to the bayou to retrieve her locket and clear Lee's name. Lee ignores this, until, while walking through a field, she hears voices telling her to go down to the bayou. Unlike in previous scenes where Lee has heard something Lily cannot hear, the voices are printed in plain text all around her head, indicating at this point that the voices are at least to some extent "real," even if they are not real to Lily. As Lee arrives at the bayou, she sees Lily stuck in the mud along the bank, a close-up depicting the mud as tiny hands grasping Lily's ankles. Lily is looking at Lee at this moment and only turns to see the large white man looming above her when Lee points. A repetition of the scene in which

Lily loses her necklace, she cannot see the danger, but in this case, Lee sees the danger very clearly.

In earlier scenes, the message was that to neither hear nor see evil was not necessarily to fail to speak evil; willful ignorance compromises Lily's ability to connect with and understand her friend. This scene expands the trope, illustrating that to neither hear nor see evil is not necessarily to be safe from the dangers surrounding one. Lily has turned her attention toward Lee and fails to see—and possibly save herself from—the huge man filling the bulk of the frame. At this moment, the reader shares Lee's point of view; we see the danger along with her. The man dwarfs Lily, and he is proportionally unsound. His tiny head rests atop broad shoulders, which expand into large arms and comically oversized hands. A small smile plays at his mouth as he gazes fixedly at Lily.

From Lee's perspective, we watch as the monstrous man draws Lily toward his mouth as she pleads for help, one panel showing Lee urinating on herself in fright, and the spread ends with a wide, satisfied smile on the man's face. Counter to the fear-mongering racist narrative of black men preying on young white girls, the man is not only white but is also not a sexual predator. In a more prosaic turn, rather than being a sexual aggressor, he simply consumes her whole. The man—who is later referred to as "Cotton-Eyed Joe"—becomes a symbol for the threat at the heart of traditional narratives that tell us who and how to fear. While crime statistics have consistently indicated that interracial violence is far less likely than intraracial violence,[12] because of cultural narratives about blacks' supposed "predisposition" to violence, whites are taught to focus their fear on people of color rather than the much more accurate focal point: other white people. Replicating the tension between the symbolic narrative of cultural anxieties surrounding blacks and the narrative provided by the reality of statistics, these panels insist the reader acknowledge how one fear screens a more disturbing reality. After consuming Lily, the man waves at Lee and walks away, singing, "hadn't been for Cotton-Eyed Joe, I'd be married a long time ago . . ." (1.44). An allusion to a popular folk song that was once recorded by Nina Simone and was popularized by the 1994 recording by the Rednex, the "cotton-eyed" element of the song is purported to refer either to alcohol-induced blindness or the symptoms of late-stage syph-

---

12. Truman, Jennifer L. and Rachel E. Morgan. U.S. Department of Justice Office of Justice Programs, Bureau of Statistics. *Criminal Victimization, 2015.* Web. 20 Nov. 2014.

ilis.[13] Lee watches as he wades out into the swamp, and then, clutching Lily's shoe, she flees into the forest.

Rather than a haven from the bayou, the forest has suddenly become littered with the lynched bodies of black men and women (see fig. 4.2).

She nearly runs into a pair of feet—one shoeless—hanging at her height, and the following full-page spread depicts a series of victims, all with nooses tied around their necks, hung from the surrounding trees. Of the six bodies, only one is rendered with the sketchy outline of eyes and a mouth, while the rest remain smooth and faceless. Orange butterflies flit below them, at stark odds with the scene. This facelessness recalls McCloud's remarks about the icon, that "when you look at a photo or realistic drawing of a face, you see it as the face of another, but when you enter the world of cartoon, you see yourself" (36). In this scene, opening the possibility of imaginative identification with the bodies is one level of empathic engagement, but it's a troubling one. The bulk of comic readers are white, and there is a perversity to vicariously identifying with victims of lynching. However, the reader's is not strictly the point of view through which identification takes place here.

At this moment, we are seeing over Lee's shoulder the eruption of a traumatic memory, but it is not her *own* memory. While she has seen the result of a single lynching while pulling Billy Glass's body from the bayou, an entire forest of hanged men is something distinct: this is not a reminder of something Lee herself has seen but rather a pastiche of what her ancestors have witnessed. Terrified, she runs through the feet, shielding her face with Lily's shoe. In a sense, she is already envisioning herself as *among* these bodies, and her only defensive weapon is the shoe of a white child.

Here, we see something of what the cherry blossom study can offer: it is not purely about the violence one has witnessed nor is it about the traumatic experiences passed down to individuals through culture. Instead, this is a warning of what the current circumstances could result in if steps are not taken to mitigate the danger. As Michael A. Chaney remarks in "Visual Narratives of US Slavery," watching this spectacle unfold means that "reader-viewers must become the auditors of an absent community of the ancestral dead, whose pictorial monologues cry out for out affective response in the present" (28). Her psychological response moves immediately to images of a threat to her and her father, even though the abductor was white. This is a future-focused memory—this pastiche of ancestral hor-

---

13. Noted in Dorothy Scarborough's *On the Trail of Negro Folk Songs* as a song sung by slaves on plantations, speculation about the meaning of *cotton-eyed* can't be pinned down with any more accuracy than the origins of the song.

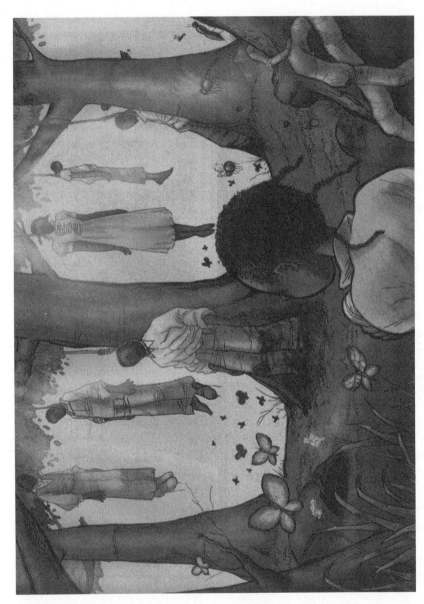

FIGURE 4.2. Lee and the lynching forest. Love, Jeremy, and Patrick Morgan. *Bayou.* Vol. 1. New York: DC/Zuda, 2009.

rors is not delivered purely as a method of displaying the traumatic experiences of African Americans in the South. It is also a matter of recentering a disavowed narrative that affects the present.

THROUGH THE BAYOU'S LOOKING GLASS

Lee's premonition comes to pass. She faints upon returning home, and during her spell, she has a vision of Lily crying out for her, wrapped in the roots of a tree. This visual metaphor indicates that Lily is in part imprisoned by her own proverbial roots, but Lee wakes to find the sheriff arresting her father on the charge of abducting Lily, a different kind of imprisonment because of a different heritage. Lily is taught her mother's racism and repeats it unthinkingly, but moreover, her actual captor does not fit the cultural script provided, and so with the flimsiest of evidence—the shoe that Lee herself had carried from the woods—her father Calvin is arrested. As she struggles to hug her father, she cries, "I ain't gon' let them do you like Billy Glass!" (1.54), but one of the posse sharply whips her with the barrel of his rifle. The scene would be horrific under any circumstances, but the reader is positioned in relative proximity to the strike, and both characters are rendered in tight detail, unlike many other scenes in which characters' faces recede to mere sketches. The men laugh about it as they drive away, one remarking, "I say we take this n***** to the nearest tree right now" (1.56), the last thing Lee hears before she passes out.

The reader is ensconced in her point of view as she wakes up to see two of her cousins and a dog, and after a brief exchange with her aunt, she fades again into a dream in which a large, anthropomorphic rabbit asks her, "Where's Lily?" As she wakes from this allusion to *Alice in Wonderland*, she hears her aunt and uncle talking about Calvin's arrest, her aunt insistent that something must be done and her uncle more pragmatic in his assertion that "You go down there raising Cain it'll be open season on every n***** in this town" (1.64). Lee decides to sneak out to try to save her father, but her uncle catches her. Instead of punishing her, he gives her his great-grandfather's axe and the story that goes along with it.

Rendered in sepia tones, the uncle describes the Battle of Negro Fort, in which Andrew Jackson was sent to capture an area around the fort in which freedmen, runaway slaves, and American Indians were living. The fort was destroyed, most of its inhabitants killed or wounded, but Lee's uncle's great-grandfather managed to escape. A Choctaw gave him the axe and told him, "Now was a time to be free. Chop wood. Build a new home. But when it was time to fight he would be ready" (1.70). The axe is described as an ambivalent symbol, as much tool as weapon, but this also describes the story itself. Because it is a story of a family, it can be used as a tool for fostering a sense of both the past and the future, but in this case, the future for Lee is primarily one of struggle. Furthermore, it demonstrates how memory is future focused. This story comes up at precisely the moment it is needed as a guiding pathway for Lee. It is not purely an event that occurred in her family's past but a reconstruction of that past in order to give her the tools—or the weapon—that she will need in the present.

Her uncle's narrative is countered with a newspaper article reporting on the arrest of Lee's father, beginning with the story of the town Charon. Describing it in glowing terms and referring to it as "one of the last bastions of Southern grandeur," the reporter recounts how the name Charon came from the ferocity of a General Bogg who defended the town during "the War Between the States." This historical interlude serves to establish the town as an idyllic replication of plantation mythology, serving as a backdrop for reporting on the crime. Lee's father is described as "a big and burly wretch, with long, sinewy, apelike arms and massive hands. His eyes are devoid of feeling and humanity. One finds it hard to empathize with this criminal" (1.73). In this reconstruction of Calvin, who, until now, the reader has seen primarily as a loving, devoted father, patient and hardworking, we instead find him filtered through a cultural script that is colored by the narrative of "Southern grandeur" built upon the backs of slaves. The representation of Calvin that the reader has seen is at odds with this account, a tension between what we know and how we know it. Throughout this passage, Lee is depicted in wordless images beside the transcript of the article, showing her journey to visit her father. By illustrating Lee alongside of the racist article, Love seeks to undermine the content of the article, which the reader is already primed to reject because they have developed sympathy for Calvin. However, this article also stands in as an allusion to the types of subtly racist rhetoric that still find its way into the pages of newspapers today, including accounts of protests characterized as "lawless" and popular media's fixation on showing looting at the expense of the peaceful demonstrations.

When Lee arrives at the jailhouse, this textual account is replaced by visual discomfort, inverting the source of tension for the reader, in which the assumed white reader in both textual and visual representations is to some extent aligned with the "bad guys." In the first three panels, the reader is put in Lee's position, the subject of the hostile observation of several older white men. Their eyes are narrowed, their mouths are either grim or shaped into a scowl, and it is clear that they view the subject of their gaze with revulsion and suspicion. The final panel shows Lee, who appears tired and has a cap pulled down to her eyes. As the shared subject of the gaze, the reader is placed in a situation of discomfort, but it is important also that the reader share the gaze directed at Lee as well. This ambivalence between the objecthood and subjectivity emphasizes the ways in which the bodies of African Americans are policed not only in the sense of arrest and incarceration but also simply in terms of existing in mixed-race spaces. The implicit assumption in the men's gazes is that she does not have a right to be there, even to visit her father. Her presence is both unwanted and is, to a certain extent, a reminder that Calvin is not merely what he was characterized as in the papers. The sheriff shows Lee into the jail, remarking, "I always been good to you people, but I ain't gettin' myself killt standing between Calvin and some fired-up mob" (1.80), indicating not that he believes that Calvin kidnapped Lily but rather that, because that is the prevailing belief, there is no way to save him. While a lynch mob would be extralegal, at this time in American history, it functioned with relative impunity. As Lee gazes into her father's beaten, bruised face, we share her perspective, but it is less a mirror or a moment of identification with Lee than it is a rendering meant to induce pain and horror in the reader. He is barely recognizable with a drooping eye and swollen lip, cuts ridging his face and a smear of blood beneath his nose. Much like the rendering of Billy Glass's corpse explored above, this is not the effect of violence posed for public consumption. He is hidden away in the jail, both for his protection and to exert power over his body, but the violence he experienced without cause is erased from the articles covering his arrest.

When Lee stands at the bank of the bayou, her face in profile, her mouth downturned in determination, we see that the journey to save Lily (and thus her father) involves accepting the world as it is. The overlap between the real and the alternate worlds is not such that they cannot be bridged, but more importantly, they exist in the same *moral* universe in which being black is enough of a crime. She swims into the bayou, retracing her route to retrieve Billy Glass's body, and while she is entering a fantastic realm, that fantasy belies a nightmarish reality at the core of this era. As she swims through the tree roots and into the other world, a dark hand grasps her foot. The creature appears to be similar to the Golliwog, a character created by Florence Kate Upton that mimicked the appearance of the blackface minstrelsy, recalling two strains of racist caricature. On one hand, the minstrelsy made African Americans out to be foolish and childlike, the object of humor and scorn, and on the other, these ideas were adapted into a doll, a human-like object you could own and play with at your whim. This creature seeks to physically drag Lee to her death, drowning her in the bayou that already took her mother, but it is a figurative burden as well, signifying the symbolic weight of caricature as a conscious element that must be counteracted. In an inversion of the white hand reaching out of the bayou to take Lily's necklace, a large hand reaches into the bayou to retrieve Lee from the Golliwog's clutches. The hand belongs the character named Bayou, a giant man with green skin who Lee mistakes for another monster like Cotton-Eyed Joe.

As she flees into the forest, she falls in a trap that spears her nearly through her heart. While Bayou stiches her up, Billy Glass warns her that it will not be enough and she will die in a few days. The inevitability of Lee's demise in seeking out her father and Lily has a nihilistic strain, but one that is perhaps not out of place in the context. While resilience, nonviolence, and passive resistance to white power have historically been cornerstones of the Civil Rights Movement and have been the qualities most honored and cited by the culture at large, the popular consciousness is quick to forget that turning the other cheek has physical consequences. Furthermore, giving recent events like the killing of Tamir Rice, a twelve-year-old Cleveland boy, it is worth considering that black bodies—even children's bodies—are considered more expendable.

"HAUNTED" OR STALKED?

The second volume of *Bayou* continues Lee's increasingly dangerous journey through the world within the bayou. Unlike the first volume, which establishes Lee as the main point of focalization, the second volume immerses her in a larger group of characters with a variety of motivations. The second volume also departs from the first in its greater integration of African American folklore, which, while referenced in the first volume, plays a subsidiary role in the first volume to illustrating the material conditions of racism. A tension between the representations of material conditions—as well as the ancestral memories—and the metacommentary that is always a part of folktales develops in this volume. The emphasis on folklore is not uniformly laudatory and often indicates the ways in which narratives restrict, as when they offer pathways of resistance or resilience. In terms of memory, the second volume is more concerned with the methods by which cultural memory can offer useful lessons for the future and, moreover, how certain tropes and character types haunt the image of African Americans to the present day.

Stagolee, a vicious, unstoppable killer, is introduced at the beginning of the volume and constitutes the main threat Lee and her friends will face. A dandy in a dapper suit, Stagolee is introduced in both name and context with American folk music. The character is clearly inspired by the song "Stagolee,"[14] which recounts the story of the title character, who kills a man because he lost money gambling. In subsequent verses, he frightens the local lawmen enough to have deputies refuse to arrest him and remarks, "I don't run, white folk, / when I got my forty one," and when he is finally ensnared and sentenced to death, the noose can't break his neck. Once he is ultimately killed, he ousts the devil from his place as king of Hell. Stagolee is also in part the story of the "uncontrollable black man," as he is able to instill fear in the authorities and to strike out against white power structures. In this regard, Stagolee would appear to some extent to be a folk hero, as he is openly feared by whites.[15] However, at the opening of the song, he is killing a man in a similar position to his own, and at the close of the song, he simply supplants the greatest evil, taking on the role of persecutor. Rather than a potential savior, Stagolee serves to stand in as one possible representation of the ways in which white supremacy can be enacted through an African American body.

The opening pages also introduce the familiar image of a chain gang, long a staple in period pieces about blacks in the South. However, rather than an *O Brother, Where Art Thou?*–esque group of men singing, the singers are instead a collection of various animals. Each animal is a visual allusion to African American folklore,[16] including Brer Rabbit, the most well-known anthropomorphic character in this genre of folktale. Stories of Brer Rabbit are categorized as trickster tales, which were "reflections of a chaotic world where wit and inventiveness were prized and victory was not assured" (Finkleman 26). One of the most interesting aspects of these tales is that they are not necessarily confined to the weak versus the strong or the good versus the bad. The moral universe and power dynamics of these folktales are considerably more complicated than what we traditionally ascribe to

---

14. Cecil Brown, in his book *Stagolee Shot Billy,* explains the origins of the song in a case in the late 1800s.

15. In some versions of "Stagolee," the character is represented as white. As with all folk orature, successive versions preserve or abandon elements of the original narrative based on context.

16. Also rendered are several less well-known trickster figures, including the Brer Gator and others.

fables, which Love preserves in his pastiche. Rather than a wily, intelligent hero, Brer Rabbit is here represented as something of a cad, having dozens of children by a number of different female rabbits. Furthermore, he is not particularly interested in Lee's plight. Suddenly, a gigantic monster storms through the forest to retrieve the fugitives, and he flees without any regard to the safety of the girl who just rescued him.

The juke joint is a space that is a pastiche of three distinct African American cultural institutions: folklore, music, and a secret gathering space placed at both social and geographic margins. Two juke joints appear within the two volumes of *Bayou*, one within the fantastic world inside of the bayou and one in the "real" world. Within the bayou, the juke joint is populated wholly by anthropomorphized animals who were at the center of an early fable, while in the real world, the juke joint has been washed away by a flood and exists only in flashbacks.

Lee and Bayou visit the juke joint in order to find information about Brer Rabbit. They are quickly identified from their wanted poster by a possum, who leaves to find the Golliwog for help capturing the two fugitives. The possum proposes that the Golliwog release a dam in order to flood the juke joint, proclaiming that the two of them will split the reward money. Instead of helping him, the Golliwog immediately eats the possum in a three-panel spread that only hints at the gruesomeness of the scene. By allowing the onomatopoeia "munch munch munch" to stand in for the actual consumption, these panels simultaneously minimize the scene by excluding it and enhance it by depicting only the sounds that one would hear if the reader was chewing on the possum herself. The final panel, a close-up of the Golliwog, heightens the effect of proximity because of the Golliwog's already cartoonish features. Not serving precisely as a mirror, the Golliwog is instead a sort of fun house mirror in which the reader uncomfortably gazes at the face twisted and bulged to conform to stereotype.

In the ensuing scene, as the Golliwog pursues Lee out of the bayou, the reader is set slightly over the shoulder of the Golliwog, mimicking its point of view, although this rapidly switches to a third-person point of view. The visual suggestion is that the reader is accompanying the Golliwog on this pursuit, although that suggestion is brief and is retracted when the reader is positioned as a helpless bystander to the events as they unfold. Instead of Bayou intervening, Billy Glass appears with a jar of red fireflies to frighten off the monster.

Fireflies are at the center of a number of American Indian myths, many of which locate them as the source of fire, as well as various African mythologies. In the East African folktale about Anansi and the firefly, the firefly uses his light to help the trickster Anansi find eggs at night, but Anansi doesn't share those he found, so the firefly leaves him in the dark and refuses to help him again. Meant as a cautionary tale against greed, here the fireflies are placed as a warding mechanism against the creature that seeks to collect the reward on Lee. Unlike the folktale, however, the Golliwog doesn't need the fireflies and is instead harmed by their light, finally slapping Billy Glass away in her continued pursuit of Lee. Finally chasing Lee up a tree, the Golliwog's weight breaks a branch, causing her to fall almost on top of our terrified heroine, who discovers that another branch has speared the monster straight through. Rather than a moral tale of the loneliness that accompanies greed, here, the Golliwog is instead seemingly undone by mere accident. However, during the pursuit, Lee cautions the monster against climbing out on the branch because it will not bear the Golliwog's weight, which suggests that greed causes bad decision making.

This simplified moral is rendered significantly more complex by the milieu and the actors, however. Above, I discussed the origins of the Golliwog, a character from a children's story that bore a striking resemblance to blackface minstrelsy representations circulating at the time. By mapping the head of this racist caricature onto the spider body of the trickster antihero Anansi, Love is juxtaposing two distinct folkloric traditions, one white (with American and British origins) and one black (specifically East African). The Golliwog was readily adopted as a character in popular culture in the United States, while Anansi was less well known as a folk figure beyond African Americans and American Indians. The Golliwog was originally envisioned as being both ugly and kind, although the stories often depicted him as "a reflection of racist beliefs about the African's dimwittedness, [and so] he remains bound to the Eurocentric discourse of being a 'bungling imitator'" (Varga and Zuk 655). By contrast, Anansi is a "schemer who unblushingly breaks taboos for the sake of a quick meal, a cunning scoundrel, audacious, selfish, lustful, unthankful, and immoral" (van Duin 34). Anansi is astute where the Golliwog is naïve, self-seeking where the Golliwog is generous. Grafting the head of the Golliwog onto a body like that of Anansi is not simply a juxtaposition of opposites. Instead, it is a joining of two opposed characters from two distinct folk traditions, both of which harbor unattractive traits. Furthermore, in later scenes, the Golliwog also trails a tail akin to that of crayfish—much like the Orishas in African folktales, while the basic character is much the same, the form alters to fit in with the environment.[17] In the case of the Golliwog, as a stand in for

---

17. Ian MacDonald, personal communication.

white paternalism, the character represents a childish inability to compre-
hend her surroundings, while Anansi is actually a site of resistance to dominant culture. Anansi would seem to be a positive folk hero within a space
of oppression as it existed in 1930s Mississippi, but because Love chose a
character widely understood to have traits that were negative for the community as a whole, he is recreating the myth of the trickster within a space
that holds few redemptive possibilities for its African American characters.
That "All tricksters are jesters and buffoons" (39) merges with the caricature of the Golliwog to craft a monster that is threatening precisely because
it embodies contradictory racist stereotypes about African Americans. That
the Golliwog eats other characters is no accident. Eating the possum for
his greed in order to satisfy the creature's own greed plays off of the idea
of the Uncle Tom, and the Golliwog's ultimate failure to capture Lee during either of their encounters suggests that Lee is not so much escaping a
mere physical threat but is also escaping integration into a social order that
demands people adhere to the prevailing stereotypes.

BILLY GLASS AND THE BUTTERFLY WINGS

Billy Glass's intervention on behalf of Lee in her flight from the Golliwog
recalls for her the beginning of this narrative. As Bayou races over to Lee
to help her, she begins coughing, and the facing page picks up the same
magenta color scheme, depicting only a face—momentarily very similar to
Lee's own—bruised and bloody but nonetheless angrily remarking, "Thu-
that the best you peckerwoods can do? Why don't you loose me, d'en we
see" (2.66). Only on the following page does it become clear that this face
belongs to Billy Glass and depicts the moments leading up to his death. As
with elsewhere in the comic, Love chooses to use asterisks to replace the
n-word as the reader views a four-panel spread simply showing a white
fist punching Billy Glass's face again and again. Even during this assault,
Billy tells them "Y'all ain't nuthin but a bunch o' pink fat hogs! No wonder Miss Maylene was givin' me the eye!" This moment of resistance stems
from either an inability to see the danger that he is in or, more likely, an
acknowledgment that they will kill him whatever he does.

Billy's decision to at least verbally resist the impulse to placate his
attackers, instead inciting them, is perhaps the only act of power and control available to him. The men do indeed drag him to a tree, hang him,
and mutilate his corpse (they threatened to "make [him] a woman" in the
previous scene, and while this is not depicted directly, it is suggested in
the blood pouring from the ankles of his trousers). However, as they fit

the noose around his neck, a grandmotherly woman with butterfly wings appears to tell him, "Hush child . . . Be Brave. Don't cry . . . They will not prevail" (2.70), giving him the strength to stutter, "T-tuh hell . . . tuh hell wit' y'all cra—" (2.70). However, the lingering question remains: What does it mean that "they shall not prevail" when Billy Glass is indeed lynched and the reader has already seen his remains? While this is meant to be an inspiring moment of hope and faith in the eventual triumph of good over evil, it is not without its dark irony, given that she is reassuring him at the very moment of his pointless death at the hands of men who are never prosecuted for their crime.

During this scene, the reader is largely positioned in the third person, especially starkly at the point when the white man begins to pull the rope through the flexure of the tree. The reader views this scene as if from across a field, both Billy's and the man's face without distinguishing features. This follows, however, the clearly rendered panels in which the grandmother approaches. The arrangement suggests that Love wants the reader to feel their distance from Billy's experience, and indeed, the positioning of the characters is both familiar and strange—familiar because most American readers would be familiar with the concept of lynching but estranged because few of us have been asked to imagine how such a thing would take place. Implicit in the grandmother's phrasing, too, is a sense of safety for the reader—"*They* will not prevail" (2.70, emphasis mine), effectively distancing the reader from the actions of the lynch mob as well. This is, however, undercut on the following page, which shows a sketchily rendered photograph mimicking the postcards that were once sold of lynchings (see fig. 4.3).

Lynching photography was popular during the lynching era, approximately 1882–1968, and was remarkable for several reasons. First, lynching and other forms of vigilantism were illegal, but because of the fear of black power and the marginalization of black citizens, the black community was vulnerable not only to violence but also to having the violence done against their bodies documented in perverse commemorative postcards. Unlike many other atrocities that occurred around the world during the same period, wherein perpetrators of violence frequently tried to hide their violence,[18] lynch mobs gathered around the mutilated corpse of an African American (usually a man) in order to pose for the camera. There is something particularly eerie about both the prospect of posing for such a photograph and about the postcard itself. In the case of the former, it suggests not only pride in something perceived as an "accomplishment"

---

18. Perhaps most notably, Nazis did not issue commemorative postcards of gassed Jews, and other atrocities during the period—when they were documented at all—were generally presented in a negative light.

FIGURE 4.3. Love's rendering of a lynching postcard. Love, Jeremy, and Patrick Morgan. *Bayou*. Vol. 2. New York: DC/Zuda, 2009.

but also an assumption of action with relative impunity. In the case of the latter, the photographs becoming postcards, the relative impunity is clear in that a postcard is a public sort of photography and is sent through a governmental organization. Direct, clear evidence of a crime is emblazoned across the front of the postcard of a lynching, yet most postcards only recognize the supposed "crime" of the person being lynched. Furthermore, the postcard—even during this period—was not equivalent to a letter. It was not painstakingly crafted with a clear recipient in mind. The postcard has always been (relatively speaking) an item of kitsch representing a truncated and partial correspondence.

In the postcard, the image is meant to stand for itself. There is only a narrow strip on which to write on the reverse side, so it communicates in its very structure the primacy of the image and the subsidiary nature of the text. Photographs, and the postcards that bear them, are artifacts of memory. They visually memorialize a particular instant in time and disseminate that image beyond those present, reaching beyond the individual point of view to offer a person's perspective to a broader audience. However, lynching photography seeks to disseminate a warning as well—a warning to blacks to "stay in their place"—as well as an encoding of socially acceptable (if technically illegal) behavior. In *Without Sanctuary: Lynching Photography in America*, the exhibit and book focused on the photograph as what James Allen called "a document of proof, an unearthing of crimes, of collective mass murder, of mass memory graves excavated from the American conscience" (*Without Sanctuary* n. pag.). The lynching photograph represents precisely the type of memory that has been marginalized and forgotten as images of Southern grandeur have been foregrounded and the Rebel flag has been reimagined as somehow not about slavery. The anxieties represented by the popularity of lynching—and its documentation—have been equaled only in the anxieties produced by those seeking to remind the greater population that those horrors were not simply "an awful part of the past" but rather emblematic of attitudes about the right to control black bodies that extends into today.[19]

Facing the page of the lynching photograph is an image no one saw: that of Billy Glass's body, weighted down by a stone and a chain, descending into the depths of the bayou. Mapped over the gutter between the two images is a rendering of a press clipping merely proclaiming that a lynching had occurred and that the victim had assaulted a woman. Placing this press release in the gutter textually reintegrates the lack of concern for black bodies within a series of images meant to reintegrate them at the center of our perspectives. The tension between word and image and between the images and the series of panels, wherein the text is undercut by what has been depicted in the narrative, and the series of images disrupts the "celebratory" form of the postcard. In addition, it serves as a reminder of the way in which violence that takes place "between panels"—or at the margins of society—is often ignored or minimized within media representations. That the news item occurs in the gutter is meant to signify not what we imaginatively project into that space but the ways in which dominant narratives *shape* our imagination.

The grandmother attempts to get Billy's spirit to leave his body as it molders in the bottom of the bayou, but Billy is reluctant because, as he says, "It's my body!"—a statement that sadly draws attention to his lack of control over being ejected from himself. While it is his body, his distance from it is stark in that the body is subject to the prevailing rules of the time. The grandmother cautions him, "Honey, that body is just a vessel. If you cling to it, bad things will happen" (2.74), a problematic statement to

---

19. Best discussed in Ta Nehisi Coates's book *Between the World and Me*.

be sure in an age where black people's bodies were subject to the whims of the whites surrounding them rather than to their own souls. However, the transition panel is telling in that it depicts the beginnings of a Golliwog, the bluish blackface and amplified, florid red lips turned into a frown. Here, the suggestion is that overinvestment in the body is in itself a part of what led to this bodily insecurity. Not on the part of those who are victimized, however—the idea that the Golliwog forms in part through white power parting the body and soul indicates that it is not only African American souls at hazard. Overinvestment in vengeance, rather than justice, turns a soul into the monster they were made out to be. However, this is layered with a certain irony, as Billy Glass remarks that his mother will be upset if he is not properly interred. Rather than focusing on the fact of his death, he worries about his mother's distress over the ceremonial rites. It is not that his mother *would* be more upset about the lack of an appropriate funeral than the death of her son. Instead, it is an indication that the body is meant to be sacred, which reflects back on the panel of the possibility of becoming a Golliwog to illustrate how racist caricature is a profane, violent act upon the body.

EMERGING

Throughout the first and much of the second volume, the relationship between the "real" world and the world beneath the bayou is unclear. We understand that, in stepping into and swimming through the bayou, Lee has entered an alternate universe where not all (but some) of the normal rules apply. Both the "real" world and the world beneath the bayou are controlled by a violent white patriarchal structure, both have consequences for rebellion on the part of people of color, and both take place in a version of Charon. The first volume suggests that the world on the other side of the bayou is an afterlife of sorts for the residents of Charon, but the second volume elaborates on how the characters are altered in their transition into this world.

When they were still alive (and human), Bayou and Rabbit played at a juke joint on the bayou, the same that washed away with Lee's mother inside. At the outset, the scenes switch between the warm and lively interior of the run-down club and the pounding rain in exterior shots. This cycles between an intimate view of a social institution usually hidden from the eyes of the assumed white reader to establishing panels that suggest trouble brewing. While the inside of the club is filled with music as Tar Baby, Lee's mother's stage name, sings, outside Stagolee is confronted by a jealous husband, and Stagolee baits him into a fight in the pouring rain and surreptitiously pulls a knife. After killing both the woman and her husband, Stagolee then threatens Rabbit and Tar Baby. Bayou is out-side beneath a tree and sees the juke joint being swept away, leaping in to save Rabbit, at which point the flashback abruptly ends, shifting back to the world within the bayou where Rabbit is looking in shock at the "Wanted" poster advertising for the capture of Lee and Bayou.

This background indicates that the world through the bayou is not the commonly understood version of an afterlife in which each soul reaches its just rewards but is instead merely another iteration of the power struc-tures that exist in the real world. In the flashback, Lee is not the primary focalizor, and instead of using characters' points of view to draw the reader into the experience, we are rapidly shifted between third-person points of view, gazing at a variety of different scenes from outside a character's per-spective. This limits our sense of identification with the characters, instead inviting us to see what transpires in these pages as a sort of fable—replete with a sea monster—of competing sources of danger. Stagolee represents a danger inherent in systems of systemic oppression, existing as a violent sort of "Uncle Tom." Typifying the stereotype of ruthless, vicious black men, Stagolee exists primarily to keep other African Americans in line with the desires of the "Bossman." He is balanced in this scene by another type of violence, however: that of the natural world. Because it has no sentience or desires of its own, it cannot be combatted and instead threatens both blacks and whites. However, Love is careful to show how the vulnerability charac-teristic of marginalized positions leaves the African American characters at greater risk than those who have power.

Crossing back into the land of the bayou, Stagolee is depicted pulling snakes out of the water whose bodies combine to form an ax, while he him-self dissolves into a cloud of insects. Overlaying these scenes are two dis-tinct fonts, the "cleaner" of the two representing, apparently, the Bossman's directions to Stagolee. The Bossman remarks, "You please me and perplex me. Working so diligently against your own people. . . . You are the sav-age id. The primal instinct of an inferior race" (2.127). This characteriza-tion employs the Freudian model of consciousness in which the id is the instinctual drive, the superego is the moral function, and the ego is the lim-inal space between those two that attempts to mediate between the desires of the id and the demands of the superego. This model was frequently employed in racist caricature to argue that African Americans represented the id of the human race, while whites were the superego that must con-trol the destructive desires of the id.[20] The Bossman's assertion reframes

20. William McDougall and others were instrumental in establishing "scientific" "evidence" for African American interiority using psychology.

the mentality of blacks as entirely separate, of which Stagolee represents the impulsive drive, an assertion that makes little sense given that the Bossman himself has set the man to his task. To whit, Stagolee objects to this characterization, asserting, "No. I just don't give a shive. Rabbit. His stories are mine" (2.128), dismissing the pop psychology argument that he exists as merely a concept made manifest. Furthermore, it is not a drive to work against his own people that prompts him but rather a desire for the stories of Rabbit, which are the embodied folklore of African Americans. Instead of the hatred toward his own race as ascribed to him by the Bossman, it is instead a desire for the narratives that create a shared folk culture. To what purpose he desires these narratives remains unclear at the end of the second volume.

Notably, while the stories that Stagolee desires are attributed to Brer Rabbit—they are contained by him, indicating a sort of ownership—these stories also represent a cultural memory that is situational and perspective oriented. African American folktales were altered significantly according to context, and characters may play different and contradictory roles from those originally intended at different times and in different places. Stagolee's desire for the stories is in itself a deep misunderstanding of what stories—and memories—are. Rather than possessions, they are negotiations between the past and the present, contextually informed and embedded in both an individual's ideas, desires, and circumstances and the cultural setting at large. Stagolee's desire for the stories is paired with his conversation with a disembodied voice—the voice of the Bossman—which in its lack of embodiment is emblematic of the phantasmal circulation of white power and provides a counterpoint to the embodied nature of the story.

FORGETTING

At an encampment with Bayou, rabbit, and the raccoon, Lee remarks, "I think I'm forgettin' Daddy and Lily's faces. I wonder if they forgettin' my face too . . ." (2.133). Lee's vulnerability in this moment lies in her fear of the deterioration of both her own memory and the memories of those she loves. Memory is, as mentioned above, less like an archive than a practice of narration, and while the ostensible purpose of Lee's quest has remained finding Lily and saving her father, the journey has taken her much further afield. Rather than simply a detective narrative, her journey has been a trip through the cultural consciousness of African Americans, a journey that is fraught with the same types of dangers one would expect in the "real" world, even though many of the threats wear a folkloric face. In forgetting the faces of those closest to her, she is also remembering a heritage of oppression and brutality that she has witnessed only in truncated forms.

In the final pages of the second volume, she encounters two villains: Stagolee, who has been tracking her for the duration of her journey, and Uncle Remus, the narrator of the African American folktales collected by Joel Chandler Harris, a white folklorist, in the late 1800s and popularized in Walt Disney's *Song of the South* in 1946. The Uncle Remus character was a kindly former slave who tells children stories of life on the plantation, and contemporary objections to this character center around the benign way in which slavery was portrayed in many of the stories.[21] Lee sees Uncle Remus after being drugged into a dream state by Rabbit, and Remus shows her that she can be with her father forever and she can have "pretty" hair if only she will abandon her search for Lily. Lee, after consideration, rejects the offer both because of Lily and because she is scared that more blacks could be hurt, prompting Uncle Remus to transform into a giant rooster who attempts to kill Lee (murdering a kindly protector spirit named Mother Sister in the process).

This scene recalls the opening pages of the first volume, in which the nostalgic and violent images of the past are depicted as both distinct and imbricated. While Mother Sister exists as a sort of angel for Lee and other black children (particularly those who have died as a result of racism), she cannot completely "save" them with her variety of wisdom. Unlike the panels elaborating the contrasts embodied by Charon, Mississippi, violence is always embedded within even the most cherished, sentimentalized images of the past.

All of these characters and situations are repetitions of African American experience, but with difference. From the seemingly benign incarceration of folktales within white narratives (Lee releases them) to the Jim Crows that kill through a thousand tiny pecks to the Golliwog, a racist caricature that seeks to physically drag Lee down into the depths, it is less a museum of racism in the United States than a retelling, in which generations' worth of experiences of violence and trauma are cast through the lens of memory as it evolves for the demands of the present. Love does not want the reader to *recall* what happened to the enslaved, the lynched, the marginalized. He wants us to understand that these memories have a clear and obvious place in the present.

Jeremy Love has yet to complete the third and final volume of this series, so I cannot say how this arc is resolved. As of yet, however, the work

---

21. Harris asserted that these stories were directly from slaves and that he did not alter them. He envisioned his work as a supplement to Harriet Beecher Stowe's *Uncle Tom's Cabin.*

melds Lee's own memories of violence along with traumatic flashbacks of events that are her heritage rather than her own memory. If the reconstructivist model of memory means that memories are less an archive than a creative project crafting from raw materials how we should deal with present demands, Lee's journey represents a powerful contribution to intergenerational memory or trauma because these reconstructions do not incapacitate our heroine. The eruption of the past into the present—whether real or reconstructed through transmission in her memory—galvanizes Lee. These are *not* ordered memories—they are disruptive and terrifying. But Lee hasn't set out to order them into an easily palatable narrative for the reader—she is instead using them to manage what is still happening.

Furthermore, in a period of increased awareness of the persistence of racism emblematized in the Black Lives Matter movement, Lee's story is all the more essential for its integration of how circumstances that do not square with a person's sense of self as it is established by memory can disrupt their narratives of history. In a material sense, intergenerational memory or trauma stands as a stark contrast to the institutionalized remembrance of the museum. The museum is a structure of enforced memory—these artifacts represent what *should* be remembered, and *how* our memories should be shaped around them. Intergenerational trauma, on the other hand, represents a disavowed history—what is *not* memorialized and *why* we don't memorialize it. It represents a past that is constantly erupting into the present through our culture—but a past that can be utilized to combat racism in the present. As Müller-Funk says, "Every culture is based on acts of common remembrance and forgetting. However, this forgetting does not cause an irreversible deletion from memory but produces a latent memory, that can in principle be reactivated" (215). The reactivation of memory is an ethical project in *Bayou,* in which the reader is asked to consider the cultural memories depicted in its pages as presences, not necessarily the "hauntings" or "possessions" sometimes metaphorically referenced in trauma theory but memories as narratives attached to material realities. The next chapter takes up this issue of the material consequences of attempts to understand in relation to a different historical atrocity, the genocide of the Tasmanian Aborigines. Continuing the line of questioning relating to point of view in a more temporally distant atrocity than those explored in the previous chapters, it is important to understand as a further tension in the genre in its meditation on geographical and cultural distance.

CHAPTER 5

TELLING THE WOUND

Framing and Restricted Narration in
Hellblazer

THIS CHAPTER will consider the most geographically, temporally, and affectively distant atrocity of the book, and because of this, it is the most difficult to frame. The genocide of the Tasmanian Aborigines is demanding to represent, discuss, or describe from whatever vantage point one chooses to approach it. If I edge toward its representation with postcolonial studies, one might ask where the "post-" is: Tasmania remains colonized, and the genocide was nearly "successful." If I approach it from the perspective of genocide studies, the first question is invariably if genocide as such existed prior to Lemkin's coinage, and if it did, how then do we assess intent when historical documents are sparse? Furthermore, how is the concept of cultural memory complicated by the fact that pre-Holocaust genocides are often minimized or forgotten? Rothberg asserts that "debates about collective memory and group identity are primarily struggles over injustices of recognition, over whose history and culture will be recognized" (20), emphasizing that remembering can itself be an ethical commitment. This ethical commitment had more obvious connections in each of the previous chapters, wherein the traumatic history discussed was either one intimately related to American history and culture or, in the case of *Deogratias*, was a recent American foreign policy failure present in the cultural consciousness. This chapter departs considerably from this framework, instead examining a work that makes no claims to immediate relevance to an American audience.

Without immediately legible ethical claims on an aspect of the assumed reader's identity, what is the core project of justice in such a work? In part, of course, it is simply the reintegration of a lost history and a lost people. However, the project is more complicated than a mere historical account because "realigning the methodological lens to bring into view the centrality of 'marginal,' transnational phenomena also allows insight into the importance of the categories of the 'human' and the biopolitical for an understanding of extreme violence and genocide," as Rothberg argues (47). A forgotten genocide is not merely a blip in the historical record but rather, as much of this book illustrates, a semiconscious process of cultural forgetting that rejects claims about the link between memory and justice. The historio-metagraphics I have examined thus far have used point of view and representation in order to comment on the erasure of these memories and perspectives, and the culminating chapter adds to this by highlighting how geographical and temporal distance may still provide an important ethical foundation for memory.

Indeed, this chapter poses a question that has haunted the edges of previous chapters: how distant does an atrocity have to be to cease to matter? The "distance" in this question is manifold: I mean to encompass the perceived (and/or lived) gulf between the sexes, between racial categorizations, between contemporary concerns and the historical processes that created them, between nationalities, and between other categories of identity that—at a surface level—seem to forestall or derail attempts to connect. By centralizing the marginal, as Rothberg frames it, one can better understand both the possibilities and limitations in narrating memory and history in a fictional context in graphic narratives. A major concern in this chapter, as in previous chapters, remains the question of what stories get told, but here, a further question is what stories get heard and how they are heard. What is it to identify with, or to empathize with, such a distant historical experience? Such an atrocity? Is it ethical to do so? Does identification or empathy miss the point of the history?

CONTESTED SPACE: THE ANNIHILATION OF THE TASMANIAN ABORIGINES

Mike Carey and Marcelo Frusin attempt to create a fictional account of the genocide of the Tasmanian Aborigines that will both represent the atrocities that occurred and gesture toward the problems such an undertaking generates. In addition to a fictionalized Tasmanian Aboriginal woman (*Palawa* is an alternate term for the people), Carey and Frusin construct a world in which the perpetrators are locked in a dream of their own aggression. They also utilize a third-person omniscient narrator who appears at only two points in the text and who is of indeterminate relationship to the characters in the story. These multiple levels of mediation and commentary are at the core of Carey and Frusin's ultimate suggestion that the reader cannot recognize the story at the heart of this comic. The historical context of the genocide of the Tasmanian Aborigines in particular lends itself to this metacommentary.

The genocide of the Tasmanian Aborigines was conducted on multiple fronts in a conflict that the British refer to as the "Black War," lasting over ten years from 1825–36 (the dates are approximate and vary according to the source; these dates are noted in H. Ling Roth's *The Aborigines of Tasmania*, first published in 1890, fourteen years after the death of the last surviving full-blooded Tasmanian Aborigine). Other scholars locate the origins of the Black War at the colonists' arrival in 1803, citing early conflicts between settlers and the indigenous population, but these clashes escalated in intensity in the 1820s, during which the colonial state declared martial law and removed the indigenous populations to outlying islands, arguably after series of attacks on colonists. There has been significant contention over the history of this "war," including the disease introduced by colonists that killed the indigenous population and whether this constituted germ warfare or was merely an unfortunate side effect of colonization. The Black War was not remarkable in the cruelties inflicted by either side, and there has been significant contention about whether or not the destruction of the Tasmanian Aborigines can properly be termed *genocide* because, as A. Dirk Moses argues, "to call something 'genocide' rather than 'extermination' was somehow seen as far more serious to modern Australians; the questions of intent and responsibility were much closer to home" (241). Roth notes that George Augustus Robinson "succeeded in bringing in, by persuasion alone [. . .] two hundred and three persons" (3) for removal to various camps on the surrounding islands, and eventually to the grotesquely named "Civili-sation Point" on Flinders Island, where most of the remaining population died.

In 1847 the last remaining Aborigines were removed to Oyster Cove, where the population dwindled to several dozen (Roth 6). Moses notes that this removal plays a role in the debate about whether or not the annihila-tion of the Tasmanian Aborigines did in fact constitute genocide. He asserts that "On the basis of a very limited knowledge of Tasmanian history, and interpreting the Black Line and the removal to Flinders Island as an exam-ple of state-led and planned desire to destroy a whole people, this scholar took the view that Tasmania constituted a clear case of genocide" (241). Moses suggests that the case of Tasmania came to be seen as genocide for two reasons:

> First, there seems to be some slippage between two distinct ideas, extinc-tion and genocide; everyone "knew" that Tasmania was a clear case of colonial *extinction*; therefore it seemed to follow that it must be a case of *genocide*. Second, as Henry Reynolds points out, the central role played by the government in controlling relations with the Aboriginal people in Tas-mania (in contrast to mainland Australia, where settlement and its destruc-tive consequences frequently ran far beyond government boundaries of control) fitted well with, and seemed to exemplify, the emphasis on the role of the state in much genocide theory and scholarship at the time. (241)

These distinctions are important in the discussion of the historiographic metafictional representation of genocide in the graphic narrative form because they underscore the slippage between what *happened* and what *terms* may be used for it. The term for an event is a representation that may or may not encapsulate the reality of the event. In Mike Carey and Marcelo Frusin's "The Pit," the final installment of the "Third Worlds" story arc of *Hellblazer* collected in *Black Flowers,* terminology is replaced with the repre-sentation of an Aboriginal woman's ghost, a mimicry of a shadow, which gestures at how these debates surrounding how to term an extinction event fail to reflect the embodied experience of the victims.

The mitigating factors outlined above are cited to indicate that the events in Tasmania remain a contested historical and intellectual space. Moses's suggestion is countered by other scholars, including Tony Barta, who in his landmark "Sorry, and Not Sorry, in Australia" argues that, in the UN definition, the word *intent* becomes particularly disruptive in the case of Australian Aborigines. However, Barta argues that child-removal policies,[1] along with the "breeding the colour out" doctrine of the time,[2] when set alongside the actual deaths, clearly denote intent. This examination of the boundaries of terminology reflects the way borders played a central role in this history and is replicated in "The Pit." However, rather than a discussion of terminology or explicit demarcation of borders, Carey and Frusin's meditation on boundaries takes place along three fronts. The first is formal; Frusin regularly depicts the characters crossing the boundary of the gutter. The second concerns content; Carey is careful to draw attention to how Constantine and the reader are denied entry into the Tasmanian Aboriginal spirit realm. Furthermore, he emphasizes the limits of what is (and what can be) told. Third, both Carey and Frusin subtly draw attention to their own distance from the story they depict. Carey is a British comics writer and Frusin is an Argentinean artist. Carey's British identity connects with that of Constantine, but both Carey and Frusin are careful within the narrative not to overplay their hand in regard to the representation of Aboriginal experience.

The arbitration of whether or not the virtual extinction of the Tasmanian Aborigines constituted genocide serves as a political commentary on how histories are policed in the contemporary age during reflections on atrocity. Geographical borders and the physical removal of the Tasmanian Aborigines are significant historical intertexts in "The Pit," which functions as a metacommentary on the form. In addition to terminological and physical boundaries, there are nonphysical borders at stake as well. The space of "The Dreaming" was, for the Aborigines, an "expression [drawn from] *Altjiringa,* meaning 'to see the eternal,' for Aborigines believe that they are in touch with fundamental truths while asleep" (McIntosh 38). "The

---

1. Barta notes in his conclusion that he met Margaret Tucker, an Australian Aborigine. He asserts that "Margaret was taken away so that she, and we, could forget there ever were Aborigines in Australia. 'I feel,' she wrote, 'that soon our ancestors won't even be a memory'" (11). While Barta's article predominantly concerns the Australian Aborigines, in this regard his reflections are particularly important, given that no Tasmanian Aborigines survive to articulate the atrocities they suffered.

2. Interestingly enough, this has in the current century resulted in hostile debates about who is and isn't an Aboriginal descendant. While Tasmania is (perhaps erroneously) cited as the only "successful" genocide in history, descendants of Tasmanian Aboriginals persist to this day and are often fair skinned and light eyed. In a strange twist, those who were darker skinned, who may or may not have been descendants (though not "full-blooded") were subject to systematic discrimination that denied their possible heritage. *The Guardian's* Richard Flanagan wrote in 2002 that "A people who suffered so completely from a racist ideology, and whose very existence was denied for over a century, now have to face once more their recurrent, mocking fate: the derision of a world that, in the end, still thinks they don't exist."

Dreaming" is a construction that relates to the mythic, an "expression of symbolic thought" (41), which explains problems within both the physical and spiritual world. As it is a realm composed of symbolic significance, the introduction of "empty" symbols like the pit becomes especially problematic in relation to dream space.

The fictionalization of victim testimony in literatures of genocide raises important questions about a victim's "story." Holocaust scholars have variously argued against excessive sentimentalization[3] and that turning suffering into an aesthetic work is disgraceful,[4] but nonetheless, demand for accounts by survivors of genocide persists. This demand has, in America, largely been limited to accounts of the Holocaust, while accounts of other genocides, including those that occurred on American soil, are relegated to the place of historical embarrassment similar to that described by Australians in their attitudes toward the atrocities committed against the Aborigines. Written survivor testimonies are, as argued by Langer, subject to literary conventions that mediate the experiences described; and survivors craft their stories, selecting and omitting various details according to time, audience, and other concerns. However, what happens when a testimony is fictional because there were no survivors, and therefore, a victim's voice must be crafted out of historical accounts? Is a genocide that left no survivors "tellable"?

VIOLATED MARGINS

"The Pit" is the final issue in a *Hellblazer* three-part story arc called "Third Worlds," collected in an edition entitled *Black Flowers*. John Constantine, the main character, is the subject of the *Hellblazer* series, which has run since 1993 and boasts over 250 individual issues. "The Pit" was written by Carey, who was responsible for the second-longest run of the series, including six collected editions, and illustrated by Frusin. The character John Constantine has developed over time from a slick, overconfident magician into a man all too aware of his own failings. The flippant attitude that was his trademark in the early years of the series remains, but after the deaths of dozens of friends partly due to his own mistakes, he has balanced this cheek with a healthy dose of guilt, often manifested in

---

3. Bernstein, Michael Andre. "The Schindler's List Effect." *American Scholar*, 63.3 (Summer 1994): 429–32.

4. Langer, Lawrence. *The Holocaust and the Literary Imagination*. New Haven: Yale UP, 1977.

the comic as a collection of ghosts that cling to him as he tries to solve supernatural problems in his native London. Without delving too far into the cosmology of the *Hellblazer* universe, a brief history of the character is necessary.

The character John Constantine was created by Alan Moore, Rick Veitch, Steve Bissette, and John Totleben and first appeared in *Swamp Thing* in 1985. Constantine was quickly recognized as a popular character, which resulted in the publication of the *Hellblazer* series, which ran from 1988 to 2013. He is reputed to be a very potent magician, but the series rarely depicts Constantine actually working spells. In spite of the general absence of magic, per se, Constantine frequently visits landscapes that, because of mystical forces, are rendered fantastic. Constantine generally remains in the U.K. The "Third Worlds" story arc departs from traditional *Hellblazer* fare as it follows Constantine travelling through Juliema, a fictional location in South America, to Iran, a location reputed to be the physical space nearest to the Garden of Eden. When he finally goes to Tasmania, where "The Pit" takes place, Constantine is in search of information about the Shadow Dog, a being said to hearken the coming of the apocalypse, which has apparently been moving through the veils between worlds. Up to this point in the larger story arc, he has not been able to gather much information about this creature, but during his attempts, several of his magician friends have been destroyed.

"The Pit" opens with a panel depicting several British soldiers standing atop a trench, text box overlays explaining, "Every night they dig the pit. They dig it for the first time. Its sides almost vertical. Stakes just below the edge, pointing down, to stop anyone from climbing out" (121). This first panel (see fig. 5.1) already gestures toward what is ventured in the plot: the conflation of temporalities and the crucial dimension of point of view.

In terms of temporality, while this is a fictionalized account of a past event, it is recounted by a nameless third-person narrator in the present progressive tense, indicating a continuous action. The narrator aligns himself neither with the soldiers nor the Aborigines, referring to both as "they," while the reader views the ditch from inside, looking upward toward the men standing at the top edge, already ensconced within the potential victims' perspective. The second and third panels show the Tasmanian Aborigines being forced down into the pit from holding pens, the narration shifting in focus between panels. The second panel shows the Aborigines from the perspective of the British soldiers, the point of view including their shadows as they look down into the holding pens, the external focalizor remarking that "they say to the prisoners 'move quickly,

FIGURE 5.1. Point of view and the pit. Carey, Mike, Marcelo Frusin, Tim Bradstreet, Lee Loughridge, and Clem Robbins. "The Pit." *Hellblazer—Black Flowers*. Issue 186. New York: DC Comics, 2005.

jena, jena. We're taking you to a new place'" (121), while the third panel depicts the Aborigines being forced down into the pit. The narrator tells us, "They don't want to go down that steep slope. But there's a wall of men with guns" (121). The shifting point of view in the first three panels coupled with the externally focalized narration destabilizes the reader's identification with characters at the outset. Rather than offering an individual's perspective of the massacre that is represented, the images are framed by a textual recounting. The pictorial element serves to illustrate the textual but simultaneously, through perspective, offers brief windows into a variety of points of view.

The final two panels on the page emphasize this instability as the reader is shown the pit from the point of view of an Aborigine during the massacre, coupled with an ambivalent narrative that asserts, "Every night, for two hundred years. Wearing and wearing at the soul, grain by grain, like sea against the cliffs. Do cliffs never tire? Do cliffs never beg the sea to take them whole?" (121). The melodramatic tone of the questions satirizes the circumstance, in which the large group is slaughtered, ostensibly "taken whole." The rhetorical questions posed do not directly map onto the Aborigines but rather onto the soldiers, who are acting within the first panel and recall cliché constructions of extreme experience, but rather than explicitly linking that with the bloodied corpses of Aborigines depicted in the final panels, the narrator is instead remarking on how "wearying" it is for the soldiers to repeatedly enact the massacre. The first and second panels both refer to the actions of the soldiers, while the third refers primarily to the resistance of the Aborigines and the activity of the soldiers. In using a slightly indeterminate pronoun, the narrator is mocking the effacement of the gulf between the experiences of the perpetrators and the experiences of the victims. The ambivalence of the metaphorical references in the questions stubbornly resists the reader's desire to take an ethical stance in relation to the obvious massacre that is depicted, as the victims' narratives are entirely erased in this, and the narrator instead expresses a parody of sympathy for the perpetrators. At the outset, Carey and Frusin work against a stable readerly position. While the images appear to merely depict what is related in the textual, instead the textual operates to complicate the focus of empathy. The reader is offered the point of view of both the soldiers and of the Aborigines, and the violence experienced by the Aborigines naturally functions to promote sympathy and horror in the reader. However, the referent in the series of metaphorical questions seems to be both groups, implying that perpetrating violence wears on the soul in a similar way as experiencing violence as a victim.

Positing this equivalency at the outset complicates the ethical position of the reader because the page likely communicates the only information that the reader has about the genocide of the Tasmanian Aborigines, and this information is already obscured by the sympathetic referents, as well as the temporal location. The digging of the pit and the experience of the massacre take place "every night," but it is not a new pit that is dug, or a new group that is slain: the same pit is dug "for the first time" every night. Notably, the narratorial voice that opened the comic disappears immediately after the first page. The textual component of the rest of the comic takes place either in dialogue bubbles or in text box narration that is directly attributable to a character presented in the comic, but the initial narratorial voice is clearly distinct from the voices of the characters. First, it indicates proximity through its knowledge of both the actions of the perpetrators and the feelings of the victims, which would suggest an omniscient narrator not present elsewhere in "Third Worlds." In fact, the only time that this disembodied voice returns is on the penultimate page, which will be explored later.

The scene of the pit and the massacre are abruptly shifted on the following page to a depiction of Constantine and Angie Spatchcock, Constantine's love interest at this point in the series. They converse over the remains of a fort, specified as "Fort Adams, Tasmania. Now," although the first page had no such time stamp. In response to Angie's question about why they have come to Tasmania, Constantine tells her, "This was a prison camp, Angie. Then after that it was a sort of concentration camp. In 1833, then they decided to wipe out the Aboriginals to make more room for the sheep" (122). Angie's reaction to this circumscribed history is predictable: "Same question, slightly more pissed off emphasis" (122). Angie embodies the normal reaction to long-ago atrocities, a mixture of annoyance and disdain at the intrusion of history into contemporary experience. In particular, this attitude is common among whites in both America and England in regards to slavery, the genocide of the American Indians, and other iterations of brutal colonial conquest from which they are the beneficiaries, although this status is often invisible to them.[5]

Constantine tells Angie that he must go on a dream walk in order to discuss the Shadow Dog with the spirits of the Tasmanian Aborigines. Since there is no "full blooded" community remaining on earth, Constantine assumes that he needs to go into their *Altjeringa* in order to speak with

5. Interestingly, this strange tension between guilt and anger exhibited by those who seek to exonerate themselves from blame for anything that occurred "long ago" is absent from the American mindset when it regards the Holocaust.

the "authentic" Aborigines. The choice to seek them out in their own land rather than call them to him bears an eerie, if subtle, resemblance to the settlement of the island, and he chooses, furthermore, to use the Aborigine's rites of consuming hallucinogens in order to depart on the dream walk, leaving Angie to guard his body.

As Angie waits by the fire with Constantine's body for his spirit to return from the dream walk, the flames erupt into human shapes, and the final panel on the page shows three Palawa, two men and one woman. The woman's hair breaks the line of the frame, but unlike the transition to the dream walk, which will be explored later, in this case, the frame is a clear straight line denoting the "real" world. The woman's violation of the frame, unlike the other example, takes place in a non–dream world perspective. Angie's point of view is not placed within an environment induced by hallucinogens, but her perspective is nonetheless subject to the same visual disorientation as Constantine's. While the first three panels of the scene slowly approach Angie from behind, the final panel depicts the Aboriginal woman and men from Angie's perspective. By closing in on Angie's point of view, these panels give the sensation of an approach from behind, of walking up to the fire.

The following page shifts immediately to the Aboriginal woman's perspective as Angie tells her, "Okay. *Your* call" (128). These shifts serve to disorient the reader. Generally, in *Hellblazer* comics, the reader is invited to sympathize with Constantine, the main character, who appears in most scenes throughout the comics series. It is a rare moment in which the narrative is not focalized through his consciousness, by depicting his actions in images and often by having accompanying text boxes that relate some of his internal monologue. However, he is mostly absent in this scene (although we do briefly see his body next to the fire), and the point of view shifts between Angie's perspective and the perspective of the Aboriginal woman.

When Angie attempts to dismiss the woman's threats, she realizes that the gun that the woman carries is in fact corporeal, and a panel depicting a third-person point of view ends the page, as the Aboriginal woman tells Angie, "I am strong ghost. You like stories, bone woman? You tell stories with me?" (128), suggesting that narratives in this context will function as a transaction. The stories Constantine sought within the dream world are denied to him, while the Aboriginal woman erupts into the conscious world in order to tell stories with Angie, the less sympathetic of the two whites to the plight of her people. In the earlier scene in which Angie asks Constantine about their purpose in Tasmania, he tries to elaborate on the history of the Aborigines, information that she rejects as unnecessary to their purpose. Her disinterest is reminiscent of contemporary claims to "colorblindness," which largely seek to discredit historical circumstances as affecting contemporary life.

This scene lays vital groundwork for how we are meant to understand memory and the narration thereof in the context of forgotten genocides. Rothberg writes of recent debates that trouble the divide between history as a narrative of victors and victims, including engaging Pierre Nora's idea "that contemporary society is 'menaced by the rewriting of history from the point of view of the victims'" (269). Rothberg focuses on texts that construct memory as threatening in order to reveal "already existing, unresolved divisions" (272). Similarly, this scene gestures toward the unsettled past's propensity for eruption into the present. While Constantine is actively searching for specific stories of the Aborigines, Angie is merely "along for the ride," largely uninterested in the historical context for their journey. That the Aboriginal woman appears to her, rather than the person seeking knowledge, seems to suggest a return not of the repressed but of the completely annihilated. Angie represents a distinct Western attitude toward the legacy of colonialism and genocide that seeks to exonerate the self based solely on temporal distance as an expression of guiltlessness. The Aboriginal woman's appearance to Angie emphasizes a universal culpability in forgetting and in not being particularly interested in remembering. What does it mean to be confronted with a dead but still animate history?

The Aboriginal woman takes the lead in the storytelling, the first panel depicting a lynching with an embedded panel depicting her in the present day (see fig. 5.2). In the embedded panel, she articulates an extended metaphor, telling Angie, "You call me ghost, but to us, your people are ghosts. Your skin is white like bone. And death is like a bone you swallowed, that you can't spit out" (131). While the Aboriginal woman is indeed a ghost, haunting the present from a position of the past, she begins her narrative by specifically rendering an alternative cultural viewpoint: what has the capacity for haunting is not the dead but rather those in power, the invaders. Structurally, the embedded panel as a representation of the present is surrounded by a representation of the past, but it also overlays the panel illustrating her memory of a hanged man surrounded by a mob. The present here, the moment of storytelling, is a part of the past but also serves to obscure it, to focus on parts of the past while erasing other elements. The simultaneous use of two distinct temporal moments suggests that the present must indeed be contained within an image of the past in order to be

FIGURE 5.2. The Aboriginal woman begins her story. Carey, Mike, Marcelo Frusin, Tim Bradstreet, Lee Loughridge, and Clem Robbins. "The Pit." *Hellblazer—Black Flowers.* Issue 186. New York: DC Comics, 2005.

decipherable. The hanged-man image bears two functions as context. First, it is reminiscent of lynching photography in the Southern United States during the late 1800s and early 1900s. Most Americans would recognize the basic makeup of the image—a hanged man with a crowd of people carrying torches and pitchforks surrounding him—as recalling the Lynching Era in their country. However, why would an intertext from a different nation be used? In part as a cognitive sleight of hand in which one disavowed history is linked with another. Second, the position of the image suggests that, rather than watching the story unfold from the Aboriginal woman's point of view, since she is the focalizor in this narrative, the reader is instead positioned within the mob.

The following panels illustrate a litany of abuses visited upon her people by the colonists. While these scenes are clearly focalized through her consciousness, her specific, individual point of view is conspicuously absent; there is no indication that these are direct illustrations of scenes she has witnessed. The woman narrates these abuses in the historical present tense, saying, "You tell us you bring laws. And then you tell us we break laws. We have to die. Always we have to die." (131). Her language is stilted, possibly to render her account more "authentic" but simultaneously imparting a sense of being colonized by language. Her employment of the historical present enhances this sense of linguistic colonization, as it indicates that her people's past is experienced perpetually. While the woman is narrating the various modes of death delivered by the whites, she is also abandoning teleological markers like past tense to emphasize the persistence of similar narratives. Furthermore, in each panel, whites are positioned in some proximity to Aborigines. The first describes a number of different laws imposed that the Aborigines would regularly break inadvertently, in part because of their cultural differences, although the woman narrating specifically links these laws with purpose: "*Always* we have to die" (131). The reader is in close proximity to an Aborigine in this panel, but he is dead. The second panel shows a line of Aborigines in the background, a pile of blankets being unloaded from a ship in the foreground. The reader is positioned in this scene more closely to the white sailors rather than to an Aboriginal point of view.

Similar to the first panel, the final panel shows a familiar image in the past with an embedded moment in the present. The panel from the past depicts men dying of smallpox under infected blankets, the shadow of a British soldier cast on the wall behind them, suggesting that the reader is sharing the nameless, faceless soldier's point of view as he surveys the suffering patients. The woman continues to use present tense when describing this scene, while the embedded panel shows Angie saying, "Smallpox. I read about that. They didn't have a name for germ warfare back then, but they knew how to do it" (131). Angie's assertion that this was a circumstance she knew about through reading emphasizes a measure of distance between the reception of historical knowledge and the witnessing of it. Furthermore, Angie's remark reintroduces the past tense, and by mirroring the first panel on the page, this panel suggests that the mediation of the memory being narrated is taking place between the two women. Neither is entirely responsible for the images that ostensibly illustrate the story told by the Aboriginal woman, rather, they are the result of a shifting point of view that suggests the history at stake is in contest between the embodied experiences of those who can no longer speak and the contemporary experiences of those who no longer care.

The Aboriginal woman includes herself in the narrative on the next page, in which the first panel depicts the twisted corpse of a man foregrounded, lying supine in the grass. In the background, the woman is being led away from the corpse by a man with a gun. Interestingly, her face is completely undefined—only the curves of her body visually link the teller and the shown—while she describes how a white man abducted her after killing her husband. By framing the Palawa woman at a significant distance, the implied Carey and Frusin deploy two significant commentaries. In the first place, her undefined face and the physical space between the character and the reader suggest that her experience, no matter how it is witnessed by the reader, is so distant as to be nearly unrecognizable, underscoring the importance of the historical and cultural context and the limits of empathy in this regard. The reader is in fact placed more closely to the twisted corpse of her husband, which is rendered in detail, his face a mask of pain, one hand falling back into the grass while the other is twisted outward from his body at an awkward angle. Second, her specific identity, as it is defined partly through the face and the reader's recognition of that face, is subsumed in a larger narrative. Rather than the projective identification of the reader with the character's experience as that which takes place during closure as defined by McCloud, there is instead an erasure that suggests a lack of specificity. So, on one hand, her story is not unique but, on the other, that generality suggests an uncomfortable proximity to this history.

Unlike the clear distinction between her own and the reader's experiences implied by her placement and rendering, the Palawa woman's husband's warped body in the foreground recalls Christian imagery of Christ as he was taken down from the cross. The reader's recognition of Christian iconography of course takes place without cognitive engagement and suggests a sacrifice made for specific redemption, which is hardly accidental given Carey's devout Christianity. However, the sacrifice is made, but the redemption suggested is replaced by another man's corpse in the following panel, mirroring the position of her husband in the first. The woman narrates that the "white man die too. I wait until he sleep, and I find knife by his stove. Cut his throat and take his balls. Take his gun and his coat, too" (132). This panel reiterates the structure of the previous one, depicting the woman in the background, her face obscured by shadow, while the body of the man is foregrounded, a long knife protruding from his chest, his hand clutched in rigor. In these two panels, why is the dead body always closer to the viewer than the depiction of the ghost woman's memory? With whom are we meant to identify?

Bhabha theorizes identity as a construct deeply attached to the image. In "The Pit," the reader is alternately visually encouraged to and foreclosed from identifying with various characters, communicating an ethics of empathy that resists the impulse to articulate victim experience as accessible. Bhabha writes, "Each time the encounter with identity occurs at the point at which something exceeds the frame of the image, it eludes the eye, evacuates the self as site of identity and autonomy and—most important—leaves a resistant trace, a stain of the subject, a sign of resistance" (71). Bhabha is speaking in terms of the consolidation of the Western viewpoint in the face of the postcolonial other, a useful metaphor for the examination of a postcoloniality in which few Others remain. The framed image, Bhabha argues, does not reveal all, and indeed, in graphic narratives the frame is used partly to present the appearance of a window into the action but also to exclude; not only to exclude unnecessary elements of the scene, but to exclude reader identification. While the woman's use of the present tense lends the story the sensation of temporal proximity, the choices the implied Carey and Frusin make in relation to perspective pointedly emphasize that focalization is taking place along two lines while she recounts her narrative. She is the teller, but the observer is an unmoored external point of view, wandering through the scenes she relates, and that point of view dwells somewhere closer to approximating the colonizers' viewpoints than those of the Aborigines. The resemblance between the woman's husband and the white man in terms of physical position posit a relationship but not an ethical equivalency.

These two panels visually demonstrate this gulf between the identities of the assumed reader and of the narrator, who is focalizor only of the verbal plane of her story. The final panel(s) of her story show her raising the stolen gun high over her head as a house burns to the ground in the background. At a distance, we look over her should as she tells Angie, "I talk to ours. I say we fight now. Give them back this death they give to us. We burn their houses. Not let them come out. Watch them blacken like wallabies on spit. Children too. Women. All them" (132). This over-the-shoulder view would seem to indicate that the reader is placed among the Aborigines, positioned in league with the heroic victims. In fact, the brutality described in her narration loses its horror since the reader has been primed with images of dead bodies for the previous two pages.[6] Those she kills are not shown in this panel—only the burning structure of the house—and our positioning in relation to the scene is disrupted by two panels showing the present exchange between Angie and the woman that are embedded in the larger panel.

By embedding two present panels in the past that include both of the women speaking, the implied Carey and Frusin again illustrate the contest between competing narratives of history, and suggest an alternate reading of the panel structure. Rather than simply being "embedded," which is the way in which such panels are traditionally described, it should also be noted that all of the embedded panels *overlay* specific parts of the scene. Each embedded panel is simultaneously functioning in two ways. First,

---

6. This woman's story may have also been based on that of Tarerenorerer, a woman in the North tribes of Tasmania who, after being abducted by sealers, escaped and led a revolt against settlers in 1828 in Emu Bay (Matson-Green).

they represent the way in which the present is entirely surrounded and mediated by a history that is essential to the decipherability of the present. Second, they suggest that excessive preoccupation with the present, and with the process of narrating, necessarily obscures details in the past.

The competing functions of the embedded/overlain panels also operate at the level of content. Angie's response to this violence is predictably ambivalent, "But you gave them something to think about, anyway" (132), once again, distinctly marking the woman's experiences as *past* tense. The woman's reply, however, is more rhetorically complex, as she asserts, "I give them what they already have. I come where they already are. They happy enough with that" (132). The woman resituates her narrative in the historical present that distinguished her narrative. In addition to the disagreement between tenses in the two women's statements, the images support this temporal disjuncture because the panels depicting the present are set inside the panels depicting the woman's memory, suggesting that the present frames the testimony even as the events of the past subsume the present. There are no signs that what is depicted in the previous panels takes place at any time but the present, but the reader is aware that these are narrated memories. In spite of this awareness, how does the woman's insistence on maintaining the historical present tense inflect the reader's connection to her story? After all, she is a ghost. She was likely killed during the genocide or, at the latest, died by 1876, as her story bears some resemblance to that of Truganini.[7] But what does it mean for her to narrate the story of the death of her people in the historical present tense, particularly when she does not include her own death and she seemingly persists beyond it?

The woman's story precludes the reader's vicarious access to her point of view, but her insistence on maintaining the historical present undercuts this by indicating that her act of vengeance against the whites only constitute a continuation of their own story. The idea of giving the settlers "what they already have" points toward a persistent strain of violence in this history, violence that is only made obvious when it comes from outside. As individuals embedded in a network of violent relations (particularly in

---

7. Truganini was purported to be the last full-blooded Tasmanian Aborigine, and she died in 1876. She was part of the group who, in 1830, were moved to Flinders Island by George Augustus Robinson as a measure to protect and preserve their culture. The relatively small group was mostly wiped out by disease over the next two decades. Truganini, while on Flinders Island, was involved with a group of fugitives who stole from and murdered settlers. Recently, Aboriginal groups have increasingly called attention to their continued existence, and contested the idea that the Tasmanian Aborigines were completely annihilated.

terms of territorial expansion), her violence toward the settlers is framed as nothing more than business as usual. Rather than emphasizing her own role in an uprising, or painting herself heroically, she frames the revolt as a portion of the continued negotiation in how this story may be told. When she says, "I come where they already *are*," she is demonstrating how the past is informed by the future. Use of the present tense for both her movement and their existence indicates that fictionalized narratives can access multiple temporalities simultaneously. But what does her assertion mean for the reader? While readers are nominally exhorted to empathize with survivor narratives, in this case the empathetic impulse is foreclosed partly through the perspectives adopted within the panels and partly through the woman's speech patterns, which are stilted. She is not a survivor. She is a narrator of an experience, but her experiences, as a murdered ghost, are so distant from the reader that the reader is left without a place to attach herself.

In demanding that Angie also narrate a story, and Angie's story of pain is specific, the reader's attention is drawn to the problematic portrayal of those who *cannot* speak for themselves, those who have been so thoroughly abused that they cannot pass along the stories that may bring at least the catharsis of telling. This story arc seems to give more dimension to both Angie and the characters with whom Constantine comes into conflict than with Constantine himself.[8] Angie's story is more familiar to the Western reader. She describes her brother Jason, formerly a funny, outgoing young man who descended into madness, was misdiagnosed, went to prison after a violent episode, and was finally diagnosed schizophrenic. Beginning with a scene prior to his illness, the panels depict his strange and increasingly violent behavior, but interestingly, unlike in the Palawa woman's story, a character (Jason) is regularly foregrounded. The over-the-shoulder point of view repeats at points at which his illness makes him most violent or at points of hallucination but never offers his interior experience and instead shows him how Angie must have imagined his experience. Angie's story is not her own but is instead the story of her brother, and unlike the wandering viewpoint of the Aboriginal woman's story, which shows scenes without a specific character-bound point of view and without following only the woman herself, Angie's story is firmly attached to Jason in particular.

---

8. Story arcs that focus primarily on minor or tangential characters are generally met with significant resistance by the *Hellblazer* audience. However, story arcs of this kind have been becoming increasingly common within *Hellblazer*, as well as multiple other long-running comics series.

The final panel of her story reiterates the structure of the final panel of the Palawa woman's, a broad panel with two panels inset. The larger panel shows the woman and men in the midst of the flames in the present day, Angie standing, explaining Jason's continued deterioration and eventual relocation to an asylum. The first inset panel shows Angie crying, the woman's hand and gun in the corner of the frame, as Angie says, "We both know what it's like to be screwed. And we both know we're nothing special," which equates her witnessing of her brother's story as a sort of institutionalized violence, positing a problematic congruence between the two women's narratives. However, given the fact that the reader has already witnessed the lack of interest Angie showed in the story of the Tasmanian Aborigines, the reader is, perhaps, less inclined to see this supposed equivalence. While Angie's story is designed specifically to mobilize empathy on behalf of her brother's and her family's plight, the Aboriginal woman's story in contrast seems matter-of-fact. Furthermore, when compared, the Aboriginal woman's narrative is significantly less elaborate and wordy than Angie's. Rather than describing her experiences in detail, the Aboriginal woman chooses instead to give only broad outlines of the story. Angie, on the other hand, narrates as many specifics as she can, and in the second inset panel, she grabs the muzzle of the gun and points it at her chest, saying, "Let's have it then, love. We've taken the getting to know you stuff about as far as it'll go" (137). Of course, given that Angie has delivered a much more exhaustive account, her statement stands in stark contrast to the bare suggestions the woman made about her own narrative.

These two passages raise a number of questions. First, why is the narrative of the Palawa woman more generic, more general, than that of Angie? Angie is the character least interested in the story the woman has to tell, and in fact, her own story of her pain takes up more space in the narrative than the Aboriginal woman's. Second, how is the reader positioned in relation to receiving these stories? The reader is less a narratee than a bystander, overhearing what transpires. Third, what judgments about the two narratives do the implied Carey and Frusin intend to elicit? Finally, why does the Aboriginal woman choose to tell her story to Angie while Constantine is dream walking? He was the one who wanted to hear the stories of the Aborigines, while Angie was merely along for the ride.

The first question, why the Palawa woman's story is less specific and detailed than Angie's, suggests on a surface level that the story of the Aborigines should be told in a general way. Perhaps this is particularly true when the author and artist bear no ancestral relationship to the story, and attempting to tell this story at all required a complicated set of ethical negotiations that limited not only how they told the story but what they could tell. However, the story is not narrated from a Western character's perspective, and choosing to tell the story through the ghost of a Tasmanian Aboriginal woman who was there to witness the genocide would suggest that the author and artist had more latitude in terms of what to include than if the account was framed as second- or thirdhand. It is, in another light, highly problematic to put words into the mouth of a victim, fictionalized though she may be. While the memoirs and accounts of survivors from other genocides may be examined as historical documents, a fictionalized testimony from a genocide that left few, if any, survivors occupies an entirely different place in the constellation of literatures of witness.

The Aboriginal woman's narrative and the images that accompany it bear more than a passing resemblance to accounts by survivors of other genocides. The first panel depicts a lynching recognizable as a revision of the lynching photography that helped Walter White[9] bring attention to the practice in the early 1900s. The panels that show the blankets off-loaded from a ship that then infect the Aborigines with smallpox clearly reiterate the biological warfare conducted by settlers against indigenous peoples in the early years of colonization. The other panels recall images associated with the slave trade. These visual historical intertexts, focused almost exclusively on recognizable American atrocities, bear the stain Bhabha references above; the past is placed alongside of the present, but moreover, the past is *active* both within the present and encompasses it. Rather than a linear structure, this story uses cross-cultural visual intertexts in order to demonstrate the way in which the present is embedded in a range of histories. These histories are in contest with one another and are a stain at the center of the heart of the American identity. The use of recognizable American images placed outside of an American cultural context is a method of working around the cognitive barriers many readers set up when asserting that violence in history no longer bears a relationship to present circumstances of marginalized groups.

In contrast, Angie's story specifically recounts individual instances in her family that led to her brother's incarceration and subsequent institutionalization. Her story is marked by an excess of talk and explanation. The accompanying images illustrate her brother's and family's experiences from both an externally focalized point of view and from Angie's perspective. In addition to the detailed explanations, Angie's story is automatically more familiar to the average Western reader because it takes place in a recogniz-

---

9. Longtime leader of the NAACP who used his ability to "pass" as white to document lynching in America.

ably modern context, the content focuses on mental health, which has been of concern in Western cultures in recent decades, and the narrative itself is familiar partly because of the proliferation of television shows dedicated to exploring criminology. Her story is one of easy identification, and in the process of recounting it, Angie also tells the listener how to interpret it. The Palawa woman's story ends when Angie interrupts and the Aboriginal woman demands Angie's story in return. Angie, by contrast, ends her story by creating an equivalency between her own pain and that of the woman. While Angie herself seems convinced of the similarity between their stories, the reader is cued to how ethically problematic this formulation is by the intervening narrative of Constantine's experience in his dream walk, which will be explored in depth in the following section.

In the case of the second question, how the reader is positioned in relation to these stories, I mentioned above that the reader was less the narratee than a bystander. Angie and the Palawa woman are telling their stories to one another, but the broader audience peers over their shoulders as they face off. Additionally, the reader is given a window into the narration that may function in several different ways. The images that accompany each incident that is recounted are framed within the process of telling the narrative, but it is unclear whether these are the images that come to the narratee's mind when hearing the narrative, images that come to the narrator's narrative as they recount, or whether the images are offered outside of the parameters of the textual narrative as illustrative accompaniments. The wandering point of view associated with the woman's story in fact seems to more closely approximate the perspectives of British soldiers and settlers, or, perhaps, the narrator who briefly recounted the scene on the first page of the comic.

In Angie's story, her point of view is a part of the narrative. One panel depicts her looking in on her brother in his room as he writes at a desk, and another may portray her point of view as Jason and her father fight. The other panels show incidents she could not have witnessed herself, however, and so function more as illustrations of what is being recounted. In this respect, her narrative has a slightly redundant quality between word and image that distinguishes it from that of the Aboriginal woman. Another important contrast between the two stories is that Angie twice interrupts the Palawa woman's narrative. In the first case, she inserts her own present-day knowledge into a story of the past, and in the second, she offers a trite truism as response to the woman's fight against the whites. By having Angie interject herself into the woman's narrative, the implied Carey and Frusin are reminding the reader of the levels of mediation at stake in this recounting. Furthermore, they are explicitly demonstrating the way in which historical accounts of atrocity are interrupted or intruded upon by contemporary voices.

In the Palawa woman's narrative, the panels also function illustratively, but rather than merely being images of what is recounted, the content of the panels fill in the story, showing scenes that explain the woman's more generalized utterances. For example, in the first panel, when the woman says, "Then you tell us we break laws. We have to die" (131), she does not specify how they are put to death. Instead, the panel shows us a lynch mob surrounding a hanging corpse. In addition, the Palawa woman's panels uniformly foreclose her point of view from the readers. On the first page, markers, like a row of Aboriginal men in the background or a helmeted shadow cast by a soldier, firmly indicate that what is depicted is not shown from her point of view. This suggests that, rather than functioning as illustrations, the images may represent what appears in Angie's mind as the woman recounts her story. Further evidence for this is the final inset panel on the first page when Angie remarks that she had read about germ warfare. Her remark, an interruption in the story, hints that the familiarity of the images comes from the same history books that the reader has also read. On the second page, which directly relates the Parlevar woman's own experience, she appears within each panel, which again implies that what we are seeing is Angie's mind busily filling in the narrative with images so that she is watching the woman's actions as the woman narrates them.

Phelan's use of the term "restricted narration" is particularly useful for examining these two passages. He defines *restricted narration* as "narration that records events but does not interpret or evaluate them" (29), which falls in line with how the Aboriginal woman formulates her story. Angie, on the other hand, is overly concerned with evaluating her own story against that of the woman. While Phelan uses this term to refer to autobiographical accounts that involve "the authorial audience to infer communication from the author beyond what the narrator tells the narratee" (29), I find it relevant here for distinguishing between the way in which the Aboriginal woman and Angie narrate their stories differently and, furthermore, to add dimension to the discussion of the irregularly appearing third-person narrator.

I will return to the third and fourth questions after an exploration of Constantine's experiences on the dream walk while the women exchanged their stories. Constantine is separated temporally and (seemingly) physically while he searches for Tasmanian Aboriginal ghosts to speak with about the Shadow Dog. His experiences are structured differently than those of Angie and the woman; rather than straight-edged panels with white gutters and a color scheme dominated by oranges and blacks, the world Constantine wakes to on his dream walk is composed predominantly of greens, the panel edges are jagged, and the gutters colored a pale blue. These alterations of form suggest that Constantine is entering a sick environment, but what this means for the comic as a whole is clarified only through its relation to the stories of Angie and the Palawa woman.

CONSTANTINE IN THE PIT

In contrast to the sharing of stories taking place between Angie and the Aboriginal woman, Constantine's search confronts not the spirits of the Aborigines he hopes to learn from but rather the ghosts of the dead British soldiers dreaming the camp where they slaughtered the remaining Aborigines over two hundred years before. One problem in terms of telling the stories of genocide is that, by and large, the ending is the same; there is an implicit inevitability, a loss of control in the face of "great" events, a sense of history as a tide that can be predicted but not stopped. The centrality of narrative to identity—and of identity to perspective—are the key features of Constantine's journey into the Dreaming. Foreshadowing, as a formal question, is interesting in regards to "The Pit." The initial scene in which Constantine crosses over to spirit walk is remarkable partly for its self-reflexive irony. Constantine awakens into his dream walk dressed as a British soldier of the period, on the ground being kick by a sergeant and excoriated for being asleep on the job. The two panels depicting this offer first the sergeant's perspective and then that of Constantine, but the third and fifth panels both show the men in silhouette, through the grates of the wire fence, as if the reader is observing the exchange from within the prison of the Aborigines. As Constantine is attempting to get his bearings, he asks what his post is, to which the sergeant responds, "Watching them, you whey-faced fagger! What do you fucking think?" (125). The vulgar language, coupled with Constantine's point of view, lend the scene the sensation of imminent threat to the main character. The whole yard is depicted in black, with a background of sickly green. By shifting from the "safe" point of view of the Western characters to the perspective within the prison yard, Carey and Frusin unmoor the normally focalizing consciousness of Constantine in the *Hellblazer* series.

There is a striking visual shift when Constantine enters his dream walk. The frames are unstable; rather than crisp, clean lines separating the panel from the gutter, the frames are slightly wavy and jagged, and the gutter is cast entirely in light blue. While the frames are still solid, the use of rough borders gestures toward a feeling of disorientation, and occasionally, characters are extended partly beyond the frame. The first page shows that Constantine has entered this dream walk as a British soldier, the first panel showing him in uniform, and the second showing two other soldiers. In the second panel, while the reader shares his perspective, this point of view is also disrupted by the fact that the commander's helmet extends outward above the frame and in fact is cut off only by the top of the page. This violation of the frame enhances the effect of disorientation.

The page ends with a panel that depicts Constantine and the two British soldiers in silhouette from within the enclosure occupied by the Aborigines. On the following page, Constantine turns to talk with the Aborigines contained within the tall, barbed fence. An over-the-shoulder panel depicts him approaching the enclosure, the silhouetted Aborigines beyond the lattice, a foregrounded bayonet poised over all of their heads. In the following two panels, from a point of view inside the enclosure, the reader views Constantine at the fence, saying, "Christ. Listen, this might not be a good time—but I came here to get some questions answered, and you're the only ones who can help me. See, there's something called the Shadow Dog. It came here once. A while ago now, but I was thinking you might have some stories about—" (126). He trails off and the following two panels approximate Constantine's point of view as he looks carefully at the Aborigines in the enclosure, who all have empty, white eyes. While Constantine is gazing inward at the Aborigines, their blank gazes directed outward at him emphasize absence. The reader shares Constantine's point of view as the object of gazes that do not exist.

The narrative picks up with Constantine's conversation with another one of the British soldiers. The panels vacillate between distance and proximity as Constantine explains to the man, "I came here because I know a lot of the aborigines were brought here. But this is the last place they'd want to hang around in" (129). The reader is cued into an interpretation of the panels depicting the Aborigines with blank eyes. While the soldier says, "It's not as though they've got much choice now, buck," Constantine explains, "When they were alive they had no choice. The dead have got loads of options. Although they don't always know it" (129). This exchange takes place in the penultimate panel, wherein Constantine and the soldier, Maine, are barely visible, silhouetted at a distance. In the foreground, a shovel looms over the lip of the pit, which boasts the angled spikes, recalling the first page. The final panel is from Constantine's point of view and shows Maine holding a match, Constantine's hand behind it casts Maine's face into shadow as Constantine tells him, "You light a match, you get a shadow, right? [. . .] Your mind is more like a bonfire than a match" (129). This metaphor is explained on the following page, which opens with an approximation of the two men's viewpoints, the Aborigines silhouetted through the fence. Constantine explains, "When the dead dream about a place they used to know, they furnish it. They make it look right. So this fence, and those people, they're here because you remember them as being here [. . .] Have another look at those faces. They're not real—they're not even real ghosts. This isn't their dream, squire. It's yours" (130). This scene is a metacommentary on the way in which atrocities are remembered, in which the historical realities of the colonialist enterprise function also to colonize the mind of the colonizers. A more obvious iteration of the intertextual traces represented in the Aboriginal woman's narrative, Constantine's metaphor suggests an ironic haunting of the past by the past.

While the reader is not shown the enclosure after Constantine's explanation, Maine's reaction is sufficient. He is depicted opening his eyes and asking, "Where?" then turning to strike Constantine and calling for help. When the narrative picks back up after the Aboriginal woman's story intervenes for two pages, Maine is frantically telling the other soldiers that Constantine "was talking to me. Some old palaver about dreams. And then he said the Abos weren't really there. And I looked. And they weren't" (137). A gigantic empty enclosure stretches out in the foreground, while the men are depicted as tiny silhouettes in the background, barely visible against the vast, wasted expanse. The sergeant decides that Constantine must have released the Aborigines, and they decide to throw him into the pit. Angie's narrative intervenes at this point, and when the narrative picks back up three pages later, Constantine is being held at gunpoint at the edge of the pit. The sergeant asks him if he still thinks this is a dream, and Constantine responds, "It's a sodding nightmare. And you deserve every bastard ounce of it. Bit of a pisser for us innocent bystanders, though" (138). Constantine is thrown into the pit, and the men prepare to shoot. Constantine's remark is meant to indicate that he is not a part of this, but instead, his situation is ironic because he is placed at precisely the area that was occupied by the Tasmanian Aborigines and continues to disavow his relationship to the men who are about to kill him. Rather than accessing the Tasmanian *Altjeringa*, he was directed into the dream of the soldiers on the cusp of a massacre, and he is unable to reflect on why he was directed there instead of his intended destination. He specifically refers to himself as a bystander rather than a descendant or inheritor, which, rather than exonerating him, instead suggests a simultaneous rejection of direct responsibility and acceptance of a complicated historical relationship in which his contemporary self is, to some extent, implicated.

The following page is composed of four long panels, each the width of the page. In the first, the sergeant is shown giving the order to fire. The second shows the balls leaving the muskets, and the third shows the musket balls paused in the air. The final panel on the page depicts two of the soldiers frozen, the bullets still poised in midair, as the Aboriginal woman approaches from behind. The faces of the British soldiers are shaded under their hats, literally becoming faceless. The face of the Aboriginal woman is also darkened but for two white eyes. While her specific features are effaced, her blank eyes stare out at the reader, who is approximately occupying Constantine's point of view. Unlike the soldiers, she is moving. This movement is indicative of the resistance to generic colonial rules of narrative within this story, as it draws attention to the inversion of the normative convention in which non-Western characters are paused in time while Western characters are capable of forward movement. In contrast, "The Pit" is preoccupied with how Western characters' disavowals of historical atrocities, and their inability to see beyond their own narratives and goals, creates stagnation.

The Aboriginal woman pulls him out of the pit as the bullets remain paused in the air, the dead British soldier's ghosts still frozen in time. As she reaches for him, she says, "You want to come with me, white bone man. Or them little blunt-nosed wasps they sting you bad" (140). His response, "Yeah. Uh . . . Thanks" is uncharacteristically awkward, but it is unclear whether he is reacting to her phrasing or to the fact that she appeared at all. It would seem, at first glance, that he is undermining her advice to avoid the bullets, in part because they are termed *blunt-nosed wasps*, an anachronism he is unprepared for, coloring his response with a slightly condescending tone. He asks her if the following night will be the same for the soldiers, to which she replies, "I not come into their dream. It narrow and dark. They dream it a long, long time now" (140). The woman and Constantine are depicted in the background, a saber diagonally bisecting the panel. Constantine takes a moment to look back at the men paused in the process of shooting into the pit, and he asks, "Who needs Hell?" Rather than meditating on this potential afterlife, he immediately turns and tells the woman he needs to ask her about the Shadow Dog.

In a reiteration of the narratorial voice that only occurred on the first page (see fig. 5.3), the following panel depicts Constantine following the woman over the landscape toward Angie, and text boxes read, "So he

FIGURE 5.3. Who speaks and who fails to speak. Carey, Mike, Marcelo Frusin, Tim Bradstreet, Lee Loughridge, and Clem Robbins. "The Pit." *Hellblazer — Black Flowers.* Issue 186. New York: DC Comics, 2005.

asked her about the Dog. And she told him all that he asked. And then she brought him back to the fire, to his mortal body" (141). The second panel on the page depicts a silhouetted Constantine's spirit standing over his body, the woman's gun and legs foregrounded, the weapon once again shearing the panel, with text boxes narrating, "But staring down into his own face—he found he had one question left" (141). While the rest of the textual component of the narrative takes place in dialogue, the text boxes formally and rhetorically suggest a third-person narrator who only exists on the first and the penultimate pages of the comic. Why would the narrator intervene again at this point? Why was their conversation not related in word bubbles rather than being summarized in text boxes? After all, the ostensible purpose of this installment of the comic was to find out information about the Shadow Dog from a Tasmanian Aborigine.

Note the formulation on the first panel of the page; Constantine asks her questions, but the narrator explains that she *only* "told him all that he asked." This suggests that Constantine's questions may not have covered all that he needs to know about the Shadow Dog and further indicates that the woman knows more about the Shadow Dog than what she told him. This cryptic reference could be interpreted as a nod to the myth of indigenous peoples having "special knowledge," but the construction also suggests that her knowledge of the Shadow Dog is available and can be communicated, if only one poses the right questions. Ultimately, this panel once again gestures to the misunderstanding first outlined in the tension between Angie and the Palawa woman's stories. The implied Carey and Frusin here seek to emphasize that the ostensible goal of the narrative was not in fact its aim, and they specifically exclude the information that was sought. By replacing actual information with "she told him all he asked," a mediating layer of narration intervenes at the point that would normally serve as denouement in an issue of *Hellblazer*, wherein Constantine finally receives the knowledge he seeks after a climax in which he is in danger.

Constantine's question, "Why did you do it? Why did you pull me out? You must hate the whites for what they did to your people" (141), is posed in hopes of an explanation of her perspective. Why would she choose to save him from his own people? She was not simply saving him from being killed during the dream walk but was altering the very fabric of their dream in order to save him. She responds, "Hate is a starting place. Lots of ways you can go from there. Lots of places it can take you" (141), an enigmatic contention that reminds the reader of the close of her story, when she remarks, "I give them what they already have. I come where they already are" (132). When reading these two lines alongside one another, the ambivalence about both time and point of view is clear.

The response the implied Carey and Frusin intend to provoke in the reader could perhaps be sympathetic identification with either the story of the Palawa woman or with the more familiar narrative of Angie, but both of these reactions are clearly undercut by the ambivalence of the Aboriginal woman. She is clearly positioned as the character with whom the reader *should* empathize, but her story is generalized and does not interpret the story for the reader. Unlike works like Speigelman's *Maus*, which is marked by explanations of the confusion and difficulty inherent in relating such a story, no such obsessive self-reflection occurs in the Aboriginal woman's narrative. Instead, this excess of explanation marks Angie's account, but between these two narratives lays a gulf in both degree and kind. Does the reader take the stories as equivalent as Angie seems to suggest they should? Does the Aboriginal woman's ambivalent response to Constantine about the nature of hate complicate our reaction to her story? Her final words to Constantine before departing are that he should ask Angie about hate because "she know." Are the implied Carey and Frusin suggesting that the Aboriginal ghost woman would herself see equivalence between her story of genocide and Angie's story of the consequences of mental illness?

Perhaps, instead, the implied Carey and Frusin intend for the reader to take into account all of the cues on the page. Because graphic narratives are read not only panel to panel but are also taken in as an entire page as the reader moves through the text, the initial panel on this page must be taken into account in the narratorial layering. The unnamed third-person narrator who appears only twice in the text as a whole suggest that the woman has not told Constantine everything but only "all that he asked." This indicates that what the Aboriginal woman told Angie during the course of her story was not the "whole" story. In fact, the woman did not include any evaluative language that would cue the reader into a specific affective response, and her purposefully stilted English suggests a wider gap between herself and the reader as well. Furthermore, the lack of evaluative language in fact cautions the reader against an expression of intimate understanding of the woman's experience, and instead of explaining her perspective to Constantine, she directs him back to Angie, who has a more identifiable form of hate than does the woman. But does this complicate the project of bringing a historically distant atrocity into closer proximity to contemporary readers? Perhaps not, as the entire issue is devoted to the negotiation of competing narratives from multiple temporalities, and the only narrative that is pronounced to be "the whole story" is the one that is not shared with the reader: the Aboriginal woman's explanation of the Shadow Dog.

In spite of the woman's direction for Constantine to ask Angie, when they awake to the morning on the following page, rather than asking her about her experience, he tells her, "I got what I needed. The whole story" (142). Their brief exchange ends in a passionate embrace, and the incidents of the previous night are apparently completely forgotten and in fact are not referenced again in the story arc (nor have they been in the series as a whole). However, Constantine's confidence in having the "whole story" is misplaced. The woman told him only what he asked, and when she gave him advice, he failed to follow it. Instead of recounting the knowledge or sharing their own stories, they embrace in a clichéd repetition of filmic conclusion, wherein the "natives" have served only as a backdrop for the drama and romance of the main (white) characters.

THE "WHOLE STORY"

The fourth question, why the Aboriginal woman chose to tell her story to Angie rather than to Constantine in spite of the fact that he undertook a journey purely in order to hear her story, rests at the center of the narratorial and authorial complexity at stake in "The Pit." Constantine set out on his journey in order to enter the Tasmanian Aborigines' Dreaming, to walk in spirit among them and ask for their stories. He adhered to the rituals, he took care to ingest the appropriate substances, but instead of reaching their dream space, he is unceremoniously dumped into the dreams of the dead British soldiers. Unlike most issues of *Hellblazer*, the reader is not solely given Constantine's experience and scenes that depict other characters talking about Constantine. The focus is instead on the story he is searching for and the stories that are told instead.

As to why the Aboriginal woman told her story to Angie, perhaps it is in part because of Constantine's eagerness to violate the boundaries of the Aborigines' afterlives, a sort of iteration of "teaching him his place." Given that he engaged in the rituals but was nonetheless directed into a different space points toward a message of cross temporal complicity. The Aboriginal woman saved him, and he had to ask why. Of course, how was he directed into a different space? Why did she appear at the moment he departed into that space? The reader can infer that she was (or, at minimum, her people were) responsible for denying him access to their *Altjeringa*, the place that was the point of his journey and instead directed him into a place where he would be put into the uneasy situation of being a perpetrator of genocide. He lives out an afternoon in the life of one of the soldiers who assisted in the slaughter of an entire race, and while he does not kill any Aborigines himself, it is clear that because of his placement, he is, as a modern white man in the U.K., always closer to the role of the perpetrator than to the role of the victim. To paraphrase Charles Mills, even as he attempts to reject his beneficiary status, he is reintegrated into the machinery of massacre.

The most significant moment in the text—the point of the story arc—is denied to the reader. While the narrator suggests that information has been withheld from Constantine himself, the reader does not even have access to what Constantine asked and what the Aboriginal woman said in response. In place of their conversation are the text boxes relating only that "she told him all he asked." By replacing a conversation, a dialogue that could have easily been depicted, the implied Carey and Frusin are suggesting that access to the information Constantine sought must be earned. Furthermore, by reducing that point in the text where knowledge is gained to a single panel, and simultaneously having the woman's and Angie's stories stretch out over several pages, perhaps the implied Carey and Frusin indicate that both the reader and Constantine have missed the point of the story.

Clearly, Constantine has not acquired the "whole story," and the reader does not know what was said, but rather than a move to build tension toward a future drama, the purpose of the journey is overlooked. But if this is true, why does the woman save Constantine, aside from the fact that he is the main character in a long-running comics series? One could contend that, in spite of its inappropriateness, Angie's creation of a metaphor between the two stories was necessary. This does not make her attempts at equation between her own experience and that of the woman's any less vile and ludicrous, but rather it points toward content that was missing in Constantine's initial ritual. When he initially removes his clothing, and Angie mocks him, he is unable to explain why he did so beyond it "feeling right." Angie, on the other hand, actually actively engages in the rites of Aboriginal culture, however unwillingly.

Sharing stories generally means that the stories are about the same thing. One person's story responds to what is raised in another's, so Angie's story already maintains a posited equivalence in the mind of the reader. However, the split between the stories that shows Constantine struggling in a hostile environment dissimilar to the one he expected to enter exposes a gap between the stories he meant to access and the lives that both he and Angie have lived. In addition, the two stories differ in their accompanying imagery. The panels depicting Angie's story illustrate her narrative, and the Aboriginal woman's appear to do the same at first glance. However, the panels depicting the Aboriginal woman's story are also, in a sense, generic representations of what happened in colonization and genocide around the world. Even her own specific story in this context, of her abduction and escape, are general.

To achieve a better understanding of these differences, I return to the first page of the narrative, in which the third-person narrator describes the scene of the pit. Of course, the scene is not described as if it represents a historical occurrence. Instead, the narrator indicates that the scene she is describing is in fact of the dreams of the dead British soldiers, rather than a window into the past. It appears at first to indulge in the trope of a collection of non-Western characters occupying an anachronistic space, in which the indigenous people are merely the backdrop for the Western hero's narrative. However, in the first panel, when the narrator says, "Every night they dig the pit. Dig it for the first time" (121), the *they* clearly refers to the soldiers. In the third panel, the narrator tells us, "They don't want to go down" (121), and the *they* refers instead to the Aborigines. The final two panels emphasize this ambivalence in the use of *they*. They place the reader within the pit in a shared point of view with the Aborigines as they are massacred, but the narrator, rather than remarking on the slaughter as it occurs, remarks instead, "Every night, for two hundred years. Wearing and wearing at the soul, grain by grain, like the sea against the cliffs. Do cliffs never tire?" (121). But which characters are the cliffs in this metaphor? In fact, aside from the Aboriginal woman who speaks with Angie *in the real world of the story*, no Aborigines speak for the duration of the text. The narrator is positioned as a third party, outside of the cast of both Western and indigenous characters, while Constantine enters the dream world of the soldiers and Angie is suspicious of the entire enterprise.

The reader assumes some empathetic responsibility toward those who are killed, rather than those who are doing the killing. But is this empathy ethical in the context of the stories that are later revealed? Where does the narrator stand in relation to the scene? Where does the reader stand in relation to these competing narratives? The first page operates as a sort of prologue, the narrator's preachy opening is dominated by hyperbolic metaphors, stressing, "Do cliffs never *tire?* Do cliffs never *beg* the sea to take them whole?" (emphasis in original). With an opening like this, the reader may expect a simple reiteration of the lessons to be learned from genocide, particularly in regard to the importance of treating other people well. However, this expectation is immediately undercut when it becomes clear that this is a melodramatic account of how the soldiers must feel, enacting the same violence again and again. What we find over the course of the issue is a range of attitudes: an abnormally sympathetic and concerned Constantine, a barely interested Angie, disengaged from the purpose of the trip, and a survivor who is not one. Rather than a narrative of the genocide wherein the white Western characters come to learn about the lost culture led by an indulgent, pedagogical native, Constantine and Angie learn nothing at all.

The final page offers no resolution to the narrative begun on the first page. The story does not return to a perspective of the pit, of the soldiers' repetition of their massacre, of the Aborigines' experience of being mowed down. Instead, the final page shows Angie offering Constantine a cigarette, John telling her he got "the whole story," and Angie making a suggestive comment. The penultimate panel shows Angie and Constantine locked in a passionate embrace. The conclusion of the story arc ends with Constantine and Angie's first kiss, an echo of the traditional conclusion for detective and action films and stories. This choice of ending suggests that "The Pit" resides firmly within conventions that invite sympathy for the suffering of the native while keeping the Western body positioned within a safe zone. However, Constantine's assertion, "I got what I *needed*. The whole story"

(142), stands in clear contrast with the absence of his actual exchange with the Aboriginal woman. Neither he nor the reader has the "whole story," both in fact misunderstand what the story *is*.

The dreaming of the Aboriginals was never accessed in the narratives. The Aboriginal woman related a narrative to Angie of the death of her people, Constantine accessed the dream of the British soldiers, and the Aboriginal woman "told him all that he asked" (141), but the actual space that Constantine was attempting to access through his mimicry of the rituals remains inviolable. By ending the story on a tender note, the implied Carey and Frusin suggest that both the characters and the implied reader have missed the "point" of the story. Discussing the Shadow Dog is abandoned in favor of a romantic interlude, which retrospectively repositions Angie and the Aboriginal woman's narratives and Constantine's experience in the dream world of the dead British soldiers. These passages of the narrative are no longer the path along which one must walk to gain knowledge but in fact constitute the knowledge that was available.

So what does identification contribute in this fictionalized testimony? "The Pit" makes an implicit argument about the limitations of empathetic identification and disputes the claim that boundaries are bridgeable through "telling" alone. Instead, empathy is in this respect a relational, but not equitable, construct. Identification as the vector through which the reader is infected with the trauma experienced by the teller is an unsustainable model, as "The Pit" demonstrates, because "tellability" is not the equivalent of "shareability." Feeling with victims articulating their experience is a necessary outgrowth of literature; many would say that it lies at the very center of the point of literature and, particularly, of fiction. But what characters are open to identification? J. D. Trout discusses a range of studies in *Why Empathy Matters* that demonstrate how

> we help those we know, and those like them, more readily because our experience with them decreases the social distance between us. So we feel more responsibility for their well-being [. . .] At the same time, it is hard to achieve genuine understanding of others' hardships while studying them from a distance. Reading fiction, or narratives about people unlike us, goes only so far. We don't learn the joys of love, the pain of cancer, the frustration of unfair treatment, or the ravages of chronic hunger merely by imagining it. (36–37)

Trout is particularly critiquing our reluctance to act even when we feel for those suffering, arguing that empathy as affect is not enough, but rather must include substantive action on the part of the empathizer. In the case of "The Pit," the implied Carey and Frusin are also critiquing how we "hear" and "see" narratives of suffering. At the historiographic metafictional level, the play between intertexts and Constantine and Angie's disavowal of the real aim of the story suggest that the reader self-reflexively question his own consumption of narratives that deal with extreme experiences. In particular, Carey and Frusin are intent on incorporating recognizable images from difficult periods of American history alongside two important narratives. One is the Aboriginal woman's, which is both familiar because of the interexts and unfamiliar because the genocide has been largely forgotten. The other is Angie's, which, when put alongside the woman's, looks more self-indulgent and privileged than she intends.

Fictionalized testimonies open up possibilities not only for constructing narratives that may not be told, but also for critiquing the nonfictional narratives that are told. "The Pit" clarifies that narratives of atrocity are provisional and also emphasizes the way in which they are often "heard." Rather than seeking a greater understanding of the woman's story, Angie is exhorted to respond with her own. Rather than seeking a more generalized knowledge of the people, Constantine approaches the stories he seeks in a utilitarian fashion. In contrast to nonfiction graphic narrative memoirs of atrocity, "The Pit" is limited in its speech acts. Works like *Maus* and *Persepolis*, autobiographical graphic narratives that deal with violence and social upheaval, are marked by their excess of self-reflexivity. "Talkiness" and self-analysis is an accepted part of the genre. By contrast, historiographic metafictional graphic narratives like *Hellblazer* are often accused of perpetuating many of the social ills critiqued in autographics. However, as "The Pit" makes clear, this charge is often leveled without a close reading of the careful ethical positioning deployed by writers and artists of such comics series. Angie and Constantine's approaches to the narratives they receive are clearly lacking. Neither reflects on the experience of speaking with the Parlevar woman, and in Constantine's ensuing bout with the Shadow Dog in future issues, it becomes increasingly clear that he has misunderstood entirely. The average reader of *Hellblazer* is already cued into this by Constantine's frequent misunderstandings, which often result in the death of his friends.

Taken out of the context of the ethical universe of *Hellblazer* as a series, a reader may be inclined to view it as a perpetuation of stereotypes about "special knowledge" held by indigenous peoples, about the "never again" lessons genocide is supposed to teach, and about the accessibility of trauma through the sharing of narratives. However, the intrusion of the narratorial voice both at a moment of extremity and at a moment of reflective questioning undermines the characters' attempts at knowledge acquisition and also demonstrates how little of the story has been told. This engages the reader with questions about what *can* be told in narratives of genocide and colonial conquest and particularly focuses on how memory and cultural positionality can complicate the project of empathetic engagement with distant experiences. Just like Constantine, we are not always aware that others' subjectivities operate within a network of cultural forces and ethical negotiations similar to, but not the same as, our own. The way in which we seek these stories may be problematic, and the lessons we receive from them may be provisional, but it is difficult to recognize that in the full throes of living. Historical projects related to empathy and cultural guilt are complicated further by temporal and social distance, so that the human becomes nearly unrecognizable through the lens we have adopted since to view experience. Historiographic metafictional graphic narratives' structure highlights these contesting positionalities and produces space for ethical interrogation of the gaze.

CONCLUSION

(THE) MOVING PAST

[. . .] trauma often doesn't make us kinder and more compassionate.
It also has the potential to make us tougher and harsher.

—Shankar Vendantam

THE PURPOSE of this volume has been to illustrate how a particular genre
of graphic narratives prompt readers to engage in complex ways with ethics during the reading process. Because the graphic narrative form has two
features—multiple points of view and the gutter—that are distinct from
other forms, I believe they offer a different "window" into questions surrounding the representation of historical atrocity. Other comics scholars
have discussed at length the representation of violence in autographics,[1]
but given their position in terms of memoir and personal memory, these
works did not engage with the same range of questions about historical
representation and empathy as those that animated my study. In part, I
was curious about the ways in which a fictionalized approach from a person not directly involved as either perpetrator or victim would differ from

---

1. Attention has also been paid to spandex titles. I bracketed this aspect of the
scholarship in part because of concerns over length but also because a spandex title
can also be a historio-metagraphic; these genres are not mutually exclusive. I also
consciously excluded further discussion of spandex titles because the scholarship has
focused on different aspects of the representation of violence than I wished to focus on
in this volume.

212

the representations of those with more intimate knowledge of an atrocity. Furthermore, I was fascinated with the way authors and artists who did not "own" a story in any sense of identity or heritage could craft nuanced works that exposed problematic ideologies, explored willfully forgotten memories, and reincorporated lost voices into the ongoing global conversation about violence. These fictional works were intervening at a new angle into ongoing conversations about the representation of violence; historical truth and facticity; the ethics of the gaze; the tensions between accounts by victims, perpetrators, and bystanders; and the way in which people emotionally engage with accounts of atrocity. Perhaps most importantly, they were intervening in ways that both avoided the objectifying operation of historical accounts concerned primarily with fact and that honored the ways in which the experiences of those who were "there" were unique and separate from their representation.[2]

Point of view is an important term in this conversation, as it is the point of entry for readers in graphic narratives, and focusing on it also emphasizes that all narratives are told from a particular perspective. Graphic narratives, because of their wandering point of view, have the possibility of telling from a complex range of perspectives in the space of one volume without the awkward shifts necessitated by changing narrators in prose. Furthermore, each point of view rendered bears a distinct ethical and affective relationship with the reader. As I mentioned in the introduction, to be prompted to identify with a perpetrator is very different from being prompted to identify with a victim, and neither of those vantage points nor others should necessarily be foreclosed because they may offer a way of engaging with a conflict that necessitates new questions be asked of our own commitment to justice, our own relationship to history, or our own understanding of what it is to think of and feel about violence.

In the preceding chapters, I selected works that would highlight the ethical relationships at stake in point of view, historical representation and memory, and affective relationships. Because of the focus on historical fiction, I began in the recent past, examining atrocities that occurred in living memory for most. Beginning with *Deogratias* signals the importance of covering atrocities beyond those in the United States to illustrate how the historio-metagraphic genre is useful beyond Western concerns. More importantly, it shows the way in which the genre can appeal in productive ways to Western readers in relation to conflicts with which they may be unfamiliar. The Rwandan Genocide is somewhat familiar to Westerners

---

2. For further discussion of this, see Raul Hilberg's "I Was Not There."

because it occurred so recently and because it was so relentlessly covered in the media, but as I argue in the chapter, the media often failed to capture the complexities of the conflict and frequently elided victims and perpetrators, creating an ethical morass in terms of representation. *Deogratias* can be understood in part as a corrective against this elision, as Stassen uses the assumed reader's tendency to identify with the main character in order to comment on the way point of view can undermine our ethical commitment to victims. Arguably the most ethically complex of the graphic narratives covered in this book, *Deogratias* highlights the potential ambivalence of viewing images of atrocity and the empathetic connection they may produce.

In the second chapter on *Watchmen*, inarguably the most well-known of the texts I covered in this book, I sought to frame historio-metagraphics as not as a new genre but a lens already embedded in many of our discussions in comics scholarship. The legitimacy of studying Moore and Gibbons' masterwork is unquestionable, and my intervention offered another way of framing questions about historicity and the representation of violence in this text. Furthermore, beginning with *Watchmen* provided the opportunity to illustrate how a graphic novel with an existing body of scholarship and a well-established history of appealing to readers at both intellectual and affective levels could be productively placed in conversation with questions about historical representation, point of view, and feminist theory.

The third chapter moved from a contemporary cast of predominantly white characters in a mostly American landscape to a mostly contemporary cast of mostly Native characters in an American landscape.[3] Building on the concept of disavowed knowledge and history immanent in the first chapter, my reading of *Scalped* highlighted questions about authenticity and representation in relation to both stereotypes and marginalized historical accounts. By focusing specifically on passages that variously represented an event that was both a personal memory for several characters and was based on an actual historical episode, the events of which are still in question, I sought to question how the tensions between various remembrances were a commentary on the negotiation of historical truth. While the first chapter focused on the perspectives left out of an event of private violence and the public violence that may marginalize even pervasive private violence, the second chapter highlighted how the historical record may fail to capture the complexity of cultural and individual memory.

---

3. My article "Jason Aaron's *Scalped*, Historiographic Metafiction, and Authenticity," which appeared in John Cameron's *Narrative is the Essence of History*, examined its historiographic metafictional elements.

The tension between registers of memory and enshrined historical accounts carried over into the fourth chapter, which dealt with a further level of complexity in terms of temporality. The first two chapters dealt with stories placed in the near-past, while *Bayou* is set in the early twentieth century. Though *Scalped* deals with the distant past, the bulk of the narrative concerns the present, while *Bayou* is set wholly in 1933 Mississippi (and the alternative world of the bayou, of course). Focusing more specifically on the way in which the individual is embedded in cultural memory, this chapter also explored a period less immediately legible to contemporary audiences. This issue with legibility is in itself a metacommentary on the way in which the lynching era is a disavowed aspect of American history, but moreover, Love's use of events from the slavery era as eruptions of memory in the present insists that whether or not a historical event is memorialized, it still affects the present.

The ambivalence of the first chapter is also taken up in the final chapter, which along with being geographically distant from the assumed audience, also takes up an atrocity that is so far removed from our contemporary context as to be virtually forgotten. *Hellblazer*'s "The Pit" resurrects a Tasmanian Aborigine to tell the story of the genocide of her people, which, while problematic in terms of co-opting another's story, is also an illustration of the potential for historio-metagraphics to "fill in" areas in the historical record that have been annihilated. Furthermore, my reading illustrates also that the language—the textual component—is vital in historio-metagraphics, as the Aboriginal woman only tells Constantine what he asks for, highlighting the way in which some stories, and therefore some knowledge, is left outside of the frame. This is also a metacommentary on the consumption of texts about atrocity, in which the atrocity, to make narrative sense to a reader who did not experience it, must necessarily be shaped by forces outside of the context. The "truth" is always shaped by what is "tellable" and what is "hearable," as Greenspan warns us.

By arranging chapters that moved backward from the relatively contemporary, I sought to illustrate how historio-metagraphics were a highly flexible genre with a range of possible uses. Furthermore, I chose works that explicitly engage with the question of what is offered by specific perspectives and by this relationship between proximity and distance, used texts that visually depict horrific events. My interest in genocide and sexual violence stems from questions about the ethical representation of extreme experiences: to what extent is the "unrepresentable" a coded term for the real ethical demands of empathy, namely that to feel as another person feels is an immense intellectual, emotional, and experiential undertaking?

To what extent are we able to empathize, identify with, or at least engage with experiences different from our own, and what type of engagement best prompts social action? In addition, I felt that it was vital to reflect on works that compromised the reader's ethical integrity as they identified with certain characters and to examine works that overtly reflect on what it means to identify with a character in situations of extremity.

There are many other historiographic metafictional graphic narratives that deserve similar attention. A number of graphic novels fall neatly into this category, including Will Eisner's *To the Heart of the Storm*, an account of the era surrounding World War II that Eisner himself described as "fact and fiction [. . .] blended with selective recall" (xi). A graphic novel more clearly distinct from autographics, and showing some of the pitfalls of historio-metagraphics, is Craig Thompson's recent work *Habibi*, which follows two characters through a disturbing present-day Orientalist fantasy that intersperses the Koran alongside of grotesque indulgences in racism and sexism. Conversely, Jason Lute's masterwork *Berlin* trilogy carefully represents the waning days of the Weimar Republic. It is a broad genre, but DC's Vertigo imprint has perhaps added the greatest range of titles. Vertigo has published a number of historiographic metafictional graphic novels like *Pride of Baghdad*, which recounts the experiences of the lions that escaped from the Iraq zoo, and *Incognegro*, Mat Johnson's fictional account of Walter White's decision to "pass" in order to document Southern lynching. Vertigo also boasts the broadest range of long-running historio-metagraphic titles. Alan Moore can be credited with bringing this type of narrative into wide circulation with *Watchmen*, *V for Vendetta*, and *Swamp Thing*, but a number of writers and artists have taken up the construct and provided their own innovations. Garth Ennis and Steve Dillon's *Preacher* is a landmark example, which follows Jesse Custer across America as he searches for God, the plot foregrounded against the heritage of Southern racism, the Vietnam War, and a variety of other historical and cultural intertexts. Warren Ellis's superb *Transmetropolitan* was also published under the Vertigo imprint and follows Spider Jerusalem, a latter-day Hunter S. Thompson, through the streets of the City, a futuristic version of New York City. The range of topics alone is remarkable,[4] but the longer-running series are important in part because of the vast array of intertexts that are included. Furthermore, all of the titles mentioned above, and many others, are preoccupied with marginalized experiences and explicitly examine perspective in terms of both

---

4. Other historio-metagraphic series titles from Vertigo include *The Unwritten*, *99 Days*, *Adventures in the Rifle Brigade*, *DMZ*, *American Virgin*, *Army at Love*, *Doom Patrol*, *Fables*, *Loveless*, *Northlanders*, *The Books of Magic*, and *The Exterminators*.

form and content. Establishing the range of historio-metagraphics is critical to the worth of the term, but how that term plays out within the pages of a work is what makes it valuable to the exploration of ethical relationships within and between texts.

Briefly, I would like to return to Denise Mina's *Hellblazer: The Red Right Hand*, which was discussed in the introduction. The story follows Constantine as he, Steve Evans, Chris Cole, and a few others race to defuse the empathy engine that is infecting Glasgow residents with the feelings of their friends and neighbors. In the final issues in the series, Constantine visits the Third Place in order to find out more about the ruler, and the city continues to spin out of control.

When Constantine asks the Master of the Third Place why he would choose empathy to bring him more souls, the monster responds, "It amplifies the sensations. Gives a new flavor to the flesh of my sheep. They crave nothingness. As much as those with no connection. Those who feel everything. The skinless. They come willingly" (94). The Master feeds off of emotions, so the empathy epidemic seasons his meals with a greater variety of emotions than the nihilism normally associated with suicide. Empathy, rather than a pathway to understanding, is instead a flavor booster which may be consumed. The emphasis here should be on the *consumption* of emotions and experiences, a metacommentary on the process whereby the reader takes in the suffering of these fictional and largely faceless characters. The reader is connected with Constantine, Evans, and a few others in this work, but the bulk of the suffering is distributed among people who are not given names. The bodies depicted in panels throughout *The Red Right Hand* are not identified or given stories, and the souls shown fleeing those bodies in Glasgow and lining up to be consumed by the Master of the Third Place are not even granted distinct facial features.

Ultimately, the cure for the empathy epidemic comes through a specific series of visual and verbal relationships. The first of these is when the characters come across a gallery devoted to the work of Joan Eardley, a Glasgow-based painter whose later work consists of portraits of street children of the local slums. In spite of the "coarse" nature of her subject matter, Eardley's work is characterized by a lushness of color and brush stroke, the expected vulgarity of common people strongly countered by a blocky, rich style akin to Gaugin. Chris Cole, an artist himself, remarks that the paintings are "Beauty from the gutter" (68). The spell that blocks the infectious empathy begins to wear off as the group stands vigil, but they discover that the negative effects can be counteracted by positivity, including gazing at an Eardley painting. The intertextual Eardley reference recalls again how important the object of the gaze is to the gazer. Furthermore, the reader is cued into an even more complex relationship with the image. As Evans holds a painting before the eyes of a woman suffering the negative effects of empathy, another character tells her to "Look at how much she loved those kids" (79), demonstrating that, in this case, it is not the object of the gaze but rather the *producer* of that object who is the focus of empathy. In this scene, the character affected by empathy weeps as she looks outward, slightly to the left of the reader, her gaze ostensibly directed at the painting but depicted as an observation of something outside of the panel and beyond the comic itself.

The Praexis demons are held at bay using pornography, long enough for Evans to get on television and put out a call for positive people to come into the hot zone of empathy. The streets of Glasgow are flooded with devoutly religious people from a variety of faith traditions, upsetting Constantine because, as he says, "They're not here to help. Most of them are here to prove that their religion is the right one" (116). Evans, however, tells Constantine that this is fine because "there is no such thing as selflessness. Self-seeking is a condition of goodness" (116). As he explains this, the reader is alternately positioned as sharing Constantine's point of view and being part of the crowd of the pious surrounding Evans, suggesting that the readers are a part of this throng.

In the final tally, the good thoughts and prayers are not enough. A spike of positive energy from the soldiers guarding the city thwarts the negative effects of empathy. This positive energy comes not from religious devotion but rather from the outcome of the World Cup quarterfinals of England and Portugal. Evans and Constantine assumed that the soldiers were English, and at the moment Portugal secures the victory, those left in the city brace themselves for the end. But this assumption was incorrect; the soldiers were Scottish and were rooting against England from the beginning. The source of their joy is in negative feelings for another. However, it is too late for Cole, who projects himself into the Third Place as he dies. Cole is able to defeat the Master of the Third Place, not through empathy or emotion but through imagination, recreating the Third Place as he sees fit. Imagination is the cure for this formulation of empathy. In *The Red Right Hand*, empathy is simply being bludgeoned with the images and emotions of another, rather than a complicated ethical maneuver of imagining a situation *as another would feel*. The treatment for the epidemic is not the annihilation of emotion or connection with others; instead, it is a more robust engagement with different experiences, one which distinguishes and allows for a variety of situations and perspectives. The connection between images of violence, empathy, and the gaze provides the resonance in *Hellblazer: The Red Right Hand*. It is not empathy itself that is the problem but rather that empathy prior to this was largely unimaginable. This surplus of affect is directed not toward outward social good but inward, toward a vast gulf of shame for not recognizing the surrounding unhappiness.

My concern with empathy arises not simply from its ethical ambivalence but also from the way in which it is leveraged in contemporary culture. There are the "empty" empathetic gestures Kaplan explicates, situations in which one has insufficient knowledge to truly feel from another perspective, while there is also the emptiness of prepackaged "empathy" seen in tear-jerker commercials, in which our propensity to feel for one another is leveraged to sell a product. Furthermore, as LaCapra notes, empathy can be seen as an enemy to objectivity,[5] while Goldie notes that empathy is not necessarily positive.[6] Indeed, at the historical and emotional levels of my argument, I hold with Goldie's contention that "*intelligibility can outstrip imaginability*" (*The Emotions* 209, emphasis in original). He asserts, "It is when our imagination fails us like this that we are particularly inclined to resort to the blanket, default use of trait terms, especially morally loaded ones" (209), wherein we cannot imagine how a "good" person is capable of a horrific act. Our failure of imagination is an ethical problem: that we cannot imagine the scenario in which a good person commits an atrocity is the first step in a range of disavowals. In terms of sexual violence, this takes the predictable form of victim blaming or absolute refusal to believe that an otherwise "good" man is capable of rape. Regarding the history of American Indians, it can be seen in our unwillingness to contemplate genocide as a part of American heritage. The rejection of the lingering effects of slavery and racism on African Americans is partly an attempt to understand ourselves (we assumed white readers) as "good," because the "good" cannot be complicit. The Rwandan genocide is distorted from a horrific act of planned mass violence that could have been averted if Western powers intervened into another example of "Africa as usual." The genocide of the Tasmanian Aborigines is so long ago, and we know so much better now.

---

5. In *Writing History Writing Trauma,* LaCapra argues that "One reason for the eclipse of concern with empathy was the relation of the ideal of objectivity to the professionalization of historiography along with the tendency to conflate objectivity with objectification" (38).

6. It is worth noting that Goldie outlines a number of emotions that are often confused for empathy and that only sympathy "involve[s] motivation to alleviate the other's difficulties" (*The Emotions* 215).

Historio-metagraphics expose the complicated ethical claims the past lays on the present, and they do so in part through what Hatfield called the tension between "codes of signification" (36) and in part through the space of imaginative possibility metaphorically opened by the gutter. How we collaborate in the reading process is a significant part of the magic of comics, but it also places ethical and intellectual demands on the reader that are different from other forms of art and literature. Furthermore, the fictionalization of history also elaborates a complicated ethical realm. Hutcheon insists that "Postmodern fiction suggests that to re-write or to re-present the past in fiction and in history is, in both cases, to open it up to the present, to prevent it from being conclusive and teleological" (*A Poetics of Postmodernism* 110), and comics open history to the present in both image and text, exposing the tension at stake in these forms of representation. At the close of *Regarding the Pain of Others,* Sontag describes "Dead Troops Talk," Jeff Walls' transparency of Russian soldiers in Afghanistan in 1986. "Engulfed by the image, which is so accusatory, one could fantasize that the soldiers might turn and talk to us," she writes, going on to ask, "Why should they seek our gaze? What would they have to say to us?" (125). These questions, also accusatory, lead Sontag to assert, "Can't understand, can't imagine. That's what every soldier, and every journalist and aid worker and independent observer who has put in time under fire, and had the luck to elude the death that struck down others nearby, stubbornly feels. And they are right" (126).

The "rightness" of that feeling, however, does not stop us from seeking to understand, seeking to imagine, seeking to connect with those who have faced extremity, whether or not they survived it. On one hand, we are truth seekers; we want to know what an experience was "really" like; we want to understand. We're prompted in part by our desire to help and in part by our desire to avert future disasters. On the other hand, there is a mystique of violence that maintains a hold over the human imagination that is perhaps less savory than our altruistic impulses.[7] While it may be true that these experiences remain remote, historio-metagraphics give us an opportunity to both access a form of that truth and to reflect on the ways in which it is—and perhaps should be—deficient. After all, as many of the works I survey implicitly argue, to be able to imagine is to collaborate in the violence. However, their ethical argument is not neatly summarized in a pat phrase about the dangers of emotional overinvestment or a tawdry account of audiences reading for a sordid thrill. At the moment we

---

7. Julia Kristeva's *The Powers of Horror* admirably outlines the ways in which we are both repelled by and attracted to the revolting.

think that imagining could be its own little violence, we are confronted in graphic narratives also with what it is *not* to imagine, however imperfectly: an eternal present, in which the atrocities of history and (hopefully) a better future are equally illegible, obscured by the inability to see the connections between word and image, between fiction and truth, between thought and action, and between past and possibility.

WORKS CITED

Aaron, Jason, and R. M. Guera. *Scalped — Casino Boogie.* Vol. 2. New York: DC Vertigo, 2008. Print.

Abumrad, Jad, Robert Krulwich, and Karim Nader. "Memory and Forgetting." Audio blog post. *RadioLab.* WNYC, 2010. Web. 05 Jun 2016.

"An Act to Provide for the Allotment of Lands in Severalty to Indians on the Various Reservations (General Allotment Act or Dawes Act)." Statutes at Large 24, NADP Document A1887. Web. 388–91. 20 Dec. 2014.

Allen, James, and John Littlefield. *Without Sanctuary: Photographs and Postcards of Lynching in America.* Last modified 28 Mar. 2000. Vienna: James Allen and John Littlefield, 2000.

Ankersmit, F. R. *Historical Representation: Cultural Memory in the Present.* Stanford: Stanford UP, 2001. Print.

Bal, Mieke. *Narratology: Introduction to the Theory of Narrative.* 3rd ed. Toronto: U of Toronto P, 2009. Print.

Barta, Tony. "Sorry, and Not Sorry, in Australia: How the apology to the stolen generations buried a history of genocide." *Journal of Genocide Research* 10.2 (2008): 201–14. Web.

Bergen, Benjamin. *Louder Than Words: The New Science of How the Mind Makes Meaning.* New York: Basic Books, 2012. Print.

Berntsen, Dorthe, and David C. Rubin, eds. *Understanding Autobiographical Memory: Theories and Approaches.* Cambridge: Cambridge UP, 2012. Print.

Bernstein, Michael Andre. "The Schindler's List Effect." *American Scholar* 63.3 (Summer 1994): 429–32. Print.

Bhabha, Homi. *The Location of Culture.* New York: Routledge, 1994. Print.

Blake, Brandy Ball. "*Watchmen* as Trauma Fiction." *ImageText* 5.1 (2009): n. pag. Web. 4 Apr. 2011. Web.

Brown, Cecil. *Stagolee Shot Billy.* Cambridge: Harvard UP, 2004.

Brunet, Alain, Scott P. Orr, Jacques Tremblay, Kate Robertson, Karim Nader, Roger K. Pitman. "Effect of Post-Retrieval Propranolol on Psychophysiologic Responding

During Subsequent Script-Driven Traumatic Imagery in Post-Traumatic Stress Disorder." *Journal of Psychiatric Research* 42.6 (2008): 503–6.

Carey, Mike, Marcelo Frusin, Tim Bradstreet, Lee Loughridge, and Clem Robbins. "Third Worlds." *Hellblazer—Black Flowers*. New York: DC Comics, 2005. 122–44. Print.

Carney, Sean. "The Tides of History: Alan Moore's Historiographic Vision." *ImageTexT: Interdisciplinary Comics Studies* 2.2 (2006). Print.

Caruth, Cathy. *Trauma: Explorations in Memory*. Baltimore: Johns Hopkins UP, 1995. Print.

Chaney, Michael. "Not Just a Theme: Transnationalism and Form in Visual Narratives of U.S. Slavery." *Transnational Perspectives on Graphic Narratives: Comics at the Crossroads*. Ed. Daniel Stein, Shane Denson, and Christina Meyer. London: Bloomsbury, 2014.

Chute, Hillary. *Disaster Drawn: Visual Witness, Comics, and Documentary Form*. Cambridge: Harvard UP, 2016. Print.

———. *Graphic Women: Life Narrative & Contemporary Comics*. New York: Columbia UP, 2010. Print.

Coates, Ta Nehisi. *Between the World and Me*. New York City: Spiegel & Grau, 2015.

Cohn, Neil. "The Limits of Time and Transitions: Challenges to Theories of Sequential Image Comprehension." *Studies in Comics* 1.1 (2010): 127–47. Print.

Coleridge, Samuel Taylor. "Kubla Khan." *Poetry Foundation*. Poetry Foundation, n.d. Web. 30 Dec. 2014.

Conway, Martin. "Memory and the Self." *Journal of Memory and Language* 53 (2005): 594–628.

Cove, John J. *What the Bones Say: Tasmanian Aborigines, Science and Domination*. Ottawa: Carleton UP, 1995. Print.

Dallaire, Romeo. *Shake Hands with the Devil: The Failure of Humanity in Rwanda*. New York: Random House Canada, 2003. Print.

Dębiec, Jacek, and Joseph E. LeDoux. "Noradrenergic Signaling in the Amygdala Contributes to the Reconsolidation of Fear Memory." *Annals of the New York Academy of Sciences* 1071.1 (2006): 521–24.

Deitrich, Bryan D. "The Human Stain: Chaos and the Rage for Order in *Watchmen*." *Extrapolation* 50.1 (2009): 120–44. Print.

Diagnostic and Statistical Manual of Mental Disorders. 5th ed. Arlington: American Psychiatric Association, 2013. Print.

Dias, Brian D., and Kerry J. Ressler. "Parental Olfactory Experience Influences Behavior and Neural Structure in Subsequent Generations." *Nature Neuroscience* 17 (2014): 89–96. Print.

Eisner, Will. *Comics and Sequential Art*. Tamarac: Poorhouse, 1985. Print.

———. *To the Heart of the Storm*. New York: W.W. Norton & Company, 1991.

Eyerman, Ron. "The Past in the Present: Culture and the Transmission of Memory." *Acta Sociologica* 47.2 (2004): 159–69. Web. 15 Jun. 2014.

Fanon, Frantz. *Black Skin, White Masks*. New York: Grove Press, 1967. Print.

Fernyhough, Charles. *Pieces of Light: How the New Science of Memory Illuminates the Stories We Tell About Our Pasts*. New York: Harper, 2014. Print.

Finkleman, Paul. *Encyclopedia of African American History 1619–1865*. Oxford: Oxford UP, 2006. Print.

Flanagan, Richard. "Tasmanian Aborigines: The Lost Tribe." *The Guardian*. Guardian News and Media. 13 Oct. 2002. Web. 15 May 2014.

Forbes, Jack. "Blood Quantum: A Relic of Racism and Termination." *Native Intelligence*. Weyanoke.org. 2000. Web. 25 Jul. 2014.

Francis, Gregory. "Too Much Success for Recent Groundbreaking Epigenetic Experiments." *Genetics* 198.2 (2014): 449–51. PMC. Web. 18 May 2016.

Fuller, Alexandra, and Aaron Huey. "Pine Ridge: In the Shadow of Wounded Knee." *National Geographic*. National Geographic, Aug. 2012. Web. 28 Dec. 2014.

Genette, Gerard. *Narrative Discourse: An Essay in Method*. Trans. Jane E. Lewin. Ithaca: Cornell UP, 1980. Print.

Gibbs, Anna. "After Affect: Sympathy, Synchrony, and Mimetic Communication." *The Affect Theory Reader*. Durham: Duke UP, 2010.

Gibson, Andrew. *Postmodernity, Ethics, and the Novel: From Leavis to Levinas*. New York: Routledge, 1999. Print.

Giroux, Henri. *The Violence of Organized Forgetting: Thinking Beyond America's Disimagination Machine*. San Francisco: City Lights, 2014.

———. "The Violence of Forgetting." *The New York Times*. 20 Jun. 2016. Web. 21 Jun. 2016.

Goldie, Peter. *The Emotions: A Philosophical Exploration*. Oxford: Oxford UP, 2000. Print.

———. *The Mess Inside: Narrative, Emotion, and the Mind*. Oxford: Oxford UP, 2012.

Good, M. I. "The Reconstruction of Early Childhood Trauma: Fantasy, Reality, and Verification." *Journal of the American Psychoanalytic Association* 42.1 (2016): 79–101.

Gourevitch, Phillip. *We Wish to Inform You That Tomorrow We Will Be Killed With Our Families: Stories from Rwanda*. New York: Picador, 1999.

Graff, Gilda. "The Intergenerational Trauma of Slavery and Its Aftermath." *Journal of Psychohistory* 41.3 (Winter 2014): 181–97.

Gregg, Melissa, and Gregory J. Seigworth, eds. *The Affect Theory Reader*. Durham: Duke UP, 2010. Print.

Greenspan, Henry. *On Listening to Holocaust Survivors: Beyond Testimony*. Vadnais Heights: Paragon House, 2010.

Grinde, Donald A. "Taking the Indian Out of the Indian: U.S. Policies of Ethnocide Through Education." *Wicazo Sa Review* (Fall 2004): 25–32. Print.

Groensteen, Thierry. *The System of Comics*. Jackson: UP of Mississippi, 2007. Print.

Hanley, Tim. "Gendercrunching June 2014—Including Nationality and Ethnicity at The Big Two." *Bleeding Cool Comic Book, Movie, TV News*. 28 Sept. 2016. Web. 08 Oct. 2016.

Hatfield, Charles. *Alternative Comics: An Emerging Literature*. Jackson: UP of Mississippi, 2005. Print.

———. "Graphic Interventions: Form and Argument in Contemporary Comics." PhD diss., University of Connecticut, 2000.

Hayter, David. "An Open Letter from David Hayter." *watchmencomicmovie.com*. 11 Mar. 2009. Web. 10 Apr. 2011.

Hilberg, Raul. "I Was Not There." *Writing and the Holocaust.* Ed. Berel Lang. New York: Holmes & Meier, 1988.

Hilsum, Lindsey. "Reporting Rwanda: The Media and the Aid Agencies." *The Media and the Rwanda Genocide.* Ed. Allan Thompson. London: Pluto, 2007. 238–41. Print.

Horstkotte, Silke, and Nancy Pedri. "Focalization in Graphic Narrative." *Narrative* 19.3 (2011): 330–57. *Project Muse.* Web. 25 Nov. 2012.

Hutcheon, Linda. "Historiographic Metafiction: Parody and the Intertextuality of History." *Intertextuality and Contemporary American Fiction.* Ed. P. O'Donnell, and Robert Con Davis. Baltimore: Johns Hopkins University Press, 1989. 3–32.

———. *A Poetics of Postmodernism: History, Theory, Fiction.* New York: Routledge, 1988. Print.

Huyssen, Andreas. *Twilight Memories: Marking Time in a Culture of Amnesia.* New York: Routledge, 1994. Print.

Iacoboni, Marco, and Jonah Lehrer. "The Mirror Neuron Revolution: Explaining What Makes Humans Social." *Scientific American.* Scientific American, 1 July 2008. Web. 2 July 2016.

Kansteiner, Wulf. "Genealogy of a Category Mistake: A Critical Intellectual History of the Cultural Trauma Metaphor." *Rethinking History* 8.2 (2004): 193–221. Print.

Kaplan, E. Ann. *Trauma Culture: The Politics of Terror and Loss in Media and Literature.* New Brunswick: Rutgers UP, 2005. Print.

Keen, Suzanne. *Empathy and the Novel.* Oxford: Oxford UP, 2010. Print.

———. "Fast Tracks to Narrative Empathy: Anthropomorphism in Graphic Narratives." *SubStance* 40.1 (2011): 135–55. Print.

Kilner, J. M., and R. N. Lemon. "What We Know Currently About Mirror Neurons." *Current Biology* 23.23 (2 Dec. 2013). Web. 20 Jun. 2014.

Kukkonen, Karin. *Contemporary Comics Storytelling.* Lincoln: U of Nebraska P, 2013. Print.

———. "Space, Time, and Causality in Graphic Narratives: An Embodied Approach." *From Comic Strips to Graphic Novels.* Ed. Danielle Stein and Jan-Noel Thon. Boston: De Gruyter, 2013. Print.

LaCapra, Dominick. *Writing History, Writing Trauma.* Baltimore: Johns Hopkins UP, 2014. Print.

Langer, Lawrence. *The Holocaust and the Literary Imagination.* New Haven: Yale UP, 1977.

Lefèvre, Pascal. "Recovering Sensuality in Comics Theory." *International Journal of Comic Art* 1.1 (1999): 140–49.

Leys, Ruth. *Trauma: A Genealogy.* Chicago: U of Chicago P, 2000. Print.

Love, Jeremy, and Patrick Morgan. *Bayou Volume 1.* New York: Zuda, 2009.

Love, Jeremy, and Patrick Morgan. *Bayou Volume 2.* New York: Zuda, 2011.

Lyotard, Jean-François. *The Postmodern Condition: A Report on Knowledge.* Minneapolis: U of Minnesota P, 1984.

MacDonald, Katharine Polak. "Jason Aaron's *Scalped,* Historiographic Metafiction, and of Authenticity." *Narrative is the Essence of History: Essays on the Historical Novel.* Ed. John Cameron. Newcastle upon Tyne: Cambridge Scholars Publishing, 2012.

Mamdani, Mahmood. *When Victims Become Killers: Colonialism, Nativism, and the Genocide in Rwanda.* Princeton: Princeton UP, 2001. Print.

Matson-Green, Vicki maikutena. "Tarenorerer [Walyer] (c. 1800–1831)." *Australian Dictionary of Biography.* Web. 2 Jun 2013.

McCloud, Scott. *Understanding Comics: The Invisible Art.* New York: Harper Perennial, 1993. Print.

McIntosh, Ian S. *Aboriginal Reconciliation and the Dreaming.* Needham Heights: Allyn & Bacon, 2000. Print.

McNally, Richard J. *Remembering Trauma.* Cambridge: Belknap, 2005.

Meister, Mark, and Ann Burnett. "Rhetorical Exclusion in the Trial of Leonard Peltier." *American Indian Quarterly* 28.3/4 (2004): 719–42. Web. 16 Oct. 2015.

Michaels, Walter Benn. *Our America: Nativism, Modernism, Pluralism.* Durham: Duke UP, 1997. Print.

Mikkonen, Kai. "Presenting Minds in Graphic Narratives." *Partial Answers* 6.2 (2008): 301–21. Print.

Mills, Charles. *The Racial Contract.* Ithaca: Cornell UP, 1999. Print.

Mina, Denise, Leonardo Manco, Lee Loughridge, and Jared K. Fletcher. *Hellblazer: The Red Right Hand.* New York: DC Vertigo, 2007. Print.

Mina, Denise, and Leonardo Manco. *Hellblazer: Empathy is the Enemy.* New York: DC Vertigo, 2006. Print.

Moore, Alan, and Dave Gibbons. *Watchmen.* New York: DC, 1987. Print.

Moses, A. Dirk. *Empire, Colony, Genocide: Conquest, Occupation, and Subaltern Resistance in World History.* New York City: Berghahn Books, 2008.

Müller-Funk, Wolfgang. *The Architecture of Modern Culture: Toward a Narrative Cultural Theory.* Berlin: De Gruyter, 2012. Print.

———. "On a Narratology of Cultural and Collective Memory." *Journal of Narrative Theory* 33.2 (2003): 207–27. *Project MUSE.*

Mulvey, Laura. "Visual Pleasure and Narrative Cinema." *Film Theory and Criticism: Introductory Readings.* Ed. Leo Braudy and Marshall Cohen. New York: Oxford UP, 1999. 833–44.

Nietzsche, Fredrich. *Beyond Good and Evil: Prelude to a Philosophy of the Future.* Mineola: Dover Thrift, 1997.

Ngai, Sianne. *Ugly Feelings.* Cambridge: Harvard UP, 2007. Print.

Olney, James. *Memory and Narrative: The Weave of Life Writing.* Chicago: U of Chicago P, 1998. Print.

Paik, Peter Y. *From Utopia to Apocalypse: Science Fiction and the Politics of Catastrophe.* Minneapolis: U of Minnesota P, 2010. Print.

Planty, Michael, Lynn Langton, Christopher Krebs, Marcus Berzofsky, and Hope Smiley-Mcdonald. "Female Victims of Sexual Violence, 1994–2010." PsycEXTRA Dataset (n.d.): n. pag. Bureau of Justice Statistics, U.S. Department of Justice, Mar. 2013. Web. June 2016.

Phelan, James. *Living to Tell About It: A Rhetorics and Ethics of Character Narration.* Ithaca: Cornell UP, 2005. Print.

"The Pine Ridge Shootout." *Time* 105.1 (1975): 16. Web. 16 Oct. 2015.

Rancière, Jacques. *The Emancipated Spectator*. Trans. Gregory Elliott. London: Verso, 2009. Print.

———. *The Future of the Image*. New York: Verso, 2009. Print.

Roskis, Edgar. "A Genocide Without Images: White Film Noirs." *The Media and the Rwanda Genocide*. Ed. Allan Thompson. London: Pluto, 2007. 238–41. Print.

Roth, H. Ling. *The Aborigines of Tasmania*. Halifax: F. King & Sons, 1856. Print.

Rothberg, Michael. *Multidirectional Memory: Remembering the Holocaust in the Age of Decolonization*. Stanford: Stanford UP, 2009. Print.

Royal, Derek Parker. "Introduction: Coloring America: Multi-Ethnic Engagements with Graphic Narrative." *MELUS* 32.3 (2007): 7–22. Web. 30 Jun. 2015.

Scarborough, Dorothy, and Ola Lee Gulledge. *On the Trail of Negro Folk Songs*. Cambridge: Harvard UP, 1925.

"Scope of the Problem: Statistics | RAINN." *RAINN*. Rape Abuse & Incest National Network, n.d. Web. July 2016.

Singer, Marc. "'Black Skins' and White Masks: Comic Books and the Secret of Race." *African American Review* 36.1 (2002): 107–19. Web. 15 Jul. 2014.

Smolen, Lynn Atkinson ,and Ruth A. Oswald *Multicultural Literature and Response: Affirming Diverse Voices*. Santa Barbara: Libraries Unlimited, 2010.

Sontag, Susan. *Regarding the Pain of Others*. New York: Picador, 2004.

Spruhan, Paul. "The Origins, Current Status, and Future Prospects of Blood Quantum as the Definition of Membership in the Navajo Nation." *South Dakota Law Review* 51.1 (2008): 23–44. Web. 12 Dec. 2014.

Stassen, J. P. *Deogratias*. Trans. Alexis Siegel. New York: First Second, 2006. Print.

Stromberg, Joseph. *Lands of the Lakota: Policy, Culture, and Land Use on the Pine Ridge Reservation*. Saarbrucken: LAP LAMBERT Academic Publishing, 2013. Print.

Sutherlin, Matthew. "Down the Rabbit Hole." *Visual Arts Research*. 38.1 (2012): 11–33. Print.

Szabo, Erika. "An Analysis of *Watchmen*: Symmetry and the Tragic Flaw." *Destroy the Cyb. Org.* 17 Aug. 2008. Web. 10 Mar. 2011.

Taylor, Christopher C. *Sacrifice as Terror: The Rwandan Genocide of 1994*. Oxford: Berg, 1999. Print.

Toppin Bazin, Nancy, and Marilyn Dallman Seymour, eds. *Conversations with Nadine Gordimer*. Jackson: UP of Mississippi, 1990. Print.

Trout, J. D. *Why Empathy Matters: The Science and Psychology of Better Judgment*. New York: Penguin, 2009. Print.

Truman, Jennifer L., and Rachel E. Morgan. U.S. Department of Justice Office of Justice Programs, Bureau of Statistics. *Criminal Victimization, 2015*. Web. 20 Nov. 2014.

U.S. Department of the Interior, Bureau of Indian Affairs. *2005 American Indian Population and Labor Force Report*. Web. 16 Jan. 2014.

U.S. Commission on Civil Rights. *A Quiet Crisis: Federal Funding and Unmet Needs in Indian Country*. Mary Frances Berry et al. Jul. 2003. Web. 20 Jan. 2014.

van Duin, Lieke. "Anansi as Classical Hero." *Journal of Caribbean Literatures.* 5.1 (Summer 2007): 33–42. Print.

Varga, Donna, and Rhoda Zuk. "Golliwogs and Teddy Bears: Embodied Racism in Children's Popular Culture." *Journal of Popular Culture* 46.3 (2013): 647–71. Web. 27 Sept. 2015.

Vetlesen, Arne Johan. "Genocide: A Case for the Responsibility of the Bystander." *Journal of Peace Research* 38.4 (July 2001): 519. Web.

Weissman, Gary. *Fantasies of Witnessing: Postwar Efforts to Experience the Holocaust.* Ithaca: Cornell UP, 2004.

Whitlock, Gillian. "Autographics: The Seeing 'I' of Comics." *Modern Fiction Studies* 52.4 (2006): 965–79. Web. 03 Mar. 2013.

Whitted, Qiana. "Sound and Silence in the Jim Crow South." *The Hooded Utilitarian.* The Hooded Utilitarian. 19 Apr. 2013. Web. 01 Apr. 2015.

Winerman, Lea. "The Mind's Mirror." *apa.org.* American Psychological Association. Oct. 2005. Web. 1 July 2016.

Witek, Joseph. *Comic Books as History: The Narrative Art of Jack Jackson, Art Spiegelman, and Harvey Pekar.* Jackson: UP of Mississippi, 1989. Print.

Žižek, Slavoj. *Enjoy Your Symptom!* New York: Routledge, 2007. Print.

INDEX

Aaron, Jason. See *Scalped* (Aaron and Guera)

Aborigines of Tasmania, The (Roth), 179–80

adventure comics, 112

African American folklore, 164–68, 172–75

African Americans and intergenerational trauma. See *Bayou* (Love)

Alexie, Sherman, 111, 118

American Indian Movement (AIM), 114, 115, 117, 130

American Indians: boarding schools and racism, 121; Dawes Act and, 120–21; Pine Ridge Reservation and AIM, history of, 114–19; representations of, 111–14. See also *Scalped* (Aaron and Guera)

Anansi and the firefly (folktale), 166–68

animals: *Deogratias*, 46–47, 60–64; in trickster tales, 165–68; *Watchmen*, 93–94; zoomorphic tradition, 46–47

Ankersmit, F. R., 6, 6n6, 113

Annan, Kofi, 37

Arendt, Hannah, 7

art, unreflective consumption of, 52

atrocity. *See specific works*

authenticity: *Bayou* and, 145–46; *Hellblazer* and, 187, 189; historio-metagraphics vs. autographics and, 35; Native American identity and, 115–

16, 119, 134–38, 140; performance of racial identity and, 113

autographics: definition and study of, 3–4; ethics in narrative and, 78–79; historio-metagraphics compared to, 4–5, 29–30, 35, 210; talkiness and self-analysis in, 210

Bal, Mieke, 26

Barrows, Paul, 146n2

Barta, Tony, 180–81, 181n1

Bayou (Love): Billy Glass and the butterfly wings, 168–72; emerging, 172–74; folklore and "haunted" vs. "stalked," 164–68; forgetting, 174–76; memory as curation, 150–61; memory, slavery, and intergenerational trauma, 144–50; through the bayou's looking glass, 161–64

Bechdel, Alison, 3, 78–79

Bergen, Benjamin K., 6, 25, 28

Berlin trilogy (Lute), 216

Bhabha, Homi, 136, 141, 191–92, 196

Bissette, Steve, 183

Black Lives Matter movement, 157, 176

"Black War," 179

blood quantum laws, 134

Brer Rabbit, 165–67

Burnett, Ann, 125, 129

bystanders: *Bayou*, 166; bystander effect, 105; *Deogratias*, 43, 45, 59–64, 66, 70,

STUDIES IN COMICS AND CARTOONS

LUCY SHELTON CASWELL AND JARED GARDNER, SERIES EDITORS

Books published in Studies in Comics and Cartoons focus exclusively on comics and graphic literature, highlighting their relation to literary studies. The series includes monographs and edited collections that cover the history of comics and cartoons from the editorial cartoon and early sequential comics of the nineteenth century through webcomics of the twenty-first. Studies that focus on international comics are also considered.